Evaluating Alternative Law-Enforcement Policies

Evaluating Alternative Law-Enforcement Policies

Edited by
Ralph Baker
Fred A Meyer, Jr.
Ball State University

LexingtonBooks
D.C. Heath and Company
Lexington, Massachusetts
Toronto

Library of Congress Cataloging in Publication Data

Evaluating alternative law-enforcement policies.

    1. Police—United States—Addresses, essays, lectures. 2. Law enforce-
ment—United States—Addresses, essays, lectures. 3. Police—United States—
Evaluation—Addresses, essays, lectures. 4. Law enforcement—United
States—Evaluation—Addresses, essays, lectures. I. Baker, Ralph. II. Meyer,
Fred A.
HV8141.E9   363.2'0973   79-1541
ISBN 0-669-02898-3

Published simultaneously in Canada

Printed in the United States of America

International Standard Book Number: 0-669-02898-3

Library of Congress Catalog Card Number: 79-1541

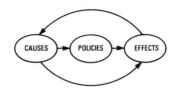

Policy Studies Organization Series

General Approaches to Policy Studies

Policy Studies in America and Elsewhere
    edited by Stuart S. Nagel
Policy Studies and the Social Sciences
    edited by Stuart S. Nagel
Methodology for Analyzing Public Policies
    edited by Frank P. Scioli, Jr., and Thomas J. Cook
Urban Problems and Public Policy
    edited by Robert L. Lineberry and Louis H. Masotti
Problems of Theory in Policy Analysis
    edited by Philip M. Gregg
Using Social Research for Public Policy-Making
    edited by Carol H. Weiss
Public Administration and Public Policy
    edited by H. George Frederickson and Charles Wise
Policy Analysis and Deductive Reasoning
    edited by Gordon Tullock and Richard Wagner
Legislative Reform
    edited by Leroy N. Rieselbach
Teaching Policy Studies
    edited by William D. Coplin
Paths to Political Reform
    edited by William J. Crotty
Determinants of Public Policy
    edited by Thomas Dye and Virginia Gray
Effective Policy Implementation
    edited by Daniel Mazmanian and Paul Sabatier

Specific Policy Problems

Analyzing Poverty Policy
    edited by Dorothy Buckton James
Crime and Criminal Justice
    edited by John A. Gardiner and Michael Mulkey
Civil Liberties
    edited by Stephen L. Wasby
Foreign Policy Analysis
    edited by Richard L. Merritt

Contents

List of Figures

List of Tables

Part I
Introduction

1

Effects of Variations on Police Policy

Ralph Baker and
Fred A. Meyer, Jr.

This volume examines evaluations of police and law-enforcement policies in the United States. Considerable funds have been expended by governmental units in the United States to generate policies that will deal with crime. However, the effectiveness of those policies is still being evaluated. This book continues that evaluation process. Like its companion, *Determinants of Law-Enforcement Policies,* it grows out of work done for a symposium edition of *The Policy Studies Journal* and for workshops presented at the 1978 American Political Science Association meeting and the 1979 Midwest Political Science Association meeting.

The book deals with public evaluations of law-enforcement policies at some length. It also looks at various analyses and explanations for public evaluations. Because of the important role of the police in generating law-enforcement policy, there is a consideration of the effects of police training on police policy as well as an examination of police community transactions. The last part of the book deals with the important part played by the media in shaping public perceptions of law enforcement.

Kingsley Game in chaper 2 presents a bibliographic essay on the evaluation of police policy. He reviews the literature on (1) the cost of policing services, (2) the measuring of the effectiveness of police services, (3) changes in police effectiveness as a result of policy change, and (4) the contextual knowledge found in the policy environment.

Part II of the book commences the examination of public evaluations of the police. Wesley Skogan in chapter 3 develops a model of individual and contextual effects upon evaluation of police roles in thirteen large American cities. This chapter leaves the reader with a series of policy questions such as,"Which police services explain variations in perception by black residents?"

Scott Decker, Russell Smith, and Thomas Uhlman in chapter 4 examine relationships of police community relations programs with public evaluations of police. They use aggregate city-level variables to measure police programs and criminal activity of the police. Their findings call into question the ability of such efforts to achieve one of their primary goals—improving public evaluations of the police.

One important factor in public evaluation of the police is public perception of the patrol function. Woodrow Jones in chapter 5 deals with the problems of efficient patrol allocation and measurement of public evaluations of patrol as an element of a patrol allocation formula.

3

Part III investigates various approaches to public evaluation studies. Elinor Ostrom, Roger Parks, Gordon Whitaker, and Stephen Percy present a model of the public service production process and apply it to police services. Their goal in chapter 6 is to facilitate the evaluation of the performance of a public agency.

Much of the evaluation of law-enforcement policy has been based on microeconomic analysis as embodied in public choice theory. In chapter 7 John Monzingo presents a criticism of public choice theory as applied to the criminal justice system.

Donald Phares also deals with economic analysis, but as applied to one topic—heroin. He analyzes current public policy in this area and then suggests an economic basis for structuring policy through the application of a supply-demand framework.

Since the police are such important actors in the formulation and subsequent evaluation of law-enforcement policy, part IV examines the effects of police training on police policy. Ralph Baker, Fred Meyer, and Dorothy Rudoni address themselves to the impact of professionalism on the delivery of police services in chapter 9. Professionalism has been cited by some as a panacea for the problems that are found in policing. However, the concept lacks clarity. Various implications of the concept are discussed in the chapter.

Stephen Wasby in chapter 10 discusses the problems involved in communicating Supreme Court decisions to the police. He examines police training programs and discusses ways in which Supreme Court decisions might be implemented in police departments.

Part V of the book deals with police-community transactions. Some alternatives to officially established policies are discussed in this section. For example, chapter 11 by Stephen Percy deals with the attempts by citizens to produce community safety on their own. These developments appear to stem from public evaluations of official attempts at the provision of community safety. Percy discusses ways to measure this coproduction and to evaluate its effect on safety and security in the community.

In some communities police-community relations programs have been developed, as well as Affirmative Action programs. These programs have a potential for bettering relations between the police and the community, particularly when there is a heterogeneous population. Nicholas Lovrich in chapter 12 presents results from his study of police-community relations and Affirmative Action programs in 161 American cities. He compares high and low police-community relations cities from 1960 to 1975 with respect to reported crimes. Also, the combined effects of Affirmative Action programs and police-community relations training on crime reduction are discussed.

In chapter 13 Robert Friedrich presents his analysis of data originally gathered by Albert J. Reiss, Jr. The data deal with racial prejudice among police officers. On the basis of the data analysis Friedrich discusses potential policies to deal with racial prejudice.

Public evaluations of the police are frequently manifested in a variety of complaints. Gerald Caiden and Harlan Hahn in chapter 14 discuss the problem of inadequate formal evaluative facilities for the public, and the lack of a system that is easily accessible, cheap, reliable, objective, and capable of instituting remedies for public complaints.

The media play an important role in conditioning public perceptions of reality. Part VI deals with effects of the media on law-enforcement policy. Doris Graber in chapter 15 presents the results of a year-long daily content analysis of four newspapers and five television news programs. In addition, data from ten interviews with four separate panels are included in the study. The chapter investigates the type of information made available to the public about crime fighting. In addition, what the public learns from this information and how the public makes evaluations of crime-fighting policies are discussed.

John Culver and Kenton Knight also deal with the impact of the media on the public. However, they focus on television portrayals of law-enforcement roles. In chapter 16 they review the images television shows project and the distortion of actual law-enforcement procedures. These distortions make it more difficult for the public to formulate accurate evaluations of law-enforcement policies.

2 Police Policy Evaluation: A Bibliographic Essay
Kingsley W. Game

Introduction

Evaluation of police policy presupposes the availability of several types of information. Information is required on (1) the cost or price of the "product"; (2) measuring the effectiveness of the product, by some discernible criterion or criteria; (3) changes in effectiveness ascribable to policy change; and (4) last but far from least, realistic contextual knowledge of the policy environment, including bureaucratic knowledge of accepted methods and formats. The purpose of this chapter is to provide a guide to the literatures that make such information available to policymakers.

Evaluating police policies is both difficult and urgent, for a number of reasons. Policing may not be an activity solely done by duly constituted, sworn police forces.[1] Most policing in the United States is done by about 40,000 separate agencies, of which only 250 or so are at state or national level.[2] (This localism is reflected in the literature: little has been written on state police since Smith's work in 1925.)[3]

Local police services are devoted to many problems other than seeking and apprehending criminal suspects, the ostensible anticrime mission. The usual estimate of the proportion of police time spent on such activities as traffic, domestic disputes, drunks, and dangerous emergencies is 70 to 80 percent. Even if direct enforcement of criminal law—the usual focus of evaluation—were the only police activity, police policy would still be a matter of frequent dispute, emotionally and politically loaded as it is with dealing in crime, emergency, and fear. Walter Miller lucidly expounds the quagmire of right- and left-wing dogmas that form the ideological context of police (and other criminal justice) policy.[4] Even if this conflict were abated, there are basic limits to the effectiveness of police:

> The police did not create and cannot remove the social conditions that lead to crime. They did not start and cannot stop the social changes that are taking place in America. They do not enact the laws they are required to enforce, nor do they dispose of the criminals they are required to arrest.[5]

Thanks for generous advice and encouragement, but no blame for sins of omission or commission, are due to Professor Susan Macmanus and Professor George Antunes, two of the best mentors one could wish for.

The Price or Cost of Policing

An indispensable element of policy evaluation is an understanding of costs. Little work has been done on the opportunity costs of particular policy changes, although many productivity reforms center on reducing off-street officer time without direct cost change, or using nonsworn personnel at fairly predictable cost savings for some tasks.[6] (The assumption is usually implicit that some benefit will result from more street time.) Larson does conclude from his review of the Kansas City patrol experiment that there is little opportunity cost in concentrating patrols according to need of the moment.[7] Most of the cost and expenditure literature, however, concerns citywide costs of operation, regardless of detailed policy, and is therefore of indirect utility in evaluating policy alternatives. This utility is real nonetheless: an understanding of the aggregate problems of police costs, and of the complexity of the relationship between crime rates and police dollars, provides a vital background for the more policy-specific cost studies that one hopes will enhance evaluation, which is still better-developed on the benefit side. Readers already familiar with this branch of political economy will be able to skip this section, but would-be evaluators unacquainted with it may find food for thought and clues for measurement.

Local governments decide for themselves, under state laws, what to spend on police budgets. What influences this decision? What makes local governments feel able or obliged to spend more on police?

Statisticians of several disciplines (tax economists, political scientists, sociologists) have used the fact that police budgets are locally written to investigate the question, using data across many states or cities. Colm and Fabricant were early pioneers.[8] It became apparent that urbanization and population density raise police costs. Brazer found police expenditures a function of income, intergovernmental revenue, population density, and size across 462 cities; density became crucial in the largest cities.[9] Wood accounted for police spending level variations among New Jersey cities with data on industrialization, housing density, population age, and poverty.[10] Where police are most needed, money is least easily spared for them: Masotti and Brown found, albeit from a small sample of cities, that high community socioeconomic status (SES) brings high police spending per capita, but low SES makes police dollars a high proportion of city budgets.[11] Pidot used factor analysis to confirm the importance of socioeconomic conditions for city police costs.[12] Shoup and Rosett explored the question of intergovernmental police cost spillovers in a Los Angeles study.[13]

Hirsch's seminal article on economies and diseconomies of scale in the search for a police cost function included property values as an input factor and allowed for service conditions expressed by street mileage, population density, age, nonwhite population, and number of businesses.[14]

Usually socioeconomic variables affecting police budgets were intuitively separated into those permitting (for example, income) and those requiring (for example, crowding) spending, the latter being putatively criminogenic conditions. In 1970 Pressman and Carol measured some relations between such social conditions in ninety-five Standard Metropolitan Statistical Areas (SMSAs) and recorded crime.[15] They did not analyze the influence of crime rates on police spending, but they did consider the other direction, and police spending did not appear to lower crime rates. It seemed as if bigger cities had more expensive police forces because of social changes accompanying city growth; crime itself was termed a diseconomy of city size. Walzer generated a police cost function based on crime rates and on geographic variables including population density; like Pressman and Carol, he detected no deterrence of crime by additional police dollars.[16]

The wavering between considering crime (or criminogenic conditions) as a determinant of police effort and vice versa may have been influenced by Becker's economic modeling of 1968, in which he had posited crime as behavior jointly deterred by risk of punishment and severity (cost to criminal) of punishment.[17] Thus analysts were torn between considering either direction of causation between crime and police budgets. Allison found demographic variables accounting for 85 percent of variance in crime rates around Chicago, with police expenditures, despite their supposed effect on risk of punishment, making little difference.[18] Jones looked in the other direction. With copious data, he could find no reliable connection between crime rate at t_1 and police spending levels at t_2 or t_3.[19]

Given the possibilities for mutual causation between crime rates and police spending levels (including changes in the rate of underreporting crime), which can confound any one-way analysis, it seemed appropriate to use simultaneous equations to resolve the enigma.[20] Dye and Pollack were among early users of multi-directional causal models to understand police spending.[21] Greenwood and Wadicki solved simultaneous equations to identify interactions among crime, police, and socioeconomic data for 199 SMSAs, and did find a positive effect of crime on police spending.[22]

The high points of this literature are reviewed pithily by Hirsch, who points out some measurement problems and strongly favors simultaneous-equation analysis.[23]

Two contributions in particular show how this literature can help with our present concern, evaluation, by their ingenious estimation of productivity. Chapman, Hirsch, and Sonenblum observed that "if prices of agency inputs are known, the production function can be used to suggest how agency efficiency might by improved."[24] They used socioeconomic data on crime "production" across California to estimate how much crime "should" occur in Los Angeles, thus getting a handle on the elusive prevented crime, and figuring its price in police dollars. Swimmer, one of those using simultaneous equations to sort out interactions of crime and police spending, was able to use his mathematical model to estimate the anticrime benefit of an additional police dollar.[25] If the estimate is under a dollar, the moral is obvious: hold spending down.

Measuring Effectiveness: Criteria, Data

The preceding section summarized a body of literature on the conditions affecting local police costs, and analyzing their relationship with "crime," usually as reported under the FBI Uniform Crime Reporting system. This leaves a number of questions still to consider, since official statistics do not always accurately reflect real crime conditions, police handle more problems than index crimes, and only one policy alternative—spending another dollar—has been assumed. This section takes up the issue of measuring effectiveness, the problem of criteria, and alternative sources of data.

Criteria for evaluation, the desired outcomes or end products of policing, are persistently centered on the ostensible anticrime mission, despite the numerous other ends, legitimate (countless babies have been born in the back of police cars) and less legitimate (improving business for auto towers and storers), often served.[26] Before we try to measure, we must define what we think we are trying to measure; hence the perennial problem of goals in evaluation—the question, "Effectiveness at what?" Even where we take rape prevention as a goal, an indisputably worthy one, there are severe problems associated with the social and legal definition of rape, let alone reporting and official recording.[27] There are also the recurrent temptations to measure output rather than outcome (for example, finding a cheap way to get more officers on the street and neglecting to inquire how much crime reduction or other benefit this brings) or to credit a coincidental improvement to a policy change, due to a lack of statistical skepticism.[28] These three problems are concisely outlined by John Gardiner, and no one should start measuring police effectiveness without reading his remarks and two informative articles by Ostrom and by Hatry.[29]

The weakness of routinely collected crime data is well known, and four articles by Ostrom, Littrel, Seidman and Couzens, and Sjoberg illuminate some institutional and economic reasons for this condition.[30] The FBI Uniform Crime Reporting program provides only a very rough index, based on reports filtered through a series of interested parties, beginning with the victim and the officer, and proceeding upward through the bureaucracy. The U.S. Department of Justice Law Enforcement Assistance Administration (LEAA) was not unduly pessimistic in its 1974 initial estimate that 50 percent of crimes go unreported to police.[31] Even if police attention is attracted, officers have considerable discretion as to whether to write a report, conditioned by social and bureaucratic circumstances.[32]

The attempt to get behind routine data to the "dark figure" of actual victimization rates for common crimes like assault and theft got under way with the 1966 U.S. President's Commission on Law Enforcement and the Administration of Justice, although as early as 1965 the Harris and National Opinion Research Center (NORC) polling organizations had piggy-backed some victimization questions onto multipurpose surveys. The Commission initiated some surveys with

victimization as a central theme.[33] The next wave of victim surveys was generated by the transfer of former U.S. Department of Commerce Bureau of the
Census personnel to the LEAA, itself the creature of legislation (Safe Streets Act
of 1968) inspired by Lyndon Johnson's Commission. The Census personnel
brought considerable skills in sampling and surveying populations to the search
for actual victimization rates, and the Census Bureau has built such surveys into
its Quarterly Household Surveys. Methodology is thus highly developed and available, as can be discovered by a perusal of the San Jose-Dayton methods test and
of Tuchfarber and Klecka's manual for low-cost telephone surveying.[34] Hindelang
presents a detailed analysis of an eight-city victimization study, introduced by a
history of previous efforts, including Small Business Administration inquiries
into commercial victimization.[35]

　　The utility of relatively cheap and reliable techniques of victimization surveying in anticrime evaluation is considerable, freeing policymakers from the
limitations of traditional crime data. Bloch's study of distribution of police services in the District of Columbia, done while the art was in an earlier phase of development, expressed an understandable impatience for better crime measures.[36]
Inciardi emphasizes the value of improved crime statistics in policy evaluation.[37]
Ostrom considers statistical vulnerability to victimization (or highway wrecks) in
the jurisdiction a key evaluation figure.[38] Bennett and associates have made sophisticated current lifetime homicide risk estimates for residents of fifty large
cities.[39] However, victimization surveys, useful as they are, have their own sources
of error. Clarren and Schwartz put qualifications on the use of such data in evaluation from experience in 1971-1975 in Cincinnati: victim-recalled crime must
be held within strict definitional limits.[40] The surveys miss transient populations.
Skogan provides a thoughtful summary of sources of error in police crime figures
and victimization surveys.[41] From an evaluation standpoint, one must remember
that police efforts are not the only influence on crime rates, however accurate
the estimate..

　　Another criterion for evaluation is consumer satisfaction, and this does not
necessarily have to be limited to the anticrime mission. A sample of citizens, or
citizens who have called the police, can be interviewed for this purpose. Gourley
looked at Los Angeles attitudes to police twenty-five years ago.[42] McGaghy and
associates, and Hahn, sought public evaluations of police service in Hartford and
in Detroit in the tense racial context of the late 1960s.[43] Ostrom led an investigation of the relation between city size and attitudes to police.[44] Some discourag-
ing but interesting findings have emerged. Furstenberg and Wellford, interviewing Baltimore citizens who had called for service, found that race affected the
perception, rather than the quality, of service; general perceptions of police
affected particular perceptions of service.[45] Smith and Hawkins, in Seattle,
found it untrue (for individuals) that less vicitmization makes for a better attitude toward police, or that fear of victimization makes for a worse one.[46] (Drawing jurisdictionwide policy conclusions from these findings for individuals requires

a mild ecological leap.) Eisenberg began the San Francisco PACE project with an attitude survey showing severe mutual misperception between blacks and police; unfortunately the project ended before this attitude gap could be checked for change.[47] Skogan discusses the growth, and methodological hazards, of surveys seeking consumer evaluations of police services and public responses to police innovations and policy experiments.[48]

Whether the simple policy of more spending can significantly deter crime is, as shown in the previous section, a matter of some doubt. Phillips and Votey call for empirical assessment of the dollar costs and actual preventability of different offenses, to counteract the practical tendency to arrest for visible but minor offenses where this is easy and where it mollifies vociferous complainants.[49] The production estimates produced by Swimmer and Chapman, Hirsch, and Sonenblum, cited at the end of the previous section, can be made more reliable with crime data based on victimization surveys. Ehrlich, who finds deterrence under Becker's risk of apprehension and conviction-cost of punishment model, finds no relationship between police spending and the deterrent value of arrest and conviction.[50] Phillips and Votey, however, did find that increased police personnel increased the chance of conviction, holding arrest rates constant.[51]

To conclude this section, it may be said in summary that the performance measurement required for evaluation is a difficult activity in which no assumption should be taken for granted or go unstated; but enough work has been done to illuminate major pitfalls and find more or less satisfactory ways around them. The technical obstacles to evaluation have been overcome to a point where policymakers trained in formal research techniques, or able to hire competent assistants so trained, will find measurement a lesser obstacle than money, politics, or bureaucracy.

Experiments, Studies, and Innovations

A number of studies, often financed and published by the U.S. Department of Justice LEAA, provide models and starting points for further police policy evaluations. Most of these evaluate policy innovations deliberately tried as controlled experiments, while a few evaluate legal or administrative changes whose consequences had been taken for granted (often unwisely) before implementation, creating quasi-experimental conditions where statistical before-and-after analysis is still possible, as in the celebrated case of the Connecticut speeding crackdown.[52] Not every previous program provides an ideal evaluation model, however; the sadly underevaluated San Francisco PACE program was cited above, and the following section will refer to the persistence of underevaluation until quite recently in some LEAA programs.

An early call for experimental testing of innovations (in hardware as well as policy) so that protection may be "wisely bought" was made by Blumenstein and associates in a 1968 Institute for Defense Analysis for the infant LEAA.[53] Already in 1967-1968 Los Angeles experimented with its motorcycle officers, varying their methods and density on different beats, and measuring effects on speeding, reported injury accidents, and crime.[54] Changes in number of personnel were only dubiously effective, but accidents were found to decrease when the method was adopted of issuing warning tickets, which enabled officers to censure truly dangerous behavior instead of those sometimes petty infractions that hold up well in court.

Another pioneer experiment that appeared to yield positive results (if costs are acceptable) occurred when the Twentieth Precinct of New York City received a 40 percent increase in personnel.[55] Press reports that demographically and criminologically similar precincts were used as controls and that neighboring precincts were checked for displacement of crime (there was little spillover). Classifying crimes as "inside" and "outside" (a custormary and revealing patrol officer distinction between on-street and off-street behavior), there was a significant reduction in reported outside crimes, with little change in the arrest rate. But some of the difference may have been due to the quality of the added personnel, or of unrecorded changes in procedure, perhaps an abatement of corruption among some "bad apples."

Kelling, Pate, and Brown reported on the most thoroughgoing single police experiment to date, the Kansas City patrol project.[56] The attempt was made, with strong support from the police chief, to determine actual effectiveness of routine patrolling on dependent variables of victimization, reported crime, arrests, citizen feelings of security, response time, self-protection by citizens and merchants, and traffic accidents. Fifteen contiguous beats were the scene of controlled variations in patrol service. The chief felt obliged to concur in the "essential finding," from plentiful and diverse data, that the changes in patrol routines and intensity, "within the range tested by this experiment," made no difference.[57] The experiment, despite the thoroughness of the analysts and the commitment of the chief, had one instructive drawback. There are ethical and political limits, however ill-defined, on the extent to which one is at liberty to experiment with protecting tax-paying citizens from each other. Larson pointed out that the "range tested in this experiment" was insufficiently broad to warrant strong generalizations but drew some practical conclusions for patrol management, perhaps overlooking some likely organizational obstacles, such as patrol beat territorialism, to implementation.[58]

A veritable mine of evaluation cases, assembled by Chelimsky from 235 criminal justice projects, many police-centered, was released by LEAA's National Institute for Law Enforcement and Criminal Justice (NILECJ) in 1976. The projects were grouped under the High Impact Anticrime program, begun in 1972, to reduce city crime and demonstrate the COPIE cycle (Crime Oriented Planning, Implementation, and Evaluation).[59] Volume Two contains copious findings and statistics.

Two subsequently released LEAA evaluations are of some interest. First, the consequences of the quasi-experiment provided by draconian Rockefeller drug legislation were analyzed with the aid of the New York City bar.[60] Given the lack of change in the actual resources and practices of the criminal justice system, and the social roots and definition of the drug problem, results of the legislation were unimpressive. There are some interesting incidental reflections on police practice. Second, in the aftermath of the Kansas City experiment, a new patrol system was tried in Wilmington. Uniformed officers in marked cars continued to respond to calls, but preventive patrol was done in plain clothes and unmarked cars.[61] Evaluation was qualified by careful measurement of selected performance criteria, overt recognition of the relation of patrol to other police activities, and questions of replicability. Replication should be tried for a more conclusive evaluation of this interesting experiment, if supportive chiefs can be found.

A digression is in order here on the question of police personality. It is too often assumed as given that a new program aimed at improving the education, training, or screening of recruits will in some way improve the force, and forgotten that "bad apples" can be made as well as attracted by police work. Thinking on this question is assisted by some available research, although there is the persistent problem of defining officer quality: civilian complaints, supervisor ratings, and attitude measures all have their biases.

Westley argued in 1953 that the enforcement role exposes officers to hostility; they are drawn to protect each other, right or wrong; rookies are socialized accordingly on the job.[62] Niederhoffer's pencil-and-paper survey showed more cynical attitudes expressed by veterans than by new officers.[63] Kroes has written with slightly popularized eloquence on the peculiar mental and physiological stresses on police, their consequences, and management policies to reduce stresses or at least legitimize their admission for the officers who sometimes suffer in alcoholic, divorce-prone, or suicidal silence.[64] He feels that psychological recruit screening alone cannot prevent personality deterioration on the job, and management must provide continuing psychological support.

Other students have questioned this line of thought concerning on-the-job personality deterioration. Brenner and Levin tested the off-duty helping behavior of veterans against that of recruits and found no difference, although the sample was small.[65] (Both groups improved on the performance of theological students.) Tift found, based on long observations of a large force, that officers generally develop an "attitude of friendliness," but while traffic officers view citizens as "ordinary people," patrol officers come to despise their clients as inferior and incompetent.[66] Whatever the effect of work, school had no effect on the attitudes of 369 officers studied by Wiener.[67] Cohen and Chaiken found the New York City background investigation no predictor of officer performance (according to personnel and complaint records), but college education indicated likelihood of better performance, along with a tendency to leave the service.[68] Chackerian used agency professionalism (training) data and citizen attitudes and found police generally popular (in the abstract.) They appeared less popular when more "professional," and more popular when seen as ready to use force. Suggestive as these findings are, they come from weak data sources and sometimes uncontrolled inferences.[69]

Much of the literature on the darker side of police psychology, awareness of which is essential to making and evaluating policy in this area, is synthesized in Toch's grim but fascinating *Peacekeeping: Police, Prisons, and Violence.*[70]

So much for the question of officer personality and the effects of selection, training, and the job. The lesson, once again, is that no policy evaluation should take assumptions for granted. This section will conclude with some works that consider sometimes inexpensive policy innovations and either provide informal evaluation only, or are unable to evaluate what has not been tried. These proposals attempt to meet the shift in public expectations of police over the last generation, analyzed by Carte, from reformism (professionalism and political independence as per the Wickersham Commission) in the 1930s, toward a combined desire for citizen and officer input into policymaking.[71] The "demilitarization" this suggests also seems to fit in with a bureaucratic liberalism that seeks either to enshrine or hive off the social-service aspects of policing.

Cumming and associates found that over half of calls to the police complaint desk were "for help and some kind of support for personal and interpersonal problems."[72] Police spend a lot of time meeting such demands, and police policy cannot be well made or evaluated without some recognition of this. Yet little work has been done on evaluating current performance or new approaches, probably because of poor data availability and the difficulty of establishing definitions and criteria. A notable exception may be in domestic dispute handling: Ostrom suggests a fairly accessible criterion of disputes handled per dollar cost in police time, and the LEAA has shown interest in evaluating its Family Crisis Intervention prescriptive package.[73] The main policy response has been to develop human-relations training, although some have recommended forming a separate, "demilitarized," service for these functions.[74]

Police social-service activities are not without their risks, however, and more police are killed on domestic calls than on any other type of mission, although they are usually peaceable.[75] Surrogate police might not in practice inspire much respect in disturbed citizens, or in "real cops" either. Further, where in a messy urban jurisdiction are the lines drawn between direct crime fighting, indirect peacekeeping, traffic enforcement, and social service? This may be why little has been done for evaluation in this area.

Caiden in 1971 described some policy problems (performance failures) of police departments, and a broad range of often low-cost and symbolic "revitalization" responses, with case studies of innovative departments. Evaluation was informal.[76] Washnis provides field reviews of block-club and community-involvement programs in thirty-six cities, but evaluation is again somewhat impressionistic in the absence of systematic data.[77] Sandler and Mintz describe, and evaluate favorably but informally, some symbolic "demilitarization" in New York City.[78] They assert that the "paramilitary style" leads to powerlessness and cynicism in the ranks and middle management, creating a we-they split between operational and administrative levels and between police and public.

Perhaps the most interesting suggested reform, and one least likely to be evaluated because of the impracticability of trying it, is recruitment of police by conscription across the community.[79]

Federal Forms and Street Realities: Contextual Knowledge

In addition to the literatures already adduced on costs, measuring effectiveness, and experiments and studies, the local or state policy evaluator requires two more kinds of information as a guide through the inferno, like Vergil for Dante. One is a knowledge of the forms and state of the cult of evaluation overhead in the federal system; the other is a knowledge of the cruel realities of the stationhouse and the street below. Most readers will have much of this knowledge already, but a quick survey of printed sources of such information may bring some useful time-saving or thought-provoking items to attention which might be missed in haste and which have not already been cited.

Police policy evaluation is but one element in the armamentarium of criminal justice planning, which has been something of a bureaucratic growth industry since President Johnson's Commission.[80] Evaluation was emphasized in the Crime Control Act of 1973, and the LEAA and its progeny, notably the National Institute for Law Enforcement and Criminal Justice (NILECJ), have responded with plentiful information on how evaluations should look and work, beyond the studies already mentioned. A brief but thorough handbook for state and local evaluators, as well as a compendium of sample research designs and reporting forms for CJS evaluations, including police, are provided by Kupersmith of LEAA.[81] The handbook is broadly applicable to policy evaluations, especially the "review questions" (pitfall checklist). Weidman, also for LEAA, produced a systematic text on methods and problems for state and local criminal justice planners, with some state case studies in evaluation strategy.[82] There are also journal articles and commercially produced manuals on seeking and keeping project funding.[83]

LEAA evaluation activities are summarized in a plan that covered fiscal years 1977 and 1978.[84] Goals for the overall program of CJS evaluation were clarified as knowledge (of effectiveness), management (aided by evaluative information), and development (of evaluation capacity in criminal justice agencies). Distinctions are also elucidated between "Phase I" studies, which run locally for some months, and "Phase II" studies of national scale, and between "Program" and "Field Experiment" studies. Some earlier work on CJS evaluation comes from the U.S. Department of Health Education and Welfare National Institute of Mental Health (NIMH) and the Police Foundation.[85]

Empey at LEAA produced a model for evaluation of juvenile justice programs that would not be a waste of time to read for a police evaluator, drawing attention eloquently to the "age-old error: assuming that change can be equated with effectiveness and that modern programs will succeed where others have failed."[86] He outlines the process of finding agreement on goals, definition of target populations, theoretical statement (making assumed causes and effects explicit), intervention, and research strategy from test of basic assumptions to future implications.

The LEAA, while indisputably leading the trend to evaluation in criminal justice, has not always found instant success. A 1973 survey of State Planning Agencies (SPAs) tied to LEAA found some agencies still "evaluating" only in the sense of traditional auditing for fiscal propriety, rather than trying to measure outcomes.[87] A 1975 NILECJ study of national Pilot Cities program evaluation revealed many measured impacts to be still within the organizational boundaries of CJS agencies, and less on external results.[88] As recently as 1976, much evaluation was still informal on the Early-Warning Robbery Reduction (liquor-store secret radio alarm and stake-out) program, due to insufficient information developed during projects.[89] The report had to establish possibilities for better future evaluation.

A word on statistics: two valuable sources were neglected in the earlier section on measurement. One is the *Sourcebook of Criminal Justice Statistics*, annually updated by LEAA.[90] The other is *Quantitative Tools*, edited by Oberlander; it is an LEAA book containing a series of expert papers on a variety of endemic CJS measurement problems.[91]

Technocratic rationality is apt to sink into stultified bureaucratic formalism, particularly under the homogenizing influence of intergovernmental subsidy, and criminal justice planning is no exception. However, the reader may be interested to know that intelligent and imaginative work is still done in this area. For example, Palumbo and associates combine a theoretical model differentiating criteria of optimality in police resource allocation with a perceptive study of crime in New York's garment district and the interests there at stake; they do not flinch from considering the interests of the security industry, law enforcers, academics, and sometimes (insured) victims, in criminal activity.[92]

Finally we come to the literature of street reality, of crime and police and politics in a law-enforcement world where things are not always as they seem. Perusal of this literature is not only a prophylactic essential for the fugitive from the ivory tower, but may also enable the hardened veteran to think more broadly about the too well known world in which evaluations must be made. The invalu-

able, rather informal, work of the "squad car anthropologists" has yielded powerful insights into the brutal, uncertain world of the street officer which cannot be
ignored if one is to make and evaluate police policy effectively. Three authors
have become near-police (or sworn police in Kirkham's case) and spent long periods involved in participant observation of street patrolling in practice, grinding
their academic training on some rough surfaces in the process, confronting the
tedium, frustration, and terror of street work, the moral universe of the patrol
officer, the rites of passage of the recruit, the organizational pecking orders and
vested interests in departments, and the insidiousness of corruption.[93] Only a
reading of the numerous odd and appalling incidents they recount can convey to
the outsider the reality (and variety—Muir's colleagues paid for their coffee;
Rubinstein's were on the take) of the police culture in which policy is made for
better or for worse.

Conclusion

A substantial literature now exists that is relevant to making and evaluating police
policies. There is no dearth of good general works, observer reports, and readers;
of manuals and examples from previous studies and projects; or of helpful texts
on formal and/or thoughtful policy planning. LEAA, the Police Foundation, and
their allied organizations, including the police departments that have served as
guinea pigs, have not labored in vain. The literatures on price and productivity of
police services are well developed, although of course not perfected, and statistical methods and availability have seen enormous improvement. Perhaps the greatest lacks are in the areas of performance of tasks not directly related to traffic
and the ostensible anticrime mission, and of the exercise and control of the discretion of the individual officer; but the nature of these problems may make this
inevitable.[94] Better data are increasingly available, and the work of Ostrom and
others provides relevant, if sometimes underused, criteria for policy evaluation.
Police policy can now be made, by those who wish to and are able, on a broader
intellectual and informational base than that of conventional wisdom or ideological dogma.

Notes

1. On policing by nonsworn persons, see Richard E. Sykes, "A Regula-
tory Theory of Policing," in David Bayley, ed., *Police and Society* (Beverly Hills,
Calif.: Sage, 1977), pp. 237-256; Harold A. Nelson, "The Defenders: A Case
Study of an Informal Police Organization," *Social Problems* 15 (Fall 1967): 127-
147; and Gary Marx and Dane Archer, "The Urban Vigilante," in James T. Curran
and Richard H. Ward, eds., *Police and Law Enforcement Annual 1973-1974*
(New York: AMS Press, 1975), pp. 153-161.

2. Donald McIntire, Herman Goldstein, and Daniel Skoler, *Criminal Justice in the United States* (Chicago: American Bar Foundation, 1974), p. 5.

3. Bruce Smith, *State Police* (Montclair, N.J.: Patterson Smith, 1969, first pub. 1925.) Thomas R. Dye, *Politics, Economics, and the Public* (Chicago: Rand McNally, 1966), pp. 223-226, found no economic influence on per capita state police; but there was a relation between urbanization and state per capita totals of state and local police combined.

4. Walter B. Miller, "Ideology and Criminal Justice Policy: Some Current Issues," in Jim Munro, ed., *Classes, Conflict, and Control* (Cincinnati: Anderson, 1976), pp. 3-38.

5. U.S. President's Commission on Law Enforcement and the Administration of Justice, *Task Force Report :The Police* (Washington, D.C.: GPO, 1966), p. 1.

6. The best starting point on police productivity, including its union aspects, is Joan L. Wolfle and John F. Heaphy, eds., *Readings on Productivity in Policing* (Washington, D.C.: Police Foundation, 1975).

7. Richard C. Larson, "What Happened to Patrol Operations in Kansas City?" *Evaluation* 3 (1976): 117-123.

8. G. Colm, "Public Expenditures and Economic Structure," *Social Research* 3 (February 1936): 57-77; Solomon Fabricant, *The Trend in Government Activity Since 1900* (New York: National Bureau for Economic Research, 1952).

9. H. Brazer, *City Expenditures in the U.S.* (New York: National Bureau of Economic Research, 1959); see also J.C. Weicher, "Determinants of Central City Expenditures: Some Overlooked Problems," *National Tax Journal* 23 (December 1970): 379-396.

10. Robert Wood, *1400 Governments Political Economy of the New York Region* (Cambridge, Mass.: Harvard University Press, 1961), chapter 2 and appendix B.

11. Louis Masotti and Dan Bowen, "Communities and Budgets: The sociology of Municipal Expenditures," *Urban Affairs Quarterly* 1 (December 1965): 39-58.

12. G.B. Pidot, "A Principal Component Analysis of the Determinants of Local Fiscal Patterns," *Review of Economics and Statistics* 51 (May 1969): 176-188.

13. Daniel Shoup and Arthur Rosett, *Fiscal Exploitation of Central Cities by Overlapping Governments: A Case Study of Los Angeles County* (Los Angeles Institute of Government and Public Affairs, 1969).

14. W.Z. Hirsch, "Expenditure Implications of Metropolitan Growth and Consolidation," *Review of Economics and Statistics* 41 (August 1959): 232-243.

15. Israel Pressman and Arthur Carol, "Crime as a Diseconomy of Scale," *Review of Social Economy* 29 (September 1971): 227-236; see also D.O. Popp and F.D. Sebold, "Quasi-Returns to Scale in the Provision of Police Services," *Public Finance* 27 (1972): 46-61; W.P. Beaton, "Determinants of Police Expenditures," *National Tax Journal* (June 1974):335-349.

16. Normal Walzer, "Economies of Scale and Municipal Services: the Illinois Experience," *Review of Economics and Statistics* 54 (November 1972): 431-438.

17. G.S. Becker, "Crime and Punishment: An Economic Approach," *Journal of Political Economy* 76 (March-April 1968): 160-167. The a priori neoclassical rational modeling of crime continues with R.W. Anderson, *Economics of Crime* (New York: Macmillan, 1976).

18. J.P. Allison, "Economic Factors and the Rate of Crime," *Land Economics* 48 (May 1972): 193-196.

19. E. Terrence Jones, "The Impact of Crime Rate Changes on Police Protection Expenditures in American Cities," *Criminology* 11 (February 1974): 516-524.

20. Ann Horowitz, "A Simultaneous Approach to the Problem of Explaining Interstate Differences in State and Local Government Expenditures," *Southern Journal of Economics* 34 (April 1968): 459-476, had paved the way, applying the mathematics to more general fiscal questions.

21. Thomas Dye and N.F. Pollack, "Path Analytic Models in Policy Research," *Policy Studies Journal* 2 (Winter 1973): 123-130. They found that increased nonwhite population generated police expenditure beyond the amount warranted by associated reported crime increases!

22. M.J. Greenwood and W.J. Wadicki, "Crime Rates and Public Expenditures for Police Protection: Their Interaction," *Review of Social Economy* 31 (October 1973): 138-151; see also L.R. McPheters and W.B. Stronge, "Law Enforcement Expenditures and Urban Crime," *National Tax Journal* 27 (December 1974): 633-644, who found that central city decay played an important role in the interaction of crime and the police dollar, and minimized Jones and Wadicki's suspicion that more police means more reporting of crime.

23. W.Z. Hirsch, "Production, Cost, and Expenditure Functions of Police Services," in Stuart Nagel, ed. *Modelling the Criminal Justice System* (Beverly Hills, Calif.: Sage, 1977.) Hirsch gives an understandably somewhat partisan account of the economy-of-scale cost function controversy he started in 1958.

24. Jeffrey I. Chapman, W.Z. Hirsch, and S. Sonenblum, *A Police Service Production Function* (Los Angeles: University of California at Los Angeles Institute of Government and Public Affairs, 1973), p. 2.

25. Eugene Swimmer, "Measurement of the Effectiveness of Urban Law Enforcement: A Simultaneous Approach," *Southern Economic Journal* 40 (April 1974): 618-630.

26. Two interesting papers that recognize police missions other than the seeking and arrest of criminal suspects are a contribution by Blumstein and associates in U.S. Department of Justice LEAA, *Performance Measurement and the Criminal Justice System: Four Conceptual Approaches* (Washington, D.C.: GPO, 1978), and Gary Marx, "Alternative Measures of Police Performance," in

Richard C. Larson, ed., *Police Accountability: Performance Measures and Unionism* (Lexington, Mass.: Lexington Books, D.C. Heath, 1978), pp. 15-32.

27. Shirley Feldman-Summers, "Conceptual and Empirical Issues Associated with Rape," in Emilio C. Viano, ed., *Victims and Society* (Washington, D.C.: Visage Press, 1976), pp. 91-104.

28. The classic exposition of the latter problem is by Donald Campbell and H.L. Ross, "The Connecticut Crackdown on Speeding: Time-Series Data in Quasi-Experimental Analysis," *Law and Society Review* 3 (1968): 33-53.

29. John A. Gardiner, "Problems in the Use of Evaluation in Law Enforcement and Criminal Justice," in Kenneth M. Dolbeare, ed., *Public Policy Evaluation* (Beverly Hills, Calif.: Sage, 1975), pp. 177-183; Harry P. Hatry, "Wrestling with Police Crime Control: Productivity Measurement," in Joan L. Wolfle and John Heaphy, eds., *Readings on Productivity in Policing* (Washington, D.C.: Police Foundation, 1975), pp. 86-128; Elinor Ostrom, "On the Meaning and Measurement of Output and Efficiency in the Provision of Urban Police Services," *Journal of Criminal Justice* 1 (1973): 93-112; and in Jim Munro, ed., *Classes, Conflict, and Control* (Cincinnati: Anderson, 1976). See also H.J. Schmandt and G.R. Stephens, "Measuring Municipal Output," *National Tax Journal* (December 1960): 369-375, and Stephen Mehay and Donald Shoup, "Models of Police Services for Program Analysis," in Ernest Nagel, ed., *Modelling the Criminal Justice System* (Beverly Hills, Calif.: Sage, 1976).

30. Elinor Ostrom, "Institutional Arrangements and the Measurement of Policy Consequences," *Urban Affairs Quarterly* (June 1971): 447-476; W.B. Littrel, "The Problem of Jurisdiction and Official Statistics of Crime," in Littrel and G. Sjoberg, eds., *Current Issues in Social Policy* (Beverly Hills, Calif.: Sage, 1976); Gideon Sjoberg, "Social Research, Social Policy, and the 'Other Economy,' " in ibid.; David Seidman and Michael Couzens, "Getting the Crime Rate Down: Political Pressures and Crime Reporting," *Law and Society Review* 8 (Spring 1974): 457-493.

31. U.S. Department of Justice LEAA, *Crime in Five American Cities, Advance Report* (Washington, D.C.: GPO, 1974).

32. Donald Black, "Production of Crime Reports," *American Sociological Review* 35 (August 1970): 733-747, provides an account of observation of the circumstances in which such discretion is exercised. Arthur C. Meyers, Jr., "Statistical Controls in a Police Department, *Crime and Delinquency* 8 (January 1962): 58-64, describes an early attempt by the St. Louis department at independent checking of crime reports. See also Richard Block, "Why Notify the Police?" *Criminology* 11 (February 1974): 555-569; John Mayer, "Patterns of Reporting Noncriminal Events to the Police," *Criminology* 12 (May 1974): 70-83; and Paul D. Reynolds and Dale A. Blyth, "Sources of Variation Affecting the Relationship between Police and Survey-Based Crime Rates," in Israel Drap-

kin and Emilio Viano, eds., *Victimology: A New Focus* (Lexington, Mass.: Lexington Books, D.C. Heath, 1973), pp. 201-225.

33. Albert Biderman and associates, *Report on a Pilot Study in the District of Columbia on Victimization and Attitudes to Law Enforcement* (Washington, D.C.: GPO, 1967); Albert Reiss, *Studies in Crime and Law Enforcement in Major Metropolitan Areas*, vol. 1 (Washington, D.C.: GPO, 1967); Philip Ennis, *Criminal Victimization in the U.S.: Report of a National Survey* (Washington, D.C.: GPO, 1967).

34. U.S. Department of Justice LEAA NCJISS, *Crimes and Victims: A Report on the Dayton-San Jose Pilot Survey of Victimization* (Washington, D.C.: GPO, 1974); Alfred J. Tuchfarber and William R. Klecka, *Random Digit Dialling: Lowering the Cost of Victim Surveys* (Washington, D.C.: Police Foundation, 1976).

35. Michael J. Hindelang, *Criminal Victimization in Eight American Cities: A Descriptive Analysis of Common Theft and Assault* (Cambridge, Mass.: Ballinger, 1976); see also Hindelang and associates, *An Analysis of Victimization Survey Results from the Eight Impact Cities: Summary Report* (Washington, D.C.: GPO, 1974).

36. Peter B. Bloch, *Equality of Distribution of Police Services* (Washington, D.C.: Urban Institute, 1974).

37. James A. Inciardi, "Criminal Statistics and Victim Survey Research for Effective Law Enforcement Planning," in Emilio C. Viano, ed., *Victims and Society* (Washington, D.C.: Visage Press, 1976), pp. 177-189.

38. Elinor Ostrom, "On the Meaning and Measurement of Output and Efficiency in the Provision of Police Services," *Journal of Criminal Justice* 1 (1973): 93-112, and in Jim Munro, ed., *Classes, Conflict, and Control* (Cincinnati: Anderson, 1976).

39. Arnold Bennett and associates, "Computing Lifetime Victimization Probabilities: Risk of Urban Homicide," in Richard C. Larson, ed., *Police Accountability: Performance Measures and Unionism* (Lexington, Mass.: Lexington Books, D.C. Heath, 1978), pp. 65-90.

40. Sumner M. Clarren and Alfred I. Schwartz, "Measuring a Program's Impact: a Cautionary Note," in Wesley Skogan, ed., *Sample Surveys of Victims of Crime* (Cambridge, Mass.: Ballinger, 1976), pp. 121-134.

41. Wesley G. Skogan, "Comparing Measures of Crime: Police Statistics and Survey Estimates of Citizen Victimization in American Cities," *Proceedings of the American Statistical Association* (1974): 44-52.

42. G. Douglas Gourley, *Public Relations and the Police* (Springfield, Ill.: Charles C. Thomas, 1953).

43. C.H. McGaghy and associates, "Public Attitudes toward City Police in a Middle Sized Northern City," *Criminologica* 6 (May 1968): 14-22; Harlan Hahn, "Ghetto Assessments of Police Protection and Authority," *Law and Society Review* 6 (November 1971): 183-194. See also Herbert Jacob, "Contact

with Government Agencies," *Midwest Journal of Political Science* 16 (February 1972): 123-146.

44. Elinor Ostrom and associates, *Community Organization and the Provision of Police Services* (Beverly Hills, Calif.: Sage, 1973); Ostrom and G. Whitaker. "Does Local Community Control of the Police Make a Difference?" *American Journal of Political Science* 17 (February 1973): 48-76.

45. Frank Furstenberg and Charles Welford, "Calling the Police: Evaluation of Police Service," *Law and Society Review* 7 (Spring 1973): 393-406.

46. Paul Smith and Richard Hawkins, "Victimization: Types of Citizen Police Contacts and Attitudes toward Police," *Law and Society Review* 8 (Fall 1973): 135-152.

47. Terry Eisenberg, Robert Fosen, and Albert Glickman, *Police-Community Action* (New York: Praeger, 1973), chapter 3.

48. Wesley G. Skogan, "Public Policy and Public Evaluation of Criminal Justice System Performance," in John A. Gardiner and Michael A. Mulkey, eds., *Crime and Criminal Justice* (Lexington, Mass.: Lexington Books, D.C. Heath, 1975), pp. 43-61. See also Fred Klyman and Joanna Kruckenberg, "A Methodology for Assessing Citizen Perceptions of Police," *Journal of Criminal Justice* 2 (1974): 219-233.

49. Llad Phillips and Howard Votey, "An Economic Basis for the Definition and Control of Crime," in Stuart Nagel, ed., *Modelling the Criminal Justice System* (Beverly Hills, Calif.: Sage, 1976).

50. I. Ehrlich, "Participation in Illegitimate Activities," *Journal of Political Economy* 81 (May-June 1973): 521-565.

51. Llad Phillips and Howard Votey, "Crime Control in California," *Journal of Legal Studies* 4 (1975): 201-211.

52. See Campbell and Ross, "Connecticut Crackdown."

53. Alfred Blumenstein and associates, *A National Program of Research, Development, Test, and Evaluation on Law Enforcement and Criminal Justice* (Arlington, Va.: Institute for Defense Analysis for LEAA, November 1968).

54. Daniel Shoup and S. Mehay, "Cost Effectiveness in Traffic Enforcement," *Journal of Transportation and Economic Policy* (January 1973): 1-26; see also their *Program Budgeting for Urban Police Services* (New York: Praeger, 1972).

55. S.J. Press, *Some Effects of an Increase in Personnel in the Twentieth Precinct of New York City* (New York: Rand Institute, 1971).

56. G. Kelling, T. Pate, and C. Brown, *The Kansas City Preventive Patrol Experiment* (Washington, D.C.: Police Foundation, 1973).

57. Ibid., Summary Report, p. 16.

58. Richard C. Larson, "What Happened to Patrol Operations in Kansas City?" *Evaluation* 3 (1976): 117-123.

59. Eleanor Chelimsky, *High Impact Anti-Crime Program* (Washington, D.C.: GPO, January 1976).

60. Association of the Bar of the City of New York and U.S. Department of Justice LEAA, *Nation's Toughest Drug Law: Evaluating the New York Experience* (Washington, D.C.: GPO, 1977).

61. James M. Tien and associates, *An Alternative Approach in Police Patrol: The Wilmington Split-Force Experiment* (Washington, D.C.: GPO, 1978).

62. W.A. Westley, *Violence and the Police: a Sociological Study of Law, Custom, and Morality* (Cambridge, Mass.: MIT Press, 1970, first pub. 1953).

63. Arthur Niederhoffer, *Behind the Shield: Police in Urban Society* (Garden City, N.Y.: Doubleday, 1967), pp. 98-99.

64. William D. Kroes, *Society's Victim: The Policeman* (Springfield, Ill.: Charles Thomas, 1976). For an early attempt to "postdict" performance from psychological tests, see Melany Baehr and associates, *Psychological Assessment of Patrolman Qualifications in Relation to Field Performance* (Washington, D.C.: GPO, 1968, LEAA Project 046).

65. Arline Brenner and James Levin, "Off-Duty Policemen and Bystander 'Apathy,' " in James T. Curran and Richard H. Ward, eds., *Police and Law Enforcement Annual 1973-1974* (New York: AMS Press, 1975).

66. Larry Tift, "The 'Cop Personality' Reconsidered," in Jim Munro, ed., *Classes, Conflict, and Control* (Cincinnati: Anderson, 1976).

67. Norman Wiener, "Effect of Education on Police Attitudes," *Journal of Criminal Justice* 2 (1974): 317-328.

68. Bernard Cohen and Jan Chaiken, *Police Background Characteristics and Performance* (New York: Rand Institute and LEAA NILECJ, 1972).

69. Richard Chakerian, "Police Professionalism and Citizen Evaluations," *Public Administration Review* (March-April 1974): 141-148.

70. Hans Toch, *Peacekeeping: Police, Prisons, and Violence* (Lexington, Mass.: Lexington Books, D.C. Heath, 1976).

71. Gene Carte, "Changes in Public Attitudes toward the Police," in James T. Curran and Richard Ward, eds., *Police and Law Enforcement Annual 1973-1974* (New York: AMS Press, 1975).

72. Elain Cumming and associates, "Policeman as Philosopher, Guide, and Friend," *Social Problems* 12 (Winter 1965): 280-288.

73. See Ostrom, "On the Meaning and Measurement. . . ."

74. This idea is considered by James T. Curran, "Emergency Human Service in the Urban Environment: Modernization of the Police Role," in Curran and Richard H. Ward, eds., *Police and Law Enforcement Annual 1973-1974* (New York: AMS Press, 1975); Bernard Garmire, "Police Role in Urban Society," in R.F. Steadman, ed., *Police and the Community* (Baltimore: Johns Hopkins University Press, 1972); and J.F. Ahern, *Police in Trouble* (New York: Hawthorne, 1972), proposes relieving police of traffic duty.

75. Richard Lundman, "Domestic Police-Citizen Encounters," in James T. Curran and Richard C. Ward, eds., *Police and Law Enforcement Annual 1973-1974* (New York: AMS Press, 1975), analyzes participant observation of nearly 2, 000 police calls, including many domestic calls.

76. Gerald E. Caiden, *Police Revitalization* (Lexington, Mass.: Lexington Books, D.C. Heath, 1971).

77. George J. Washnis, *Citizen Involvement in Crime Prevention* (Lexington, Mass.: Lexington Books, D.C. Heath, 1976).

78. Georgette Bennett Sandler and Ellen Mintz, "Police Organizations: Their Changing Internal and External Relationships," in Jim Munro, ed., *Classes, Conflict, and Control* (Cincinnati: Anderson, 1976), pp. 417-424.

79. I. Piliavin, *Police-Community Alienation* (Andover, Mass.: Warner Modular Pub., 1973).

80. David Norrgard, *Regional Law Enforcement* (Chicago: Public Administration Service, 1969), outlined fertile possibilities for coordination, consolidation, and other empire-building activities, with some examples from that early date.

81. Gerrie Kupersmith, *High Impact Anti-Crime Program: A Framework for Assessing Project-Level Evaluation Plans*, and *High Impact Anti-Crime Program: Sample Impact Project Evaluation Components* (Washington, D.C.: GPO,1975).

82. Donald Weidman, *Intensive Evaluation for Criminal Justice Planning* (Washington, D.C.: GPO, 1975).

83. See O'Neill B. Blair, *Criminal Justice Planning* (San Jose, Calif.: Justice Systems Development, Inc., 1976). Other ready-made frameworks for CJS planning are provided by Burt Nanus, "A General Model for Criminal Justice Planning," *Journal of Criminal Justice* 2 (1974): 345-356; F. Howlett and H. Hurst, "Systems Approach to Comprehensive Criminal Justice Planning," *Crime and Delinquency* 17 (October 1971): 345-354; see also Larry Hoover, "PPBS: Problems of Implementation for Police Management," *Journal of Police Science and Administration* 2 (1974): 21-30. These articles are reprinted in Jim Munro, ed., *Classes, Conflict, and Control* (Cincinnati: Anderson, 1976).

84. U.S. Department of Justice LEAA, *LEAA Two Year Evaluation Plan (FY '77-FY '78)* (Washington, D.C.: GPO, 1976). John D. Waller and associates, *Monitoring for Criminal Justice Planning Agencies* (Washington, D.C: GPO, 1976) discuss administrative and technical problems of LEAA monitoring. LEAA, *NILECJ Evaluation Program* (Washington, D.C: GPO, 1975), listed then-current evaluation projects, including model evaluation grants and projects to develop methodologies.

85. Daniel Glaser, *Routinizing Evaluation: Getting Feedback on Effectiveness of Crime and Delinquency Programs* (Washington, D.C.: GPO, 1973), from NIMH, deals with social-science issues in evaluation and questions of administrative institutionalization. See also M.D. Maltz, *Evaluation of Crime Control Programs* (Washington, D.C.: GPO, 1972), from LEAA NILECJ; *LEAA Evaluation Policy Task Force Report* (Washington, D.C.: GPO, 1974), and J.H. Lewis, *Evaluation of Experiments in Policing: How do you Begin?* (Washington, D.C.: Police Foundation, 1972),

86. LaMar T. Empey, *Model for the Evaluation of Programs in Juvenile Justice* (Washington, D.C.: GPO, 1977). For another useful LEAA nonpolice CJS

evaluation, see John J. Galvin and associates, *Instead of Jail: Pre- and Post-Trial Alternatives to Jail Incarceration* vol. 5 (Washington, D.C.: GPO, 1977).

87. W.C. Kimberling and J.T. Fryback, "Systematic Evaluation of Criminal Justice Projects: A State of the Art in the U.S.," *Journal of Criminal Justice* 1 (Summer 1973): 145-160.

88. U.S. Department of Justice LEAA NILECJ, *National Evaluation of the Pilot Cities Program* (Washington, D.C.: GPO, 1975).

89. Warner A. Eliot and associates, *Early-Warning Robbery Reduction Projects: An Assessment of Procedures* (Washington, D.C.: GPO, 1976).

90. U.S. Department of Justice LEAA (Washington, D.C.: GPO, annual).

91. Leonard Oberlander, ed., *Quantitative Tools for Criminal Justice Planning* (Washington, D.C.: GPO, 1975).

92. Dennis Palumbo and associates, "Individual, Group, and Social Rationality in Controlling Crime," in Stuart Nagel, ed., *Modeling the Criminal Justice System* (Beverly Hills, Calif.: Sage, 1977), pp. 73-78.

93. Jonathan Rubinstein, *City Police* (New York: Ballantine, 1973); George Kirkham, *Signal Zero* (Philadelphia: Lippincott, 1976); and Kenneth Muir, *Police: Streetcorner Politicians* (Chicago: University of Chicago Press, 1977). See also James Q. Wilson, *Varieties of Police Behavior* (Cambridge, Mass.: Harvard University Press, 1968). On police in city politics, see Leonard I. Ruchelman, *Police Politics: A Comparative Study of Three Cities* (Cambridge, Mass.: Ballinger, 1974). For learned consideration of fundamental and sometimes neglected police issues, see Harvey Goldstein, *Policing a Free Society* (Cambridge, Mass.: Ballinger, 1977).

94. On officer discretion, see Black, "Production of Crime Reports"; Joseph Godstein, "Police Discretion Not to Invoke the Legal Process," *Yale Law Journal* 69 (1960): 543-594; Kenneth C. Davis. *Discretionary Justice* (Urbana, Ill.: University of Illinois Press, 1976).

**Part II
Public Evaluations
of the Police**

3 Citizen Satisfaction with Police Services
Wesley G. Skogan

Introduction

Research on the distribution of government services reflects a "consumer" perspective on the relationship between citizens and their government. This perspective draws attention to equality in the distribution of public services to citizens, measured in terms of effort (expenditures), activity (delivery units), or performance (problem solving). As a consequence, social scientists have been observed lately measuring street-light lumens, road roughness, park acreage, ground litter, garbage pick-ups, and air pollution.

Herbert Jacob (1971) made an early plea for focusing these studies upon one of the key services provided by local government, order-maintenance. Most subsequent research has focused upon policing. The police deliver a spatially distributed service available more or less on demand to all citizens, one apparently aimed at dealing with a large but presumably finite set of social problems. Research on police services has utilized all three types of measures of its distribution, employing indicators of manpower and expenditure patterns, response time and clearance rates, and their deterrent effects. Recognizing that the police perform many functions other than crime control, studies of citizen satisfaction with police service also have been an important component of this research.

Some of these studies involved following up specific citizen encounters with the police in order to gauge satisfaction with that contact (Bordua and Tifft, 1971; Furstenberg and Wellford, 1973). Others have employed sample surveys to investigate the demographic correlates of perceptions of the police (Jacob, 1971: Hahn, 1971; Garofalo, 1977), the attitudinal correlates of different types of contact with the police (Walker and associates, 1972; Smith and Hawkins, 1973), or the apparent consequences of variations in the quality of service recieved by individuals who have summoned the police (Parks, 1976; Poister and McDavid, 1976). Police agencies have commissioned surveys to find out what people think about their policies (Boydstun, 1975; Institute of Policy Analysis, 1978). Researchers also have contrasted police and citizen perceptions of the police role in order to isolate sources of role conflict (Bayley and Mendelsohn, 1968; Rossi

Authorship of this chapter was supported by Grant No. 78-NI-AX-0057 awarded to Northwestern's Center for Urban Affairs by the National Institute of Law Enforcement and Criminal justice, Law Enforcement Assistance Administration, U.S. Deparment of Justice, under the Omnibus Crime Control and Safe Streets Act of 1968, as amended. Points of view or opinions stated in this document are those of the author and do not necessarily represent the official positions or policies of the U.S. Department of Justice.

and Groves, 1970) and have contrasted citizen perceptions of the police at different points in time to gauge changes in popular sentiment (Carte, 1973). These studies have been reported (in English) for the United States, England (Sparks and associates, 1978), Canada (Courtis, 1970; Koenig, 1975), and India (Bayley, 1969).

With only a few exceptions these studies have been cast entirely at the individual level, and fewer still have attempted to link individual satisfaction and dissatisfaction with variations in departmental policy or aggregate indicators of their performance. Those notable exceptions include the evaluation studies conducted by the Police Foundation (Kelling and associates, 1974; Schwartz and Clarren, 1977), the Rossi and associates (1974) reanalysis of the Kerner Commission's survey data for fifteen cities, similar work by Schuman and Gruenberg (1972), and the many reports by Elinor Ostrom and her associates at Indiana University (see, for example, Ostrom, Parks, and Smith, 1973) on the effects of institutional arrangements upon police performance. In these projects, survey data on individuals have been linked to district or jurisdictional attributes or experiments in an attempt to ferret out the impact of variations in policy and service upon citizen satisfaction.

This chapter reports a first mapping of another set of data which may be addressed to this problem. It is one step in the development of a model of individual and contextual effects upon evaluations of the police role in thirteen large American cities. I conceptualize the problem as one of partitioning the explained variance in evaluative measures, attributing it to a series of increasingly more causally proximate determinants of citizen satisfaction, and estimating the impact of each, using a block of indicators for each conceptual cluster. These clusters are sketched in their hypothesized causal ordering in figure 3-1.

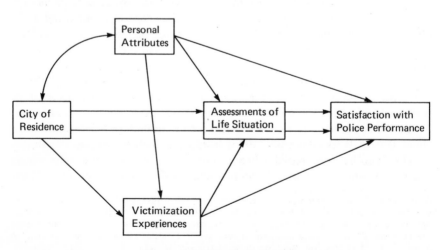

Figure 3-1. The Basic Model

In this chapter the specific policies and practices of jurisdictions which might account for variations in citizen satisfaction are not fully modeled; rather, I account for them as dummy variables reflecting the various communities represented in the data set. Analysis of the individual-level determinants of satisfaction with police services indicates that several interaction terms will have to be built into the complete model. Those interaction terms should be useful in explaining variations in perceptions of police service which do not appear to be linear and additive. Groups in the population clearly react to the police in different ways, but these differences are not the same from place to place.

The Data

The data utilized here were collected by the Census Bureau in surveys of the residents of thirteen large central cities, conducted early in 1975. In these surveys, respondents sixteen years of age and older were quizzed about their perceptions of crime and the police in addition to being questioned about their experiences with crime. Those attitudinal measures were administered in a random half of the 10,000 households contacted by the Census Bureau in each community, yielding data on approximately 9,500 respondents per city. For this analysis I have randomly sampled about 10 percent of those respondents from each city data set, or a total of about 12,000 individuals. These thirteen cities constitute one-half of all of those included in the Census Bureau's community survey program[1], and they reflect the general distribution of all twenty-six on the major variables of interest in this report.

Intercity Variations in Police Performance

In the surveys conducted by the Census Bureau central-city residents were asked, "Would you say, in general, that your local police are doing a good job, an average job, or a poor job?" There was substantial variation in citizens' ratings of the performance of their local police from community to community. In a few areas many residents indicated that the police did a good job, and in most a majority were willing to give them at least an average rating. Examining the proportion who gave their police top marks (see figure 3-2), the cities ranged from Newark (on the bottom, with less than 25 percent thinking their police were "good"), to Denver (which counted almost 55 percent in the highest rating category). Three of the five largest cities in the nation (Chicago, Detroit, and New York) fell below the average proportion who rated the police highly for the thirteen cities, 43 percent. Los Angeles was near the top of the scale, joining several smaller communities.

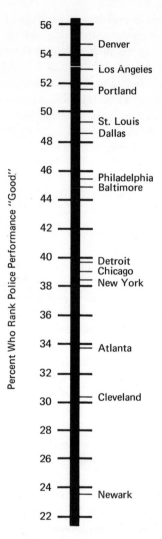

Figure 3-2. Intercity Differences in the Evaluation of Police Services

Individual Differences in Ratings of the Police

While the residents of these thirteen cities differed in their ratings of the police, part of that variation can be attributed to individual differences in the evaluation of police performance. When the personal attributes of individuals are strongly related to their ratings of the police, their distribution across cities (their "population mix") may account for aggregate differences in performance scores. This is known as a "composition effect" in survey analysis.

The strongest individual-level determinant of police ratings measured in these surveys was race, and these cities varied considerably in the proportion of their residents who were black. The individual-level correlation (theta) between race[2] and ratings of satisfaction with the police was 0.45.

It is not surprising, therefore, that cities in this group with large black populations were less favorably disposed toward the police. Newark ranked at the bottom of the scale in figure 3-2, but over one-half (53 percent) of this sample of Newark residents were black.

The strength of this distributional effect is indicated in figure 3-3, which depicts levels of police satisfaction separately for blacks and whites in the thirteen cities. The gap between the races is starkly apparent. Fifty-one percent of Chicago's whites rated the police most favorably, but only 14 percent of the city's blacks. Similar gaps can be observed in Los Angeles (59 and 24 percent), St. Loiuis (61 and 29 percent) and Philadelphia (56 and 22 percent). Much of the relatively high rating among the largest cities afforded Los Angeles's police department can be attributed to the fact that only 18 percent of the sample there was black.

Figure 3-3 suggests that the relationship between race and citizen satisfaction with the police is not altogether a simple matter, however. The police in Denver were highly rated by both black and white residents, with only a 5 percent gap between them. In Atlanta, on the other hand, blacks and whites agreed that their police were not very good (30 and 39 percent, respectively). Polarization between the races over the issue of the police varies from place to place, both in the size of the cleavage and in the level at which it is pegged. In Przeworski and Teune's (1970) terms, these cities differ *as systems* (things covary differently from place to place); the research question is, "How do policies affect both levels of satisfaction and polarization over ratings of police service?" The latter element may be a more important political question than the former.

Assessments of Life Situation

Another potential determinant of ratings of the police are citizens' assessments of crime trends and the resulting quality of their lives. However, the police perform many functions unrelated to crime control, and it is not clear that many persons blame them in particular for increases in the crime rate. Thus perceptions of the crime problem actually may not be strongly related to assessments of police performance.

The limited connection between the public's rating of the police and their assessments of the crime problem is suggested in Hazel Erskine's (1974) review of surveys since the 1960s which have asked something like, "Who is to blame for crime?" Categories like "failure of the police" or "not enough police protection" were chosen only by 2 percent of respondents to Gallup and Harris polls in the mid-1960s and "lack of proper law enforcement" (which might include the

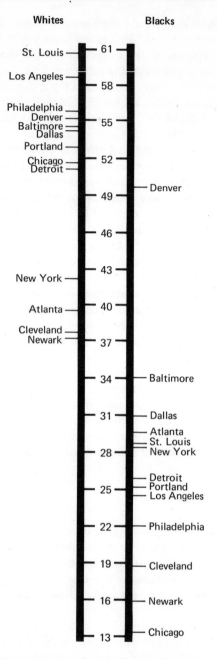

Percent Who Rank Police Performance "Good"

Figure 3-3. Race and City Differences in the Evaluation of Police Services

courts or correctional institutions) was chosen by only 8 percent in a 1972 national survey. Asked in the early 1970s to indicate "how much of a problem" various law-enforcement topics were, many more citizens (60 percent) ranked "lack of public support for the police" above "not being enough police" (26 percent).

Not surprisingly, questions about crime included in the Census Bureau's city surveys were not strongly related to evaluations of the police. For example, hopeful responses to an item inquiring whether the respondent's neighborhood was more dangerous, about the same, or less dangerous than others in the city were correlated (gamma) 0.26 with satisfaction with police service. In Cleveland (a city where the police are ranked low) 29 percent of the citizenry polled reported that they felt "very unsafe" on the streets alone in their neighborhood at night, while in more highly rated Portland that proportion was only 16 percent. Fully 57 percent of all Chicagoans felt that crime in their neighborhood was on the upswing, but only 38 percent of those in the sample from Dallas felt this way. There was a negative relationship between perceptions of crime or safety and opinions of the police. Those perceptions varied from city to city, and evaluations of police performance aggregated at the city level were affected. However, despite its hypothesized close causal proximity to police ratings, the effect was quite modest both at the individual and city level.

Victimization

The same conclusion describes the effect of the recent criminal victimization of either the respondents or members of their immediate families. The surveys were designed to produce reliable and valid measures of individual and household crime, and in each crime category those who reported being victimized during the previous year were less likely to grant the police a favorable rating.

One of the strongest individual-level correlations of this set is the relationship between living in a household which was burglarized and ratings of police performance. The nonparametric correlation between the two (gamma) was 0.19; however, the parametric Pearson's r which is employed in most multivariate statistical analyses was only .08 for the same set of data. The "difficulty" is that relatively few (12 percent) of these big-city residents lived in a home that was burglarized during the previous year. As a result, burglary victimization cannot statistically explain (in an "r-squared" sense) much variance in the more normally distributed measure of satisfaction with police performance. Victims—and especially repeated victims—were more dissatisfied than nonvictims, but few were in that category. Numerically, more nonvictims gave the police a poor rating than did repeated victims. The same problem can be observed among the victims of theft and violence, crimes which in general have a much stronger effect upon attitudes than do property crimes. Across these thirteen cities, only 2.1 percent of the respondents reported being robbed during 1974, and although they were quite unhappy about that experience the correlation between it and poor ratings of the police was only 0.06. Recent victimization and the resulting experiences of those who were involved may explain why they are more likely than others to dislike the police; however, it cannot explain why most of those who disliked the police fell into that category.

Multivariate Analysis

To this point, this chapter has focused sequentially upon the clusters illustrated in figure 3-1. It has examined the bivariate relationship between one indicator from each cluster and the dependent variable. This section of the report examines the impact of all of the measures of each conceptual cluster, taken together in a multivariate analysis of their simple linear impact upon ratings of police performance. The multivariate analysis indicates that the attributes of individuals in these samples had the strongest independent effect upon those ratings; next were the respondents' assessments of crime, followed by their city of residence and then their victimization experiences.

A number of indicators were available in the Census Bureau surveys of each of the conceptual clusters described in figure 3-1. Ten standard demographic descriptors (age, sex, race, income, home ownership, and so on) were employed in the analysis, as well as nine attitude measures (including questions on crime trends in the neighborhood, safety on the streets, and changes in behavior due to crime), eleven victimization counts (number of times robbed or burglarized, number of family members assaulted and the like), and twelve dummy variables accounting for simple city effects. Following the method described by Kerlinger and Pedhazur (1973), the blocks of variables were each entered last in a series of regression equations in order to tease out the statistically independent effect of each. This technique also allows us to specify the amount of multicolinearity in the data which cannot be attributed to any individual variable or block of indicators. The results of this preliminary analysis are presented in table 3-1.

Table 3-1 indicates, in the "addition to R^2" and "percent of explained variance" columns, the unique contribution of each block of indicators. In addition, the multicolinearity in the data—the contribution of R^2 which cannot be statistically attributed to any particular block—is indicated. It is the second most important factor in the data, reflecting the overlap between social background and attitudes. The major block of variables explaining satisfaction with police service is the social-background cluster, followed by the measures of perceptions of crime. The former contribute over 45 percent of the explained variance, the latter almost 15 percent.

Table 3-1
Variance-Partitioning Analysis of the Determinants of Evaluations of Police Service

Variable Block	Addtition to R^2	Significance of Effect	Percent of Explained Variance
Perceptions of life situation	2.1%	.01+	14.4%
Victimization	0.5%	.01+	3.5%
Background	6.8%	.01+	46.6%
City effect	1.3%	.01+	8.9%
Multicolinearity	3.9%	—	26.7%
Total	14.6%	.01+	100.0%

$N = 8,215$
$F = 34.12$

Modeling Policy

This preliminary analysis of the thirteen-city data suggests several courses of action. First, the effect of interaction terms can be modeled. For example, as I indicated above, polarization between the races over attitudes toward the police appears to differ from community to community. The correlation (tau-c) between race and attitudes toward the police varied in this data set between .02 (Denver) and .37 (Chicago). In the latter city, blacks and whites have a quite different image of the quality of service delivered by the police. This polarization is distinct from the *levels* of service delivered. Denver and Atlanta (at tau-c = .08) were polarized around race to about the same degree, yet ratings of the police by both races were twenty percentage points lower in the latter city.

This suggests that there is an interaction of some importance between city and race. To be black and live in Cleveland means to share with whites perceptions of low levels of service. In Chicago, Los Angeles, and Philadelphia, on the other hand, blacks perceive relatively low levels of service while whites are quite satisfied with what they receive. In New York, Baltimore, and Denver the races are less polarized and black perceptions of service are favorable, while in St. Louis and Dallas perceived service levels for blacks are relatively high, but so is polarization. While the simple effect of race on perceptions of the police is strong, the fit between race and service ratings could be improved considerably by inclusion in the model of interaction terms which capture these city-level differences in the explanatory power of race.

It is important to attempt to *explain* these interaction effects as well as take them into account in the individual-level analysis. To do this we must shift our unit of analysis to the city level, for polarization is an attribute of polities and not of persons. Table 3-2 presents some correlates of evaluations of the police and racial polarization over the police, by city. Although not all of them are statistically significant (which requires a correlation of about .48 for an "n" of 13), most are in the expected direction.

Three indicators of police department policy and service delivery are presented in table 3-2: black representation on the police force (the ratio of black officers per capita to blacks in the population per capita), the employment of civilians by the police, and the number of police per capita. The indicators of black representations and civilian employment are both correlated with reduced levels of racial polarization over police service (measured by the correlation between race and ratings of police service for each city), although the correlations are only modest in size. Note also the substantial effect of racial differences in experiences upon ratings of the police. Large differences between blacks and whites in the robbery victimization rate within each city are strongly related to interracial differences in ratings of police service. On the other hand, cities with relatively large police forces evidence substantially higher levels of racial polarization over police performance. This would appear to be an artifact of the fact that there are more police per capita serving cities with large black populations and high crime rates, both of which are themselves correlated with polarized attitudes about the police. Also, in cities with large black populations black residents are more underrepresented on police departments than are those in cities with

Table 3-2
City-Level Correlates of Aggregate Police Ratings, by Race, and Polarization across Racial Groups on Evaluations of Police
(N = 15)

City-Level Attribute	Correlation with Level Percent Think Police "Good"			Correlation with Polarization (tau-c)
	Whites	*Blacks*	*Total*	
Black representation on police force	.26	.49	.37	−.24
Police-percent civilian	.59	.37	.75	−.32
Police per capita	−.39	−.32	−.64	.63
City-percent black	−.34	−.48	−.74	.40
Robbery victimization group rate	−.43	−.17	−.38	.37
Difference between groups	.04	−.58	−.22	.68

Note: Correlations significant at the .05 level are boxed.

relatively small black communities, and fewer civilians are employed by those police departments. Figure 3-4 depicts the correlations between these key city and policy elements and levels of racial polarization over the quality of police service.

Variations in relationships can be observed in other components of the model as well. In some cities the relationships between perceptions of neighborhood safety and evaluations of the police are moderately correlated (tau-c's of about .30), while in other communities the two are virtually unrelated. This may be attribuatable to local politics, for cities may vary in the extent to which crime and the police have become "causally" connected by political entrepreneurs.

There also is some evidence of changes in the pattern of black and white opinions about the police over time, a change which points to greater levels of polarization over police service than in the past. In their reanalysis of survey data collected for the Kerner Commission in the mid-1960s, Rossi, Berk, and Eidson (1974) report that the city-level ($N = 15$) correlation between black and white

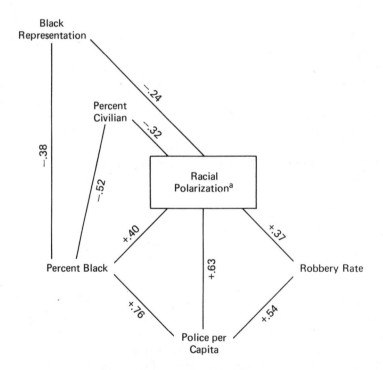

[a]Zero-order correlations. Polarization is measured by the correlation (tau-c) between race and evaluations of the police.

Figure 3-4. Relationships between Key Policy Variables and Racial Polarization over Evaluations of Police Service for Thirteen Cities

satisfaction is +.86; that is, although they differed in level of satisfaction, blacks and whites mostly agreed about which departments were the best and the worst. For these thirteen cities data collected during the mid-1970s reveal a similar correlation of only +.32, or a great deal of interracial discordance over evaluations of police service. On the other hand, Schuman and Gruenberg (1972), using the same data, also reported a *positive* correlation between police per capita and satisfaction with police service, both for blacks and whites; by the mid-1970s we find a *negative* correlation for both groups (table 3-2).

Again, the research questions which need to be answered are, "What policies explain variations in perceptions for service among blacks (and what presumably could raise those levels), and what policies appear divisive, or serve one group or community more satisfactorily than another (and presumably could be changed)? The macro effect of specific city-attribute, city-attitude, or attitude-attribute interactions (and others) can be accounted for statistically in the model sketched in figure 3-1. The long-range goal should be to replace the city terms employed there with indicators of policy and performance: hiring practices, response times, and the like. Different practices may have different effects on different types of individuals, and this signals interaction effects between city- and individual-level attributes. Blacks, for example, may be impressed by the hiring of black officers; victims, by rapid response times; the elderly, by visible police patrols. We see some evidence of this in table 3-2, which presents (weak) evidence that only blacks in these cities were affected by the racial hiring practices of police departments, while whites were primarily those impressed by the employment of civilians. This calls for specifying interaction terms for major subgroups which take into account city-level policies or practices which should affect their perceptions of the police. Modeling these effects would turn figure 3-1 into an explanatory rather than a descriptive model. An analysis model which attributes citizen satisfaction to some "Cleveland" effect is not at all useful to policymakers, while one which indicates the relative effect of nondiscriminatory hiring practices on black citizens' perceptions of the police could be quite useful indeed.

Notes

1. The cities were surveyed because they were among the five largest in the nation (Chicago, Los Angeles, Detroit, Philadelphia, and New York), or because they participated in LEAA's High Impact Cities crime program during 1972-1974 (the remainder). The cities are identified in Figure 1. The data were supplied by the Crime Surveys Branch, U.S. Bureau of the Census.

2. Whites were combined here with a small number (166) of those of "other" races (primarily Asians). They closely resemble one another in demographic and attitudinal profile.

References

Bayley, David H. 1969. *The Police and Political Development in India.* Princeton, N.J.: Princeton University Press.
——, and Harold Mendelson. 1968. *Minorities and the Police.* New York: The Free Press.
Bordua, David J., and Larry L. Tifft. 1971. "Citizen Interviews, Organizational Feedback, and Police-Community Relations Decisions."*Law and Society Review* 6 (November): 155-182.
Boydstun, John E. 1975. *San Diego Field Interrogation: Final Report.* Washington, D.C.: The Police Foundation.
Carte, Gene. 1973. "Changes in Public Attitudes toward the Police: A Comparison of 1938 and 1971 Surveys." *Journal of Police Science and Administration* 1 (April): 182-200.
Courtis, Malcolm C. 1970. *Attitudes to Crime and the Police in Toronto: A Report of Some Survey Findings.* Toronto: Centre of Criminology, University of Toronto.
Erskine, Hazel. 1974. "The Polls: Causes of Crime." *Public Opinion Quarterly* 38 (Summer): 288-298.
Furstenberg, Frank F., and Charles F. Wellford. 1973. "Calling the Police: The Evaluation of Police Service." *Law and Society Review* 7 (Spring): 393-406.
Garofalo, James. 1977. *The Police and Public Opinion.* Washington, D.C.: Law Enforcement Assistance Administration.
——, and Michael J. Hindelang. 1977. *An Introduction to the National Crime Survey.* Washington, D.C.: National Criminal Justice Information and Statistics Service, LEAA, Analytic Report SD-VAD-4.
Groves, Eugene, and Peter M. Rossi. 1970. "Police Perceptions of a Hostile Ghetto: Realism or Projection." *American Behavioral Scientist* 13 (May-August): 727-743.
Hahn, Harlan. 1971. "Ghetto Assessments of Police Protection and Authority." *Law and Society Review* 6 (November): 183-194.
Institute of Policy Analysis. 1978. *City of Eugene Public Opinion Survey: Citizen Preferences and Expenditure Priorities on Selected Public Services and Policies.* Eugene, Oreg.: The Institute of Policy Analysis.
Jacob, Herbert. 1971. "Black and White Perceptions of Justice in the City." *Law and Society Review* 6 (August): 646-668.
Kelling, George L., Tony Pate, Duane Dieckman, and Charles E. Brown. 1974. *The Kansas City Preventive Patrol Experiment: A Technical Report.* Washington, D.C.: The Police Foundation.
Kerlinger, Fred N., and Elazar J. Pedhazur. 1973. *Multiple Regression in Behavioral Research.* New York: Holt, Rinehart and Winston.
Koenig, Daniel J. 1975. "The Effect of Differential Judicial and Police Contacts upon Attitudes and Experiences with the Police." Paper presented at the Annual Meeting of the Pacific Sociological Association.

Ostrom, Elinor, Roger E. Parks, and Dennis C. Smith. 1973. "A Multi-Strata, Similar Systems Design for Measuring Police Performance." Paper presented at the Midwest Political Science Association Meetings, May 2-5.

Parks, Robert B. 1976. "Police Responses to Victimization: Effects on Citizen Attitudes and Perceptions." In Wesley G. Skogan, ed. *Sample Survey of the Victims of Crime.* Cambridge, Mass.: Ballinger, pp. 89-104.

Poister, Theodore H., and James C. McDavid. 1976. "Citizen Evaluations of Police Performance: Police-Citizen Interactions in the Context of Criminal Victimizations." Paper presented at the Annual Conference of the American Society for Public Administration, Washington, D.C.

Przeworski, Adam, and Henry Teune. 1970. *The Logic of Comparative Social Inquiry.* New York: John Wiley.

Rossi, Peter H., Richard A. Berk, and Bettye K. Eidson. 1974. *The Roots of Urban Discontent: Public, Municipal Institutions and the Ghetto.* New York: John Wiley.

Schuman, Howard, and Barry Gruenberg. 1972. "Dissatisfaction with City Services: Is Race an Important Factor?" In Harlan Hahn, ed. *People and Politics in Urban Society.* Beverly Hills, Calif.: Sage Publications, pp. 369-392.

Schwartz, Alfred, and Sumner Clarren. 1977. *The Cincinnati Team Policing Experiment.* Washington, D.C.: The Police Foundation.

Smith, Paul E., and Richard O. Hawkins. 1973. "Victimization, Types of Citizen-Police Contacts, and Attitudes toward the Police." *Law and Society Review* 8 (Fall): 135-152.

Sparks, Richard, Hazel Genn, and David Dodd. 1978. *Surveying Crime.* New York: John Wiley.

Walker, Darlene, Richard Richardson, Oliver Williams, Thomas Denyer, and Skip McGaughey. 1972. "Contact and Support: An Empirical Assessment of Public Attitudes toward the Police and the Courts." *North Carolina Law Review* 51 (November): 43-79.

4

Does Anything Work? An Evaluation of Urban Police Innovations

Scott H. Decker,
Russell L. Smith, and
Thomas M. Uhlman

The effectiveness of the police depends upon more than law enforcement. Police need to combine tangible benefits such as the suppression of crime with symbolic reassurances in order to maintain and enhance their legitimacy in the community. Recent research and theorizing has emphasized the importance of the symbolic role which the police have been called upon to play. Weninger and Clark have identified the important interrelationship that exists between the symbolic and instrumental aspects of police work.[1] In the former role, police act as agents of community pattern maintenance by providing social services that are outside legally mandated enforcement duties. The instrumental role consists of the traditional tasks ascribed to the police, such as making arrests and issuing citations.

The importance of the symbolic role has been underscored in recent empirical investigations of police activity. Bercal[2] and Reiss[3] provide evidence that police spend roughly 80 percent of their time in a symbolic capacity. Thus, citizen contacts with the police usually take place in a setting that is not enforcement-oriented. When police fail to provide symbolic support in these circumstances, their ability to function effectively in their instrumental, law-enforcement role may be severely impaired. Legitimacy may be withdrawn from one police role because of failure to fulfill the other. Rather serious consequences for both the community and the police may result if police legitimacy is eroded. Police depend heavily on citizen cooperation in reporting and solving crime. Black found that 76 percent of police responses in Boston, Chicago, and Washington, D.C., were initiated by citizen phone calls.[4] This, as well as similar findings, indicates that the importance of citizen input for the continued effectiveness of law enforcement cannot be overstated.

Awareness of the linkage between symbolic and instrumental success has resulted in efforts to improve public perceptions of the police in a number of cities. This article examines the success of two widely heralded innovations—police-community relations programs and citizen-police review boards. Public attitudes toward the police are compared in fourteen central cities. Evaluations of police services among both black and white residents are contrasted in cities with and without these programs. Several confounding factors that may affect citizen evaluations of the police are introduced as control variables in order to isolate programmatic effects.

Evaluations of the Police

Myriad evaluations of the police have been completed during the past decade. These studies can be divided into two general categories. One group has focused on the impact of organizational arrangements upon objective indicators of police performance, such as crime and/or clearance rates.[5] Variations in expenditures, training, manpower, equipment, patrolling practices, jurisdictional structures, and the like have been related to levels of criminal activity. Firm conclusions regarding the impact of police organization on performance have not evolved from these evaluations.. Research has been hampered by both a narrow view of police effectiveness and difficulties inherent in the use of official crime statistics as indicators of police performance.

A second group of studies has focused on the perceptions of the consumers of police services—the public.[6] These examinations have sought to cross-tabulate citizen characteristics such as age, race, income, and victimization with public attitudes toward the police. Representative of this research is the work of Ostrom, Parks, and Smith.[7] A critical assumption in their work is that citizen evaluations will more accurately reflect the totality of police services than will singular dependence upon crime rates. In a similar vein Furstenberg and Wellford have noted:

> Preventing crime and apprending criminals are, of course, primary goals of a police force. But to assess performance by this single standard is to discount many other services which police departments provide, services which help to maintain order but contribute only indirectly to crime control. It is our contention that both the police and the public would benefit if the criteria for evaluating performance were broadened to include these other activities.[8]

Despite differences in location, technique, and focus remarkably similar findings have emerged from the second group of evaluations. One of the principal themes has concerned race. The police are perceived positively by a majority of whites, but negatively by most blacks.[9] While generally critical, the harshest judgments are made by blacks who have had personal contact with the police. This finding is of particular importance in light of sizable black central city populations and the above average crime rates usually found in predominantly black residential areas.[10] The result is a serious law-enforcement problem: evaluations are lowest where the likelihood of contact and victimization are greatest.

Two programmatic responses to mitigate these negative attitudes will be explored here. In many cities, police-community relations programs and citizen-police complaint boards have been established on the premise that they would improve public perceptions of the police, thereby enhancing law-enforcement capability. Advocates of police-community relations programs in particular have recognized this linkage.

Police-community relationships have a direct bearing on the character of life in our cities, and on the community's ability to maintain stability and solve its problems. At the same time, the police department's capacity to deal with crime depends to a large extent upon its relationship with the citizenry.[11]

Further, police-community relations programs have maintained an explicit emphasis on improving relationships with those segments of the community who have the worst perceptions of the police and whose contacts with the police have likely been most negative.[12]

Citizen-police complaint boards have also been advocated by police reformers as a means for improving public perceptions of the police. The President's Commission Report on *The Police* gave explicit recognition to this, noting that dealing with citizen grievances in a satisfactory manner was an important step toward improving police-community relations.[13] These boards have generally been granted investigatory powers to review allegations of police mistreatment of citizens. The need for such bodies has often been seen as a key to successful efforts in altering minority perceptions of the police. Davis concludes that there must be "meaningful avenues of redress within the legal system" if the obligation to the criminal law is to be justified for blacks in American society.[14]

Both community relations programs and citizen-police complaint boards stress sensitivity and accountability to community needs as their primary goals. If they prove effective, the consequences of the apparent failure of standard law-enforcement techniques to increase public esteem while also combating crime will be circumscribed. If such practices fail to generate public trust and confidence, then law-enforcement agencies will need to reassess these programs before police legitimacy within the community, particularly the black community, is further undermined. Missing in the current inventory of studies is an evaluation of whether these reforms are associated with positive attitudes toward the police. The research reported here represents an attempt to assess the success these innovations have had in meeting their goals.

Data Base and Research Design

Two types of data are combined to test the hypothesis that attempts by police to foster community support will lead to more favorable citizen evaluations. Individual-level data on citizen perceptions of police practices, attitudes toward government officials, and evaluations of the police are drawn from a 1968 survey by Campbell and Schuman of residents in fourteen central cities.[15] Interviews were weighted in such a way that separate samples representative of black ($N = 2809$) and white ($N = 2950$) attitudes across these cities can be analyzed. Second, a cluster of aggregate, city-level variables are combined with these individual responses.[16] Indicators of the existence and nature of programs designed to improve citizen evaluations of the police, the level of criminal activity in each survey city, and the effectiveness of police in combating crime are collected for 1967.[17]

Two programs intended to have a positive effect on public attitudes toward police are examined.[18] The first is whether or not a city had a police-community relations program in 1967. In addition to its existence, the "commitment" of each department to improving community relations is measured by the year the program was started. The establishment of a citizen police complaint board is the second programmatic variable. Greater "commitment" or willingness by the police and other public officials to accept this form of public accountability is indicated if the board also has investigatory powers.

Other factors possibly influencing citizen attitudes toward police serve as control variables in the analysis. Official measures of crime were the basis for two. Threats to citizen safety in each survey city are indicated by the number of index crimes per person in 1967.[19] While these figures have shortcomings,[20] reported crime rates are useful indicators of relative differences in crime across cities and possible correlates of such differences.[21] Police effectiveness in dealing with crime is measured by the clearance rate that year.[22] Relatively high crime and/or low clearance rates may well negate the politive effects of police public relations efforts. The nature of police-citizen contacts and general citizen attitudes toward government may also influence evaluations of police. Police-citizen contacts are measured, first as the probability of arrest for blacks and whites in each city.[23] and second as a respondent's belief that police abuse occurs in his or her neighborhood.[24] Both a high probability of arrest and belief that police abuse is common should be predictive of a weakened police program-citizen evaluation linkage.

Two indicators of citizen-government relations are used: one is a measure of general trust in government officials[25] and the other measures the extent to which respondents believe public officials respond to their problems.[26] The effectiveness of police programs may well be indirectly influenced by a citizen's general reaction toward government authority and responsiveness.

The impacts of these police programs and this set of intervening variables are related to a single dependent variable—citizen satisfaction with police protection. Respondents were asked whether they are generally satisfied, somewhat dissatisfied, or very dissatisfied with the quality of police protection in their neighborhoods.[27] Because citizen protection is the basic and probably most important police function, response to this question is seen to reflect general citizen attitudes toward police.

Findings and Analysis

Since the data are ordinal in nature, gamma is used to assess the impact of the two innovations upon public evaluations of the police. The zero-order gamma coefficients portray the relationship between each of the police programs and citizen evaluations. Partial gamma coefficients illustrate the impact of the intervening variables upon the original relationship. Table 4-1 relates police-citizen programs to public evaluations for both the black and white samples.

Overall, the relationships must be judged weak, but suggestive patterns do emerge within each group. For blacks, the linkage between programs and attitudes is in the hypothesized direction; both the existence of programs and program commitment are positively, albeit quite modestly, related to more positive police evaluations. The establishment of these programs is more important than commitment level (length of time for community relations and investigatory powers for complaint boards) for black respondents. The use of control variables alters the original relationships little, if at all; police effectiveness and behavior, rates of crime, and blacks' feelings toward governmental authority, with the exception noted in table 4-1, fail to have mediating effects on the program-attitude linkage.

A different pattern is found for white respondents. The existence of citizen complaint boards and community relations programs has almost no relationship to public evaluations of police. Contrary to inital expectations, one of the program commitment variables, the comparison of complaint boards with and without investigatory powers, is inversely related to attitudes. Although tentative, this relationship may be the result of white dissatisfaction with police policies such as strong complaint boards that are perceived as primarily geared to improving relations with minority group members.

The mere existence of such programs may be hardly noticed by whites. Review boards with investigatory powers, however, are more likely to be associated with public controversy and criticism of the police. The highly publicized proceedings of these boards may project an image of excessive concern with the rights of those who have faced a history of discrimination at the hands of law-enforcement officials. There is preliminary evidence to indicate that programs designed specifically to improve police officer-minority relations engender feelings of resentment towards those minorities.[28] Such programs may be perceived by whites as an unnecessary accommodation to the black community.

In addition to these black-white differences, a noteworthy similarity across both racial groups surfaces. Police programs and citizen evaluations are higher among citizens with "low" levels of government trust. Apparently individuals who have rather modest levels of faith in government, regardless of race, can be favorably influenced by an environment where affirmative actions are taken by the police to improve their ties with the community. This finding may have important implications for other governmental agencies in urban areas, particularly in an era of general public distrust of government.

Despite these trends, one must ask why few strong relationships exist between these police program measures and citizen evaluations. Two general answers seem most germane; one is methodological; the other, substantive. Simply put, the full impact of these programs on attitudes may not be completely assessed

Table 4-1
Relationships between Police Programs and Citizen Evaluations: Black and White Respondents
(gamma coefficients)

Police Program	Zero-Order Gammas	Partial Gamma Coefficients																
		Clearance Rate		Crime Per Capita		Arrest Probability		Police Abuse			Govt. Trust			Citizen Complaints		
		Low	High	Low	High	Low	High	Low	Med.	High	Low	Med.	High	Low	Med.	High
Black Sample																
Citizen board	.14	.18	.06	.14	.15	.12	.14	.17	.13	.18	.18	.16	.11	.10	.28	.10
Community relations program	.13	.12	.09	.19	.02	.10	.14	.19	.16	.10	.32	.19	.13	.10	.22	.13
Citizen board commitment	.03	.12	.08	-.04	.04	.06	.06	.05	.04	.02	.03	.08	-.06	.02	.17	-.04
Community relations commitment	.03	.14	.00	.08	.02	.07	-.10	.01	.09	.01	.01	.07	-.03	.03	.11	.02
White Sample																
Citizen board	.02	.11	-.11	.08	-.10	.01	.16	.01	.07	.21	.33	-.02	.01	.01	.03	.01
Community relations program	.06	.11	-.06	.15	-.16	.10	-.16	.06	.10	.16	.30	.03	.07	.01	.12	.04
Citizen board commitment	-.16	.07	-.41	-.26	-.10	-.03	-.38	-.16	-.19	-.08	.04	-.12	-.24	-.15	-.25	-.17
Community relations commitment	-.02	.08	-.06	.08	-.14	.05	-.14	-.03	.03	-.11	-.04	.03	.02	-.02	-.15	-.01

by our data. Thus, the results reported here may understate the impact of programs upon evaluations of the police to some extent. Jacob has noted the impact which police contact has on citizen perceptions; negative evaluations are closely tied to past experiences.[29] To capture this relationship precisely would also require data reflective of individual perceptions of the programs themselves; final conclusions are simply not possible at present. Factors not included in the research design may also be confounding the analysis. For example, police-citizen contacts, poorly operationalized programs, and socioeconomic conditions may be suppressing the relationships. We can conclude, however, that the programs examined in this analysis have not had a major effect on the general police-community environment in this broad cross section of cities.

The second reason, substantive in nature rather than methodological, for the generally weak relationships may be that these programs are not important factors in shaping public attitudes toward police. It has been noted in this chapter that perceptions of the police, however much they may be related to other variables, are most affected by the nature of specific police-citizen relationships; a single negative contact may alter an individual's perception of the police and police programs in general. This contact may be observational in nature, or result from a personal or word-of-mouth experience. Campbell and Schuman found that blacks more than whites perceived abusive language, needless stop and frisks, and unnecessary roughness in their community, personally and among acquaintances.[30] When one of these incidents occurs, the impact of any community relations program may be severely undermined.

Furthermore it has been found that programs designed to improve citizen attitudes are neither as important nor as effective as the behavior of the individual officer.[31] Such shortcomings have been attributed to the location of these programs within separate divisions of police departments. This placement means that the responsibility for program implementation resides with a small and relatively isolated group not involved in day-to-day service delivery.[32] By way of contrast, Bordua and Tifft observe, "Police-community relations are, in large measure, a result of the every-day actions of patrolmen carrying out their duties on the street."[33] These findings may indicate that police-community relations programs do little to affect the variable most critical to evaluations of police— the individual officer.

A second reason offered for the apparent failure of these programs to meet intended goals may be found in their design and implementation. Their humanistic and benevolent nature has caused them to be broadly embraced. Although widely accepted, program design has generally failed to deal effectively with the complexity inherent in community relations. This shallowness has often resulted in programs which have been operationalized in only the most general of terms. As Kelly has noted,

> Current definitions of police community relations range across assertions
> that the phenomenon is an art, a form of race relations, a philosophy,
> public relations, image building, community service, community partici-

pation in police activities, and, in general, all behaviors and things done by police and citizens as they interact.[34]

This lack of specificity made program implementation more difficult and uneven.[35] Finally, failure to define programs in specific terms has made it difficult if not impossible to assess their impact upon the community.

In the end, it may be beyond the ability of the police to produce the changes expected. The innovations examined are clearly not going to affect basic socio-economic conditions of central cities. Some have contended that the conditions addressed by police-community relations programs and citizen review boards are not primarily law-enforcement problems, but conditions of political and socio-economic powerlessness.[36] If negative perceptions of the police are directly related to variables beyond the control of these officials, neither courteous behavior nor well-defined programs can change those perceptions.

Conclusion

Using a large urban data base, this chapter has employed the "consumer-oriented" approach to public evaluations of two police innovations. Specifically, the impact of police-community relations programs and citizen-police review boards on black and white perceptions were examined. The strong positive program-attitude linkage indicative of the symbolic benefits of both programs was not observed. Thus perceptions of the police do not appear to be related to the existence of these programs. Three interpretations were offered to account for the absence of a relationship: citizen interactions, poorly conceived programs, and the inability of such efforts to alter urban conditions that may be associated with negative attitudes toward the police. Two additional findings were suggested by the data. First, while attempting to improve relationships among minority groups, these programs may have had the latent function of creating negative reactions among whites. Finally, when control variables were introduced, greater programmatic impacts upon respondents expressing low levels of government trust were observed.

Notes

1. Eugene P. Weninger and John P. Clark, "A Theoretical Orientation for Police Studies," in Malcolm Klein, ed., *Juvenile Gangs in Context* (Englewood Cliffs, N.J.: Prentice-Hall, 1967), pp. 161-172.

2. Thomas E. Bercal, "Calls for Police Assistance: Consumer Demands for Governmental Service," *American Behavioral Scientist* 13 (1970): 681-691.

3. Albert J. Reiss, *The Police and the Public* (New Haven: Yale University Press, 1972).

4. Donald J. Black, "The Production of Crime Rates," *American Sociological Review* 35 (1970): 733-748.

5. Illustrative findings can be found in George L. Kelling and associates, *The Kansas City Preventive Patrol Experiment: A Summary Report* (Washington, D.C.: The Police Foundation, 1974); Elinor Ostrom and associates, *Community Organization and the Provision of Police Services* (Beverly Hills, Calif.: Sage Professional Papers in Administrative and Policy Studies 03-001, 1973); Richard Chackerian, "Police Professionalism and Citizen Evaluations: A Preliminary Look," *Public Administration Review* 34 (1974): 141-148; and Wesley G. Skogan, "Efficiency and Effectiveness in Big City Police Departments," *Public Administration Review* 36 (1976): 278-286.

6. For example, see Darlene Walker and associates, "Contact and Support: An Empirical Assessment of Public Attitudes toward the Police and the Courts," *North Carolina Law Review* 51 (1972): 43-79; and Howard Schuman and Barry Gruenberg, "Dissatisfaction with City Services: Is Race an Important Factor?" in Harlan Hahn, ed., *People and Politics in Urban Society* (Beverly Hills, Calif.: Sage Publications, 1972), pp. 369-392.

7. Elinor Ostrom, Roger B. Parks, and Dennis C. Smith, "A Multi-Strata, Similar Systems Design for Measuring Police Performance," presented at the Midwest Political Science Association Meetings, 1973.

8. Frank F. Furstenberg and Charles F. Wellford, "Calling the Police: The Evaluation of Police Service," *Law and Society Review* 7 (1973): 393-406. Copyright 1973 by the Law and Society Association. Reprinted with permission.

9. For example, see Ronald L. Carter and Kim Quaile Hill, "Criminals and Noncriminals' Perceptions of Urban Crime," *Criminology* 16 (1978): 353-371; Ilana Hadar and John R. Snortum, "The Eye of the Beholder: Differential Perceptions of the Police by the Police and the Public," *Criminal Justice and Behavior* 2 (1975): 37-54; Harlan Hahn, "Ghetto Assessments of Police Protection and Authority," *Law and Society Review* 6 (1971): 183-194; and Herbert Jacob, "Black and White Perceptions of Justice in the City," *Law and Society Review* 5 (1971): 69-89.

10. See, for example, Sarah L. Boggs, "Urban Crime Patterns," *American Sociological Review* 30 (1965): 899-908; and Michael J. Hindelang, *Criminal Victimization in Eight American Cities*

11. President's Commission on Law Enforcemnt and the Administration of Justice, *The Police* (Washington, D.C.: GPO, 1967), p. 144.

12. Herbert Jacob, "Black and White Perceptions of Justice in the City," *Law and Society Review* 5 (1971): 69-89; and Jack L. Kuykendall, "Police and Minority Groups: Toward a Theory of Negative Contacts," *Police* 15 (1970): 47-55.

13. President's Commission, *The Police*.

14. John A. Davis, "Justification for No Obligation: Views of Black Males toward Crime and the Criminal Law," *Issues in Criminology* 9 (1974): 69-87.

15. A detailed explanation of the sampling design and questionnaire used

can be found in Angus Campbell and Howard Schuman, *Racial Attitudes in Fifteen American Cities: Report for the National Advisory Commission on Civil Disorders* (Ann Arbor: Institute for Social Research, Univ. of Michigan, 1968). Data from fourteen of the fifteen cities in the original project are utilized in this analysis. Brooklyn was omitted because data on crime levels, police effectiveness, and police-community relations programs were not available. These data have been used previously to explore issues such as the importance of race in public evaluations of other city services, the roots of black alienation, and the impact of city size upon citizen evaluations of police. See, for example, Peter Rossi and associates, *The Roots of Urban Discontent* (New York: John Wiley and Sons, 1974), and Henry Pachon and Nicholas P. Lovrich, "The Consolidation of Urban Public Service: A Focus on Police," *Public Administration Review* 37 (1977): 38-47. Although not as recent as might otherwise be desired, these data still constitute one of the few available and comprehensive sources of attitudinal information concerning police.

16. Typically, studies of the police organization-citizen attitude linkage have utilized governmental entities as units of analysis. As a result, citizen views have often been aggregated in order to make them compatible with citywide or jurisdictionwide indicators of police performance; see Pachon and Lovrich, "The Consolidation of Urban Public Services: A Focus on the Police." In doing so, however, much of the variation among individual repondents has been lost. The alternative adopted here retains the richness of the individual-level data by ascribing to each respondent the characteristics of his environment. This approach, employed with increasing frequency when units of analysis problems are encountered, provides a contextual framework as scores on citywide variables expected to influence citizen attitudes (police-citizen programs, crime rates, police performance indicators) are assigned to black and white respondents. For a more detailed methodological discussion and other applications of this technique see Adam Przeworski, "Contextual Models of Political Behavior," *Political Methodology* 1 (1974): 27-61; and David R. Segal and Marshall W. Meyer, "The Social Context of Political Partisanship," in Mattai Dogan and Stein Rokkan, eds., *Social Ecology* (Cambridge, Mass.: MIT Press, 1974).

17. These indicators are measured a year prior to the survey to allow environmental factors time to influence citizen attitudes.

18. The data on police community relations programs and citizen complaint boards were obtained from *The Municipal Year Book, 1968* (Washington, D.C.: International City Management Assoc., 1968), p. 452.

19. The variable was computed by dividing the number of reported Index Crimes in a city by a 1967 estimate of its population. These data were drawn from *Crime in the United States, 1967* (Washington, D.C.: Federal Bureau of Investigation, 1968), pp. 177-178.

20. Marvin M. Wolfgang, "The Uniform Crime Reports: A Critical Appraisal," *University of Pennsylvania Law Review* 3 (1963): 708-738.

21. Scott H. Decker, "Official Crime Rates and Victim Surveys: An Empirical Comparison," *Journal of Criminal Justice* 5 (1977): 47-54; and Wesley Skogan, "The Validity of Official Crime Statistics: An Empirical Investigation," *Social Science Quarterly* 55 (1974): 25-38.

22. Data were obtained from the Uniform Crime Reporting Office of the FBI in Washington, D.C.

23. This measure was computed by dividing the total number of blacks and whites arrested by the total black and white population. As with clearance rate information, these data were supplied by the Uniform Crime Reporting Office of the FBI.

24. The "police abuse" indicator is a six-point index created from three questions dealing with police insults, frisks/searches without good reason, and unnecessary roughups of citizens within the respondent's neighborhood. For a complete description, see Institute for Social Research, *Racial Attitudes in Fifteen American Cities* (Ann Arbor: Institute for Social Reasearch, Social Service Archive, University of Michigan, 1973), p. 183.

25. Trust in government is measured by a seven-point index based on three items. Each respondent was asked whether government officials were "trying hard," "fairly hard," or "not hard at all." See Institute for Social Research, *Racial Attitudes*, p. 182.

26. Citizen competence is measured by a six-point index composed of two items—whether or not the respondent has called city officials with a complaint and whether or not the respondent could get city officials to act on calls about services. See Institute for Social Research, *Racial Attitudes*, 180.

27. See Campbell and Schuman, *Racial Attitudes in Fifteen American Cities*, 43.

28. John E. Teehan, "A Longitudinal Study of Attitude Shifts among Black and White Police Officers," *Journal of Social Issues* 31, (1975): 47-56.

29. Jacob, "Black and White Perceptions of Justice in the City."

30. Campbell and Schuman, *Racial Attitudes in Fifteen American Cities.*

31. See, for instance, David T. Bordua and Larry L. Tifft, "Citizen Interviews, Organizational Feedback and Police-Community Relations Decisions," *Law and Society Review* 6 (1971): 155-182; and Paul E. Smith and Richard O. Hawkins, "Victimization, Types of Citizen-Police Contacts and Attitudes toward the Police," *Law and Society Review* 8 (1973): 135-152.

32. Terry Eisenberg, Robert H. Fosen, and Albert S. Glickman, *Police Community Action: A Program for Change in Police-Community Behavior Patterns* (New York: Prager, 1973).

33. Bordua and Tifft, "Citizen Interviews, Organizational Feedback and Police-Community Relations Decisions," p. 156.

34. Rita Mae Kelly, "Generalizations from an OEO Experiment in Washington, D.C.," *Journal of Social Issues* 31 (1975): 57-86.

35. But the results of well-defined and administered programs, such as PACE

(Police and Community Enterprise) in San Francisco, have indicated even the steps noted above may not be sufficient to alter public perceptions of the police. See Eisenberg and associates, *Police Community Action.*

36. See, for example, Eisenberg and associates, *Police Community Action*; and Louis A. Radelet and Hoyt Coe Reed, *The Police and the Community*, Second Edition. (Encino, Calif.: Glencoe Press, 1977).

5 Police Patrol Allocation Algorithms and Police Effectiveness

Woodrow Jones, Jr.

Until recently there has been little effort or interest in identifying and evaluating means of improving police patrol practices. The patrol force is the backbone of all police services. It has become more important as police duties become more complex and numerous. Responsibilities of the patrol force have increased from the deterrence role of the foot patrol to the more specialized role of the special weapons and tactics squads. The patrol officer is not only responsible for the apprehension of criminals but also for such duties as searching for lost children, gathering information, and giving directions and advice. With such an overlap of responsibilities the cost of police services has continued to rise, creating an ever-increasing financial burden for city residents.

The increasing cost of policing has brought new demands for new methods and procedures for the efficient allocation of the patrol force. Since 90 percent of the police department budgets are expended for personnel and since about 50 percent of police personnel in most departments are assigned to the patrol function, it is reasonable to look to this function to furnish much of the material for improving the efficiency of the police service.[1]

The analysis of how cities might effectively deploy personnel is an important part of the planning of adequate service delivery. Planning at the patrol unit level has not been effectively integrated into the practices of police administration. Further evidence suggests that recommendations from the planning process are not very useful to the police administrator in the areas of preventive patrol, community relations, and political support.[2] However, the planned allocation of the patrol force is the only means to accomplish the policy objective of efficiency. The goal of this chapter is to provide a coherent overview of the problems of police allocation as well as current allocation algorithms. Through the critical examination of the major issues of patrol allocation it is our intent to explore areas where further experimentation and evaluation are needed.

Patrol Allocation Context

Consideration for the increasing cost of police is one among many factors in the allocation of police. Public pressures for crime prevention, property recovery, and problem solving are a part of the pressures assumed by the police administrator. Allocation decisions are difficult when the reported crime per capita in many cities has increased more rapidly than the demand on police services. The number of calls per patrolman increased by 30 to 40 percent and reported crimes per patrolman increased by 35 to 160 percent in some cities.[3] Thus the context of allocation decisions is just as important as the particular algorithm use for patrol deployment.

Patrol allocation can be defined as the entire process of determining the total required patrol units given the spatial and temporal assignments and the rules governing their operation.[4] Spatial considerations are important for the distribution of patrol units in an equitable manner. This has a direct relationship to response time, quality of service, and the ability to gather information. Spatial considerations include the spatial distribution of patrol units and the spatial design of the patrol sector. On the other hand, temporal considerations are important for the distribution of patrol units during tours of duty. Factors that are important for the temporal dimension include the availability of units, call-overload conditions, and response to nonpriority calls. Also the temporal design of the patrol sector is similar to the spatial design in that sectors can be configured to minimize travel time and distance for a patrol unit.

The rules and regulations governing the spatial and temporal dimensions of allocation decisions are made at the executive command level of the department, usually supported by the analysis of the planning department. Rules which equalize the workload, hazards, and experiences are of chief concern. Further, rules as to emergency allocations serve to routinize the crisis dimension of patrolling. The effectiveness of any manpower changes can be measured in the capabilities of administrators to use the rules and regulations to anticipate the consequences of a deployment of men and resources.

Given the complexity of the definition of patrol allocation the decision context requires a great deal of organization. The administrator must analyze and assess the needs not only of a particular sector but of all sectors simultaneously over time. It is his responsibility to reallocate and redeploy units on a regular basis. This requirement if fully implemented would result in the analysis of various types of inputs before the distribution decision could be made.

The statistical problems with such an analysis are overwhelming for a large urban city. The question of data inputs becomes paramount to the type of allocation algorithm used. The reliability of socioeconomic data can be easily questioned, as well as the availability of up-to-date crime data. Another problem is the ability of the planning unit to quantify the variables that are most useful for the analysis effectiveness. For instance, citizens' satisfaction with services is very difficult when most citizens do not have any objective criteria by which to judge the performance of the patrol officer. Finally, the epidemiology of crime and the service needs are difficult to measure over time, given the statistical data problems.

The conceptual problems are also important in any analysis of patrolling. It is difficult to transform many of the objective criteria into measurable performance criteria. For example, the deterrence of crime is not a clear objective in terms of performance. It is very difficult to reallocate units based on a criterion which cannot be measured. Another conceptual problem is the linkage between allocation policies and the reduciton of crime. Studies on allocation and deployment for prevention/deterrence and arrest are either inconclusive or indicate a low probability of impact on these goals.[5] The President's Crime Commission reported the probability of a patrol officer's observing a robbery in progress as being once in every fourteen years.[6] It would appear that there is the possibility of the impact of patrol's being negligible in regard to the major objectives of patrolling.

In allocation decisions it appears that police administrators are faced with the problem of institutional design in a turbulent environment. The conceptual and statistical problems created by the two dimensions of allocations have created political problems in regard to the possibility of experimentation in new allocation methods. It appears evident that police administrators are unwilling to make policy decisions that incorporate a sophisticated mathematical technique for allocating personnel who are expected to perform both service and prevention functions.[7]

Patrol Allocation Algorithms and Methods

A variety of algorithms and methods are used to provide preventive patrol as well as for response to calls for service. To be of maximum value, allocation methods should employ data that can readily be obtained, allocate on the basis of predicted future conditions rather than past conditions, and use several evaluation criteria, so that several policy-relevant aspects of each proposed manpower allocation can be adequately evaluated.[8] Focusing on the problems and values in analyzing the allocation processes that are currently being used will give further insight into the problems of allocation.

First, the traditional method of patrol allocation is universally based on an equalized workload formula sometimes called the hazard formula. This method utilizes the geography and crime analysis in creating a score for each patrol sector. The term "hazard formula" is most appropriate when the factors focus on crime hazards such as licensed premises, parks, and storefronts. The term "workload formula" is more appropriate when the factors focus on activities that consume patrol time.[9] In one case the formula equalizes the hazards and in the other there is an equalization of workload. Patrol sectors are designed to balance closely the workload or hazards among patrol units given the constraints of geography, natural boundaries, and preferred boundaries.

The actual allocation of patrol units is accomplished through a simple additive model. First, the citywide scores for the factors which are assumed to be important are collected from each district. To arrive at a single hazard or workload score for each area a weighting factor is multiplied times each ratio of the area score on a factor and the total score on that factor. The weighting factor usually indicates the relative importance of that factor in the total allocation of police. All weighted factor scores are then summed to get the total score for the area, which would indicate the number of patrol units assigned to the area.

The strengths of the traditional patrol allocation methods are few. The possibility of unsatisfactory allocations can be caused by the nonlinear and interactive nature of many of the variables used as factors. The ability to plan from a linear model is limited due to the lack of temporal considerations in the model. When time is not a factor the formula does not reflect future operational policies in terms of sector design. Also the nature of the weighting procedure is arbitrary in explaining in a systematic way the deployment policy which would best reduce response time, cross-sector dispatching, and preventive patrolling. Finally, hazard formulas are not relevant to determining the total size of the patrol force required to satisfy certain service-level criteria.[10]

Modifications of the basic hazard formula have been used in several police departments. Some have included time, types of calls, and shift and sector deployment in order to strengthen the basic model. A more innovative technique is team policing. Team policing is a deployment strategy based on geographical and functional assignment. The teams are usually structured along the lines of a workload formula and then are responsible for their own decisions about priorities. Another innovation is the specialized patrol. The specialized patrol is created by a mathematical technique which estimates the number of patrol units needed to answer immediately 85 percent of the predicted incoming calls for service in each sector. The rest of the patrol force is assigned to preventive patrol.[11] However, their deployment is limited by the variables used to determine the required number of patrol units. In fact, the question of the relative value of a patrol unit on preventive versus responsive patrol has not been addressed. Thus these aberrations of the basic hazards formula do not solve the basic policy issues created by the method but only suggest a reconsideration of optimization algorithms.

The second dominant factor in the allocation of police is the development of mathematical algorithms which are feasible and flexible in meeting the needs of a variety of police jurisdictions. Richard Larson's study of urban patrol analysis is a definitive work within this approach.[12] Larson experiments through a simulation with all the relevant dimensions of police allocation. Starting with a travel time estimation model applied to a simulation of the total system, Larson included Poisson arrivals, variable dispatch strategies, vehicle position simulation, and replicable call-for-service in a simulated environment.

The purpose in formulating this simulation model was to develop an alternative to the traditional models for allocation. Among the characteristics studied were the geometric shape of the beat, orientation of street grid, density of streets, and travel speeds. Given the assumptions that a patrol sector is regular in geometric shape and closely related in north-south and east-west travel speeds, then the algorithm minimizes the time in dispatch queue when constrained by the number of units available.

The allocation method developed by Larson appears to offer several advantages compared with the subjective hazard formula. Each variable that is thought to be important appears as a constraint or in the objective function. The nonlinear behavior of each variable is incorporated and can be a determining factor in any patrol sector. Finally, the stochastic nature of the police response system is fully incorporated in the model, and no assumption is made about the deterministic nature of any variable of the system.

Working from an entirely different approach, in contrast to Larson, Campbell has proposed a spatially distributed queuing model.[13] This model focuses on the design of the patrol sector and the specific travel time of a patrol unit. A specific travel-time matrix is constructed with the weighted average of the estimated travel time and historical call data of an area. By combining the service data for calls received and the travel-time matrix in a multi-server queuing model, Campbell was able to calculate the average time in queue. Thus, the travel-time estimate and the queue-time estimate give a response-time estimate which is used to demonstrate the effects of alternative geometrical shapes of different patrol sectors on (1) average response time, (2) equity of response time given the geometrical distribution of the patrol sector, (3) workload balance, and (4) average number of intersector dispatches.

Problems with Campbell's model are that it uses a matrix requiring a great deal of time-consuming calculation, use of estimations for the time matrix, and a false sense of accuracy. For increased accuracy the area under study must be subdivided so that the travel-time estimates can be handled in an efficient manner. The cost of subdivision of an area increases the likelihood of sampling and data-collection errors. To base the exactness of a queuing model on the estimations from the time matrix is defeating for a precise queuing model. Finally, the mathematical technique is far beyond the capabilities of most police administrators and cannot be quickly implemented in departments without computer facilities.

Both Campbell's and Larson's formulations for the allocation of police are not presently being used. This is not because of any decisions to avoid their use but rather because recurrent use is prohibited by the nonavailability of computer packages and there is lack of personnel to handle such sophisticated techniques. However, their conclusions tend to corroborate that knowledge of sector design and the location of patrol units are important for the measurement of effective police allocation.

Although these methods are effective in the allocation of police in an efficient manner the actual deployment of patrol units is the most important determinant of the outcome. Deployment strategies are just as important to the response time, citizen satisfaction, and overall evaluation of the effectiveness of the police in the reduction of crime. Such decisions as reassignment, repositioning, and intersector assignment are relatively unexplored areas of police patrol analysis.

Criteria for Evaluating Police Allocation Algorithms

Any strategy for the allocation of police must be consistently reevaluated for changes in patterns of crime and service calls. The systematic discussion of evaluation criteria and the methodological aspects of patrol resource allocation are only of limited value without real data from actual evaluations.[14] In surveying a number of large-city police departments, Kakalik and Wildhorn found existing evaluation methods based on data of very low quality. Further, personnel were not skilled in mathematical evaluative techniques to examine effectively the impact of a patrol algorithm.

All the algorithms we have discussed require a statement of both the policy objectives and policy constraints before any evaluative studies can be completed. Other relevant factors to consider in choosing criteria include measurability, statistical variability, policy sensitivity, degree of acceptability, and the degree to which program outputs rather than resource inputs are measured. Currently criteria vary widely and include command discretion, simple resource input measures, conglomerate hazard ratings, and the percentage of calls for service that cannot be immediately dispatched to a free patrol unit.[15]

The improved mathematical algorithms for the allocation of police can handle several of these problems simultaneously while guaranteeing that minimally acceptable levels of performance can be maintained. The comparison of values for each district can be disaggregated by time, sector, and sector demographics to assess the equitability of distribution decisions. Finally, the ability to simulate future experiences, given these previous events and allocation strategies, is entirely possible for the altering of data-collection methods, specific measures, and preferred goals.

In the examination of preferred goals we find the common political problems of evaluation that are characteristic of all policy evaluation. Traditional departments view the overall purposes of the patrol force to be as follows: (1) the prevention and deterrence of crime, (2) the apprehension of criminals, and (3) the performance of certain public services.[16] However, these goals are not clear as to the specific action that is to be taken by the patrol unit. Further, there is no correlation between a public service-type call and criminal apprehension. Thus the overall deterrence of crime is an immeasurable goal.

On the other hand, Larson's approach is geared toward the translation of all objective criteria into performance criteria that can be measurable. There are many performance criteria of patrol allocation, including (1) system response time, (2) system error probability, (3) system cost, (4) amount of preventive patrol, (5) probability of criminal apprehension, (6) citizens' subjective opinions, and (7) workload imbalance among police officers.[17] However, without extensive analytical work and experimentation, there is no assurance that these measures will actually examine the deterrence of crime or patrol activity. With the current limited knowledge it is not possible to predict how apprehension probability varies with alternative programs.

Kakalik and Wildhorn suggest an ideal set of criteria which would reflect true crime rate, true victimization rate, total social and economic impacts of crime prevented and deterred, plus criminal and public attitudes in relation to alternative police patrol programs.[18] These values would be measured citywide and would be an indicator of effectiveness. The relative efficiency of patrol operations would be indicated by the relationship between resources expended and the indicator of effectiveness.

It is apparent that the more systematic the allocation the more data collection problems planning units are likely to incur. These realities must be considered in the selection and evaluation of patrol allocation strategies. Thus the evaluation of a preferred set of criteria for evaluating patrol programs is entirely dependent upon allocation strategy and available data.

Conclusions

In the examination of patrol allocation practices we have found significant gaps in the knowledge of how to allocate patrol units efficiently. In discussing these gaps we found a conflict between mathematical explanations and the standard hazard formula. The more mathematical formulations remedy many of the mistakes which are found in the standard allocation practices. However, the limitations of present planning staffs and administrators to implement these techniques hinder the development of more effective patrol allocation practices.

Notes

1. G. Douglas Gourley, *Patrol Administration* (Springfield, Ill.: Charles L. Thomas, 1974), pp. 151-186.

2. James S. Kakalik and Sorrel Wildhorn, "Aid to Decisionmaking in Police Patrol: An Overview of Study Findings," *Police* 16:6 (February 1972): 41-46; Joseph H. Lewis, *Evaluation of Experiments in Policing: How Do You Begin?* (Washington, D.C.: Police Foundation, 1972), pp. 10-16.

3. Ibid., p. 44. See also James Kakalik and Sorrel Wildhorn, *Aids to Decisionmaking in Police Patrol*, R-593 (Santa Monica, Calif.: Rand Corporation, 1971).

4. Richard C. Larson, *Urban Police Patrol Analysis* (Cambridge, Mass,: MIT Press, 1972), p. 270.

5. See R.P. Shumate and R.F. Crowther, "Quantitative Methods for Optimizing the Allocation of Police Resources," *Journal of Criminal Law, Criminology and Police Science* 57:2 (1966): 197-206.

6. President's Commission on Law Enforcement and Administration of Justice, *Task Force Report: The Police* (Washington, D.C.: GPO, 1967).

7. Kakalik and Wildhorn, "Aid to Decisionmaking," p. 43; see also Richard C. Larson, "On Quantitative Approaches to Urban Police Patrol Problems," *Journal of Research in Crime and Delinquency* 7:2 (July 1970).

8. Lewis, *Evaluation of Experiments*, pp. 17-19.

9. Larson, *Urban Police*, p. 36.

10. Kakalik and Wildhorn, "Aid to Decisionmaking," p. 45.

11. See George L. Kelling and associates, *The Kansas City Preventive Patrol Experiment: A Technical Report* (Washington, D.C.: Police Foundation, 1974).

12. See also Jan M. Chaiken, *Patrol Allocation Methodology for Police Departments* (New York: Rand Institute, 1975).

13. See George L. Campbell, *A Spatially Distributed Queuing Model for Police Patrol Sector Design* (Cambridge, Mass.: MIT, Operation Research Center, June 1972).

14. Lewis, *Evaluation of Experiments*, pp. 17-22; also G. Hobart Reinier and associates, *Crime Analysis in Support of Patrol* (Washington, D.C.: Department of Justice, 1977).

15. Kakalik and Wildhorn, "Aid to Decisionmaking," p. 42.

16. See Frank F. Furstenberg and Charles F. Wellford, "Calling the Police: The Evaluation of Police Services," *Law and Society Review* 7 (Spring 1973): 393-406.

17. Larson, *Urban Police*, p. 31.

18. Kakalik and Wildhorn, "Aid to Decisionmaking," p. 43.

Part III
Analysis of Public Evaluations

6 The Public Service Production Process: A Framework for Analyzing Police Services

Elinor Ostrom, Roger B. Parks, Gordon P. Whitaker, and Stephen L. Percy

Interest in evaluation research is rampant in both academic and practitioner communities. This interest stems largely from increased concern about, and frustration with, the functioning of public agencies. Fiscal stringencies and political pressures have forced policymakers to reexamine both priorities and the mechanisms and structures by which policies are implemented.

Careful and complete evaluation of the performance of a public agency (or even part of its performance) is, however, no easy task. Probably the greatest hindrance to evaluating the performance of public agencies is the problem of identifying and measuring an agency's output and its effects upon community conditions. Yet we must be able to specify what is being produced and how it is being produced to evaluate agency performance.

In this chapter a model of the public service production process is presented and applied to the case of police service delivery. The model identifies a production flow through which organizational arrangements structure inputs into activities that produce outputs and outcomes. With a model of this type, the components of the production process may be identified and their impact on performance traced. Only with greater comprehension of the process by which public services are produced can we hope accurately to evaluate public agencies.

The evaluation of public agencies must be related to the process through which organizational arrangements lead to the production of specific goods and services. Organizational arrangements are the set of decision-making rules for producing goods and services. For police these arrangements include the agencies involved—the way these agencies divide up their work, their size and internal authority structure, the extent of citizen access and control, and other structural variables.

Organizational arrangements affect the particular production strategies utilized by public agencies. In choosing production strategies, agency officials make decisions concerning the inputs to be utilized and the activities to be undertaken

The research was funded by the National Science Foundation (Research Applied to National Needs Division) under Grant NSF GI-43949. The authors gratefully acknowledge this support. Any findings, inferences, views, or opinions expressed herein are, however, those of the authors and do not necessarily reflect those of the National Science Foundation.

by agency personnel. Inputs may be defined as the resources utilized in a production process. Inputs in the public sector include the number and type of employees, the physical plant, and the supplies and materials utilized. In the case of the police, common input units include police officers, patrol cars, and radios.

Activities are the processes that convert these inputs into outputs. In the delivery of police services, activities include patrolling, investigating cases, talking with juveniles, making out reports, and processing evidence. Through activities, inputs are converted into outputs, which are the direct results of some set activities. An arrest is the output of specific investigative activities—questioning witnesses and suspects, examining the scene of a crime, processing evidence, and others. Similarly, the determination of the chemical nature of a substance is the result of a series of chemical tests. Taken together, these components of the production process may be arrayed schematically as follows:

The aggregate output of a public agency is the summation of individual outputs over some specific time period. To understand a production process we need to consider the flow of outputs over time. For a year's period the number of arrests, the number of chemical substances identified, the number of traffic accidents investigated, and the number of case reports filed are typical police outputs.

Evaluation of the performance of public agencies requires more than analysis of their outputs, however. Outputs may have little impact on the citizens who are supposed to benefit from their production. Further, some outputs may make things worse rather than better. The consequences of outputs—which we define as outcomes—must also serve as a basis for evaluating public organizations.

Outcomes may be divided into two types: objective and subjective. Objective outcomes may be defined as the impact of the outputs of public agencies upon general community conditions. For example, a decrease in a community's crime rate could be an objective outcome associated with police crime-solving activities and arrests. It is important to note that the outputs of police agencies are not the only factors affecting objective outcomes. Socioeconomic conditions such as unemployment rates, income levels, and age distributions are also likely to have impact on crime rates. Also, other public agencies simultaneously influence objective community conditions. Objective outcomes, then, result from many factors that make assessment of the unique impact of police outputs on objective community conditions quite difficult.

Subjective outcomes are defined as the impact of public agency outputs and objective outcomes upon citizens. Specifically, subjective outcomes are the perceptions and evaluations of public agencies, their outputs, and their objectives by individual citizens in the community. The arrest rate of a police department may affect citizen perception of safety and/or citizen evaluation of police performance.

Considering all of these factors, the public service process may be schematically expanded to include these outcome components:[1]

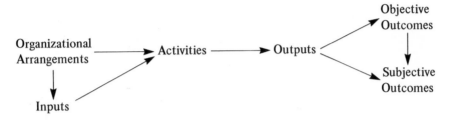

Citizen activities may affect both the output and outcomes of public agencies. Citizens in some neighborhoods may lock their doors, while those in other areas do not. In this way citizens may affect victimization rates and, thus, objective outcomes. Citizens may also call the police about a victimization in progress or give evidence that leads to the arrest of a felon. In these instances citizen activities supplement police activities in the production of an output, the arrest. Citizens, then, in some instances become coproducers with police through the contribution of their activities.[2] The activities of citizens influence public agency outputs, objective community conditions, and citizen perceptions. It should be noted that citizen activities, like those of public agencies, may not always lead to positive outcomes. Citizens may attempt to thwart the efforts of police by actively destroying evidence or giving false information.

A concrete example of the public service process in operation will be useful to tie these concepts together. A set of police activites related to crime solving is presented in table 6-1. Both police and citizen activites operate to produce outputs like arrests or the return of stolen property. For example, the arrest of a burglar could involve the reporting of the crime by citizens, the provision of information (for example, a careful and full description of the burglar), police questioning of suspects and witnesses, chemical substance analysis, lifting and comparing of fingerprints, and other activities. An objective outcome of the arrest is its affect on the crime rate. The arrest may also affect the perception of safety by some citizens and/or their evaluation of police performance in solving crime.

Several other factors also affect police outputs and outcomes. These include the service conditions in which an agency operates and the individual characteristics of citizens and of police officers. With respect to police services, service conditions include housing density, the income of residents, distribution of racial and

Table 6-1
An Example of the Police Production Process: Crime Solving

Inputs	Activities	Outputs	Objective Outcomes	Subjective Outcomes
Police	*Police*	Arrests (crimes cleared by arrest)	Warrants issued/ warrants applied for	Citizen perception of ability of police to solve crimes
Patrol officers	Responding to a victimization call	Return of stolen property	Arrests that survive the first judicial screening	Citizen satifaction with police crime-solving ability
Patrol vehicles	Questioning suspects and witnesses	Response time to the call for service	Crime rate	Citizen level of fear of future losses through crime
Detectives	Searching for stolen property			
Crime lab personnel and equipment	Lifting fingerprints			
Dispatch personnel and equipment	Crime lab analysis			
	Filling out crime report			
	Checking identification against criminal files			
Citizens	*Citizens*			
Time and effort in testifying, reporting, observing activities in neighborhood	Informing the police of a crime			
	Providing detailed evidence			
	Testifying and serving as a witness			
	Careful preservation of the crime scene			

age characteristics, traffic patterns, commercial and industrial activities, and related factors. Two departments with the same initial resources, utilizing similar production strategies, will have different outputs and outcomes if the neighborhoods they serve vary significantly in terms of service condition variables.

The individual characterisitics of citizens and of police officers affect the type of activities each will adopt. Older citizens who have previously experienced a victimization may be more likely to take self-protective activities than younger citizens without adverse experiences with crime. It is often assumed that more highly educated police officers will conduct themselves more effectively than their less educated colleagues. Individual characteristics are essential variables for any analysis of individual activity. Such characteristics may often have more impact than organizational arrangements on a person's activity.

All of these factors are synthesized in figure 6-1. Organizational arrangements for policing are posed as affecting both the kinds and amounts of police activity and citizen self-protective activity in a community. These activities pro-

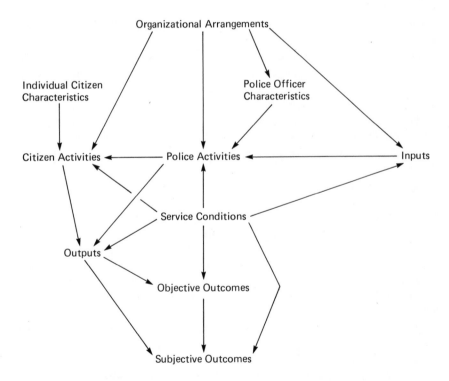

Figure 6-1. Organizational Arrangements and the Service Production Process

duce outputs such as arrests and streets patrolled. Outputs in turn are posited to influence outcomes in the community. The differences in outputs among communities should be related to differences in objective and subjective outcomes—community safety and citizens' perceptions and evaluations. Service conditions are shown to affect most components of the service production process.

Once the components of the service production process are more clearly identified and understood, then the measurement and evaluation of agency performance can be undertaken. The first step in measurement is the development of empirical indicators of the concepts in the model. Some indicators for police services are listed in table 6-2; many other types of indicators are possible. Limitations of research methodology may prevent empirical measurement of certain concepts. For example, one cannot directly measure the amount of crime *not* committed because of preventive patrol or the number of traffic accidents avoided because of traffic patrol. In these cases other measures must be used; the level of crime in the community might be used as an inverse indicator of police ability to deter and/or solve crimes.

Evaluating performance can be achieved by examining agency outputs and outcomes according to specified criteria and stipulating the relationship between these results and the activities and inputs that produce them. If a researcher is interested in evaluating performance in terms of an equity principle, the distribution of outputs and outcomes across some area or population would be examined. The performance of agencies can be evaluated according to the criteria of efficiency by comparing the benefits associated with outputs and outcomes with costs of production. Other types of evaluative criteria, such as responsiveness, can be used in evaluating performance of public agencies.[3]

Evaluation research should be more than a tool to provide an assessment of a given agency's performance at a given point in time. By comparing the production strategies and organizational arrangements of an agency over time, or of multiple agencies in a cross-sectional design, we can begin to learn about the relationship of strategies and arrangements to performance. We might determine, for example, that highly centralized and specialized police departments are more effective in investigating crimes and are less effective in handling family disputes. Departments arranged in other ways could have very different performance. Findings about the relationships of organizational arrangements to performance are of crucial concern to policymakers who attempt to achieve certain community goals and interests.

The challenge of evaluation research is to examine and compare the outputs and outcomes of agencies utilizing different organizational arrangements and production strategies. Evaluation research needs to consider performance in light of a number of criteria. With the findings from evaluation research we can design and modify public agencies so as to improve their performance according to community needs, preferences, and resources. Conceptual understanding of the service production process is an important first step to productive evaluation research.

Table 6-2
Sample Indicators

Organizational Arrangements

1. Size
   Number of full-time employees
   Number of full-time sworn officers
   Number of part-time employees and volunteers

2. Departmental Autonomy
   Number of services department performs independently from other agencies

3. Scope of Patrol Officer Activities
   Number of direct services that patrol officer provides

4. Authority Structure of Department
   Number of ranks in departments
   Proportion of personnel in each rank
   Presence and level of supervision of patrol officers

5. Citizen access to Department
   Proportion of neighborhood residents who complain directly to police regarding problem
     with police services
   Presence of precinct stations and/or storefront operations
   Citizen participation in police policymaking

Inputs

1. Revenues
   Percent of general fund allocated to police
   Amount of federal and state grants to department

2. Capital
   Number of patrol and traffic vehicles
   Number of portable radios
   Number of weapons
   Extent of crime laboratory facilities

3. Expenditures
   Total salaries to sworn personnel
   Total expenditure for police vehicles
   Expenditures allocated to types of services (for example, patrol, traffic)

4. Manpower
   Number of full-time employees
   Number of sworn personnel
   Number of part-time and volunteer personnel
   Number of employees of each rank

Police Activities
   Number of cars on patrol per shift
   Number of reports written
   Number of citizens referred to social service agencies
   Number of chemical substances analyzed
   Number of calls for service handled
   Police officer actions in encounter with citizens

Citizen Activities
   Number of calls reported to police
   Number of suspects described
   Number of homes where extra security locks added
   Percent of homes that installed burglar alarm system
   Percent of homes where property marked with ID markings

Outputs
   Arrest rates by type of crime
   Average response time by type of crime
   Traffic citation rates
   Proportion of family argument cases where argument is settled by police
   Proportion of crimes cleared by arrest
   Proportion of thefts, robberies, and burglaries where stolen property returned

Objective Outcomes
   Victimization rates by type of crime
   Types of arrests that survive first judicial screening
   Traffic accident rates
   Complaint rates about police officer actions

Subjective Outcomes
1. Citizen Perceptions
   Perceived safety of neighborhood
   Perceived response time by police when called
   Perceived safety from being robbed, burglarized, vandalized
   Perceived honesty and courtesy of police
   Perceived change in crime rate in neighborhood

2. Citizen Evaluations
   Rating of police services in general
   Rating of police services in particular case
   Rating of equality of treatment of police
   Rating of police services in the neighborhood

Notes

1. Many researchers involved in evaluation research have in recent years begun to develop similar types of input-output-outcome models. For example, see David Greytak, Donald Phares, and Elaine Morley, *Municipal Output and Performance in New York City* (Lexington, Mass.: Lexington Books, D.C. Heath, 1976); and A. Allen Schmid, "Conceptualization of Government Program Impacts: Inputs vs. Impact Budgets" (Agricultural Economics Report No. 311, East Lansing, Mich.: Michigan State University, September 1976).

2. Viewing citizens as coproducers of police (and other social) services is a rather novel and important aspect of our approach. We have discussed this coproduction in several recent works, including Vincent Ostrom and Elinor Ostrom, "Public Goods and Public Choices," in E.S. Savas, ed., *Alternatives for Delivering Public Services: Toward Improved Performance* (Boulder, Colo.: Westview Press, 1977), pp. 7-49; Gordon P. Whitaker, "Size and Effectiveness in the Delivery of Human Services" (Bloomington, Ind.: Indiana University, Department of Political Science, Workshop in Political Theory and Policy Analysis, Technical Report T-17); Frances P. Bish and Nancy M. Neubert, "Citizen Contributions to Community Safety and Security," in Mark S. Rosentraub, ed., *Financing Local Government: New Approaches to Old Problems.* (Ft. Collins, Colo.: Western

Social Science Association, 1977). See also the chapter by Stephen L. Percy, "Citizen Coproduction of Community Safety," in this volume.

3. These authors have used the concepts of inputs, outputs, and outcomes to operationalize four evaluative criteria: effectiveness, equity, efficiency, and responsiveness. See Elinor Ostrom, Roger B. Parks, Gordon P. Whitaker, and Stephen L. Percy, "Evaluating Police Organization," *Public Productivity Review* (forthcoming, 1979).

7

A Critique of Economic Analysis in the Criminal Justice System

John E. Monzingo

The application of microeconomic analysis to policymaking, known as public choice theory,[1] has grown in influence in the 1970s. This is not only true in areas of public administration but in policymaking in the field of criminal justice as well. Perhaps the most dramatic application of this type of analysis in the criminal justice system was the use of Isaac Ehrlich's article on the deterrent effect of the death penalty[2] in *Fowler* v. *North Carolina*.[3] The subsequent controversy over the validity of the findings in that article is one of the most heated in criminal justice today.[4]

As a fresh approach to the problems of the criminal justice system, the economists have much to offer in the way of new insights and untried solutions to problems. For instance, the economists' suggestion that the seriousness of the crime be measured by the harm done—while not without problems, as will be pointed out later—might furnish a much more objective definition of crime than is now available. Also, the recommendation that the level of crime-suppressing activity be determined by weighing the direct costs of crime against the cost of suppression might be helpful in making more efficient use of our limited resources. Finally, the economists' suggestion that compensation of those harmed rather than the exclusion of evidence be used to control official misbehavior might prove helpful.

These are only some of the suggestions made by economists as a result of their applying economic analysis to the criminal justice system, and they at least ought to be given serious consideration. But, once valuable contributions are recognized, it must be added that the use of economic analysis and the conclusions derived from it might be dangerous. Those who do not understand the assumptions on which the analysis is based and the biases these assumptions introduce into the policy recommendations may apply the analysis and conclusions inappropriately.

Criticism of microeconomic analysis is not new or unique.[5] However, criticisms of this approach tend to be very general. They point out that certain biases exist and that the conclusions reached are often the direct consequences of these biases, but they do not specifically indicate how these biases are introduced. The purpose of this chapter is to point out some of the more important biases and show how they are introduced into the analysis.

Bias is introduced by those who use economic analysis when they adopt methodological individualism, when they shift from methodological individualism to normative individualism, by the special meaning they give the word "freedom," by the way the assumptions they adopt regarding the existing distribution of wealth influence concepts critical to their methodology, and as an inevitable result of adopting a methodology which is rigorous and precise.

Methodological individualism is the assumption that all social phenomena can be reduced to individual behavior.[6] Group behavior, according to this view, is no more and no less than a function of individual behaviors. This view denies or ignores the facts that the social context in which the individual acts is significant for that action. It also ignores the effects which techniques of mass manipulation can produce. Ignoring the effect of the social context on individual action results in the belief that the individual is totally responsible for his actions; and this, along with the belief that individuals act on the basis of a calculation of costs and benefits, justifies the contention that punishment deters.

Whether or not punishment deters crime is not in question here. What is questioned is whether the assumptions economists make about the motivation of human behavior predispose them to accept one answer rather than another. The uniformity of opinion among economists and the vehemence with which they argue their position suggest that they do. It appears that for most economists the question of the deterrent effect of punishment is not an open one. One, after quoting Jack P. Gibbs approvingly: "The point is that some sociologists do not treat the general question of deterrence as an open one,"[7] immediately adds, "Punishment does function as a deterrent."[8]

If the adoption of methodological individualism introduces certain biases, the failure of economists to apply it consistently introduces others. Economists confuse methodological individualism with normative individualism and alternately use both. Which they use depends on their immediate purposes. They assume not only that social phenomena may be totally explained in terms of individual behavior, but also that the individual is the sole judge of what is good for him (this may be implicit in the first assumption) and that those individual preferences ought to be respected. Whatever one may think about the proposition that individual preferences ought to count, it cannot be denied that this proposition interjects a normative element into the methodology. A blatant example of the interjection of values into what is claimed to be an objective consideration of problems associated with public policymaking appears in Gordon Tullock's *The Logic of the Law*, in which he claims to have constructed an ethical system without making ethical judgments.[9]

In a society such as ours, where there is a high degree of agreement with the proposition that individual preferences ought to be given serious consideration, the inclusion of such a widely shared norm does not seem to present much of a problem for practical application. Indeed, this stress on freedom probably accounts for much of the appeal of the methodology. But there is a catch. Economists do not mean the same thing when they use the term freedom as is meant when the term is used in casual conversation. In everyday usage, the term freedom carries with it a natural rights connotation. The Declaration of Independence states that liberty is one of the unalienable rights with which God has endowed all men. For the man on the street, freedom is something which all share equally, or at least ought to share equally. For the economist, however, one is free only in relation to the wealth one possesses.

Economists arrive at this conclusion in the following manner. They start by observing that the earth is such that it cannot provide each person with everything he could possibly wish for. People prefer more than can be produced. As a consequence, some method has to be devised by which preferences are ranked according to priority. If it is agreed that the end to be achieved in allocating scarce resources is the maximization of individual happiness, and if it is recognized that one individual might prefer a particular thing more strongly than another person, then a reasonable system of allocation might be based on strength of preference, with scarce goods going to those who prefer them most strongly. A problem immediately comes to mind. How would it be possible to measure true preferences when individuals would have an incentive to exaggerate their preferences in order to gain more scarce goods? The solution to this dilemma suggested by economists is to require individuals to indicate their preferences in terms of how much of other things they would be willing and able to give up to attain the thing desired. This, simply stated, is what economists refer to as alternative costs. Note, however, that once this means of setting priorities is accepted, the preferences of each individual are no longer equal to those of every other individual. If preferences are given priority according to what one is willing and able to give up, those who have more to give up will have a distinct advantage. In other words, the preferences of the wealthy are given priority over the preferences of those who command fewer resources. This fact has led one writer to refer to the use of economic analysis in policymaking not as "public choice theory" but as "public choice-property rights theory."[10]

Economic analysis is biased heavily toward the existing distribution of wealth in other ways. This bias is intimately connected with two critical concepts used by economists in the policy area, externalities and the Pareto optimum.

Externalities are either costs or benefits imposed on individuals by the actions of others concerning which the individuals on whom the costs or benefits are imposed have no role in the decision-making which results in said costs or benefits. Another term for external costs is harm. We have already noted that economists define crime in terms of harm and that harm may be a more objective way of defining crime than the definitions now in use. The problem is that harm is directly related to existing property or other rights established by society. If I deprive you of the use of property, whether or not I have harmed you depends on which of us owns the property. Since the distribution of rights in society is determined through the political process, the definition of crime as harm is not purely objective, but has important political dimensions.

The adoption of the Pareto optimum as a standard by which the desirability of policies is judged is also biased toward the status quo. Usually economists favor the allocation of goods through a market system in which those who possess the most wealth have an advantage. But even the most enthusiastic supporter of the market will admit that the marketplace must sometimes be supplemented by public action. The problem at these times becomes one of choosing between alternative public policies. Economists reject the political process as a means of doing this.[11] They would prefer instead that the policy choices be made according to objective criteria, and they propose the Pareto optimum as such an objective measure. Simply stated, any change in policy which results in at least one person's being better off and no one's being worse off meets the definition of a Pareto optimum. The use of the Pareto test is justified because it is claimed to be a standard which does not require intersubjective evaluation of preferences. If at least one person is better off and no one is worse off, no weighing of preferences of those who will gain against the preferences of those who will lose will be required.

There are several problems associated with the Pareto optimum, but here the focus will be on two of them which introduce normative biases.[12] The first problem is one which arises from misuses of the Pareto test, and the second problem is one which questions the usefulness of the concept no matter how it is used.

Theoretically there can be three types of changes in condition: (1) those which are harmful to some and helpful to none, (2) those which are harmful to some and helpful to others, and (3) those which are helpful to some and harmful to none. It is possible without making intersubjective comparisons of preferences to say that the first type of change is bad and the third (Pareto optimum) is good. Of the second category of changes some may be good and some may be bad, depending upon what changes are made and how the preferences of various individuals affected are ranked. The correct use of the Pareto test by a social scientist with claims to objectivity implies this: changes which benefit at least one person while harming no one are good. There may be other good changes which do not meet the standards of a Pareto test (harmful to some while benefiting others), but, without adopting a normative standard by which to judge the effects of these moves, nothing can be said about them, nor can they be excluded as potential alternatives. Some advocates of public choice theory, however, would limit policy changes to those which could meet the Pareto test.[13] In doing so, they are elevating the status quo to a normative standard. They are saying that nobody, under any circumstances, ought to be made worse off even though it is quite reasonable to argue that under some circumstances there may be some people who ought to be worse off.

The second criticism is more serious. It grows out of the fact that the terms "better off" and "worse off" are not specified as either absolute or relative. The problem which results from this can be illustrated by the following example. Suppose that a very valuable meteorite fell to earth and a decision was made by the government to give it to the wealthiest person in the nation. If we assume that no damage was done when the meteorite fell, the incident described meets the criteria for a Pareto optimum. In terms of absolute wealth, no one would be worse off and the wealthy person would be much better off. Could it be assumed, however, as the economists do, that no one would object to the way the government disposed of the meteorite? It is doubtful. It seems more reasonable to assume that those who did not benefit from the incident would feel worse off relative to the person who did benefit. One might try to salvage the Pareto test by arguing that the incident described does not meet the criteria because people felt relatively worse off. If this explanation is accepted, the question is: Are there any significant changes in condition which meet the criteria for a Pareto optimum? Can you ever have anything but the most frivolous change which will not produce a feeling of relative deprivation among those who did not benefit from the change? It may be that the only way the Pareto optimum makes any sense is if those who use it are not predicting what people will do but are stating what they think people ought to do. If this truly is what the economists mean when they use the Pareto optimum, they are again introducing a normative standard.

It may be argued that the introduction of a bias in favor of the status quo in recommending policies for the criminal justice system is not to be condemned. This bias coincides with what is probably a commonly held belief, that the existing distribution of wealth, no matter how maldistributed it seems to be (if indeed it seems to be maldistributed at all), ought to be changed through political rather than criminal activity. The problem with this argument is that it is sometimes difficult to distinguish between the two. Were the riots and demonstrations of the 1960s political or criminal? Was the Boston Tea Party a political or criminal act?

The final criticism of the economic approach to setting policy for the criminal justice system is a criticism of what many think is the major advantage of the economic approach. Economists have developed a method of analysis which, for a social science, is very rigorous. The ability of economists to quantify what they study and to use mathematical models and sophisticated statistical techniques makes them the envy of quantitatively oriented social scientists in all fields. But a very heavy price is paid for this rigor. In order for any rigorous methodology to be employed, severely restrictive assumptions must be made, and the focus on the events to be studied must be very narrow. Failure to do this results in a model which is so unwieldy it would be of no use. Therefore, those who construct models must choose significant factors to include within the model and disregard all others. There is a tendency for significance to be equated with what is easily quantifiable as well as what fits the ideological predispositions of the model builder. This can be illustrated very well by using the economic analysis of plea bargaining as an example.

William M. Landers, Richard A. Posner, and Gordon Tullock all deal with plea bargaining, although not in the same depth.[14] All conclude that the public interest and the interest of the person accused of crime are served by plea bargaining.[15] They come to this concllusion because of the narrowness of their focus and the bias resulting from choices which this narrow focus requires.[16]

Landes makes the most detailed analysis of plea bargaining. His model is based on the assumption that "both the prosecutor and the defendant maximize their utility, appropriately defined, subject to a constraint on their resources."[17] The prosecutor, whose interests are assumed to coincide with the interest of the public,[18] tries to get as many convictions as possible and attempts to get the most severe sentences possible, but he must do this with limited resources. Under these circumstances the rational prosecutor will concentrate his resources on those cases where there is the highest probability of conviction and on cases where conviction carries the heaviest penalties. To do this the prosecutor must be willing to trade something (reduced charges or reduced sentences) in return for guilty pleas in those cases where the probability of conviction is low and the length of sentence, upon conviction, is low. The amount of reduction the prosecutor is willing to give in return for a guilty plea will be determined on the basis of the sentence upon conviction, the probability of conviction, and the difference between the perceived costs involved in negotiating a plea and the costs of going to trial.[19]

The defendant, on the other hand, will try to minimize the losses which result from being accused of a crime. These include the material and nonmaterial costs of being convicted and the costs of defending oneself against the criminal charges. Landes assumes that the more one invests in defending oneself, the lower the probability of conviction. This being the case, the defendant's choices run from one extreme, where no resources are spent on defense and the probability of being convicted of the crime charged is very high, to the other extreme, where all the individual's resources (assuming he has substantial resources) would be invested in the defense, with the result of lowering probability of conviction to near zero. The defendant, however, will probably not choose either of these extremes, but instead expend resources to that optimal level where additional expenditures would be more costly than the punishment upon conviction.

The defendant will accept a negotiated plea when the perceived costs of a trial (the value of the resources expended in a trial, plus the costs associated with conviction, discounted by the probability of conviction) are greater than the costs of accepting the prosecutor's offer to plead guilty (the costs associated with pleading guilty to the reduced charge or other consideration offered plus the costs of lying if the defendant is innocent).

If an offer based on the prosecutor's calculation of his advantage entails less cost than that perceived by the defendant in going to trial, then a negotiated plea will be possible. The prosecutor, the public, and the defendant will benefit from such an agreement.

What has been presented is a very condensed and simplified version of Landes's analysis. While it is sufficient for our purpose, it should be noted that it does not include much that Landes includes, such as the effect of wealth, the availability of a public defender, pretrial detention, and the present bail system. It should also be noted that the guilt of the defendant is considered only peripherally. Landes says that "the question of whether the defendant did in fact commit the crime he is charged with does not explicitly enter the analysis."[20] It does influence the outcome of the process in two ways, however. Landes assumes that the evidence against an innocent person will be less than the evidence against a guilty person, therefore reducing the probability of conviction; and, as mentioned earlier, the innocent defendant may have an aversion to lying, therefore raising the cost of a negotiated plea to the defendant.[21] Tullock also concludes that the question of guilt or innocence is irrelevant in evaluating plea bargaining. "In discussing confession, I have said nothing about guilt or innocence of the accused. There is no *real* reason why this should have any major bearing on the matter."[22]

This conclusion that guilt or innocence does not make any difference will serve to illustrate how the narrow view taken by economists along with their individualistic assumptions leads them to overlook some very important questions in considering the consequences of the operation of the criminal justice system. If one accepts the individualistic assumptions of the economists, it is quite possible to argue that the innocent person is better off by pleading guilty to a crime he did not commit. If one of the costs of going to trial is the notoriety that accompanies a public trial, an innocent person might be much better off to plead guilty if probation or a suspended sentence were offered. But if one broadens one's view to include the social consequences of plea bargaining, one might come to a different conclusion.

The most obvious flaw in Landes's analysis is his assumption that the interests of the prosecutor and the public are coincidental. It is not too difficult to imagine instances where the interests of a public prosecutor ambitious for higher office might conflict with a broader public interest in a just criminal justice system.

Landes ignores for the most part the function which a public trial may serve for the public in general. One such function is pointed out by John Griffiths:

> If a trial can be seen as a goal in itself—a lesson in legal procedure, dignity, fairness and justice, for the public and for the accused (whether he is convicted or acquitted)—we would not want to lose its potential for good by encouraging short-circuits.[23]

Of course, the benefits derived by society from trials are difficult if not impossible to measure and weigh against the benefits of plea bargaining. This fact, as well as the individualistic bias of the economic approach, may explain why such considerations are ignored.

Another possible consequence of plea bargaining which is difficult if not impossible to measure is the cynicism which the process generates. Appearances indicate that the plea bargaining participated in by high government officials in the last few years has encouraged the cynical belief that justice is defined differently for the powerful than it is for the average citizen, therefore reducing the general deterrent effect of the criminal proceeding. Specific deterrence may also be affected. Even supporters of the process are aware that a by-product may be a cynical view of the system. Arnold Enker makes the following observation relating to those who pass through the system:

> But a real vice in the procedure may be that it often gives the defendant an image of corruption in the system, or at least an image of a system lacking meaningful purpose and subject to manipulation by those who are wise to the right tricks. Cynicism, rather than respect, is the likely result.[24]

Empirical evidence to support this is conflicting. In a study published in 1972, Jonathan D. Casper concluded that the practice of plea bargaining resulted in convincing those who passed through it that the morality of the criminal justice system was no better than the morality of the streets and did not furnish a model to emulate.[25] In a study published in 1978, however, one of the conclusions Casper reaches is that "those who plead guilty are slightly more likely to accept their treatment as fair than those who go to trial, although the relationship is not strong."[26] Whether or not the process produces cynicism is not the point here. What is the point is that the economic approach does not even address itself to the problem, or for that matter even acknowledge that such a consequence might be possible.

By ignoring these types of questions, the economists, by implication, say that they do not matter. There is an implicit claim that "objective" policy decisions can be made based on the conclusions of economic analysis. This contradicts common sense as well as a great body of knowledge from other social sciences. While it cannot be argued that that which contradicts the findings of the economists ought to be accepted as more valid than what the economists conclude, it can be maintained that ignoring many factors which may have a vital influence on the conclusions reached merely because they do not fit methodological or ideological presuppositions is not a very good or useful way of making policy recommendations. This is not to say that the use of economic analysis in making policy recommendations for the criminal justice system is to be avoided. It is useful, and its finding may be valid within the sphere of its competence, but it is inadequate to answer all of the questions facing the criminal justice system, regardless of what some of its supporters may claim.[27]

Notes

1. See Vincent Ostrom and Elinor Ostrom, "Public Choice: A Different Approach to the Study of Public Administration," *Public Administration Review* (March-April 1971): 203-216.

2. Isaac Ehrlich, "The Deterrent Effect of Capital Punishment: A Question of Life and Death," *American Economic Review* 65 (June 1975): 397-417.

422 U.S. 1039 (1975).

4. See the series of articles in the *Yale Law Journal* 85 (December 1975): 164-227; and the "Comments" in the following issue: 85 (January 1976): 359-369; and Brian E. Forst, "The Deterrent Effect of Capital Punishment: Across-state Analysis of the 1960's," *Minnesota Law Review* 61 (May 1977): 743-764.

5. See Thomas R. DeGregori, "Caveat Emptor: A Critique of the Emerging Paradigm of Public Choice," *Administration and Society* 6 (August 1974): 205-228; see also the exchange between Robert T. Golembiewski and Vincent Ostrom in *American Political Science Review* 71 (December 1977): 1488-1543.

6. See May Brodbeck, "Methodological Individualisms: Definition and Reduction," *Philosophy of Science* 25 (January 1958): 1-22.

7. Jack P. Gibbs, "Crime, Punishment, and Deterrence," *Social Science Quarterly* (March 1968): 515, in *The Economics of Crime and Punishment*, ed. by Simon Rottenbert (Washington, D.C.: American Enterprise Institute for Public Policy Research, 1973), p. 21.

8. Ibid.

9. Gordon Tullock, *The Logic of the Law* (New York: Basic Books, 1971); see especially chapter 1, "Law without Ethics," and chapter 14, "Ethics."

10. DeGregori, "Caveat Emptor," p. 211.

11. For a short statement of this view see James M. Buchanan, "An Individualistic Theory of Political Process," in *Varieties of Political Theory*, ed. by David Easton (Englewood Cliffs, N.J.: Prentice-Hall, 1966), pp. 25-37.

12. For a short discussion of other problems see John E. Monzingo, "Economic Analysis of the Criminal Justice System," *Crime and Delinquency* 23 (July 1977): 268.

13. Buchanan and Tullock both suggest such limits.

14. William M. Landes, "An Economic Analysis of the Courts," *Journal of Law and Economics* 14 (April 1971): 61-107; Richard A. Posner, *Economic Analysis of Law* (Boston: Little, Brown and Co., 1972), p. 343; and Tullock, *Logic of the Law,* pp. 174-186.

15. Landes, p. 61; Posner, p. 343; and Tullock, pp. 182-186.

16. Landes, at least, does note that there is a difference of opinion as to whether a trial enhances the quality of justice (p. 85, footnote 15). Posner does mention a social function served by trial but he limits it to the development of the law (pp. 322-323).

17. Landes, p. 61.

18. Ibid., p. 63.

19. Ibid., p. 64.

20. Ibid., p. 68.

21. Ibid., p. 69.

22. Tullock, p. 182. The emphasis is mine.

23. John Griffiths, "Ideology in the Criminal Process: A Third 'Model' of the Criminal Process," *Yale Law Journal* 79 (January 1970): 398.

24. Arnold Enker, "Perspectives on Plea Bargaining," Appendix A in Presi-

dent's Commission on Law Enforcement and the Administration of Justice, *Task Force Report: The Courts* (Washington, D.C.: GPO, 1967), p. 112.

25. Jonathan D. Casper, *American Criminal Justice: The Defendant's Perspective* (Englewood Cliffs, N.J.: Prentice-Hall, 1974), p. 77.

26. Jonathan D. Casper, "Having Their Day in Court: Defendant Evaluations of the Fairness of Their Treatment," *Law and Society Review* 12 (Winter 1978): 249.

27. It may be interesting to note here that some of the predictions about what would happen if plea bargaining were eliminated seem to be wrong. A twenty-seven-month study on the consequences of the elimination of plea bargaining in Alaska indicates that the average disposition time is down, the number of trials has increased, and prosecutors claim to be working harder. But there has been no increase in staff, guilty pleas have not been substantially reduced, conviction rates have improved, but not dramatically, and the length of sentences has increased for some crimes (felony narcotics) but not for others (rape, burglary). Those responsible for the study conclude that elimination of plea bargaining resulted in a more efficient criminal justice system but not a more just one. Michael L. Rubinstein and Teresa J. White, "Plea Bargaining: Can Alaska Live without It?" *Judicature* 62 (January 1979): 266-279.

8 Heroin, Society, Public Policy: The Infernal Triangle

Donald Phares

A Perspective on the Heroin Problem

Heroisch, German for large or powerful, was the word adopted by the Bayer company as a brand name for diacetylmorphine, undoubtedly to portray its pharmacological impact on the human body. First commercially introduced in the United States in 1898 under the brand name Heroin, one of its prime proposed medical applications was as a "cure" for morphine addiction. It thus followed much the same route that morphine had taken earlier as a "cure" for alcoholism. While the literal meaning of heroin remains the same (large or powerful), the figurative object of its impact has become primarily society rather than the individual. Over the nearly eighty years since its appearance on the U.S. medical scene, it has evolved from the long hoped for panacea for the dreaded morphinism to a major social scourge. Drug abuse, particularly that of heroin, has become a newfound social panapathogen (a cause-all), with the drug itself often assigned the status of an ethical agent.[1] Like the controversy over the gun versus the person who pulls the trigger—"Which does the killing?"—heroin, per se, has been blamed for a vast array of social as well as private ills.

Were it not for the profound impact this drug and its attendant activities exert on society, and the importance this has for the rational formulation of policy, the ethical question would be "interesting" but hardly earthshaking. It is the pragmatic spin-offs from the use of heroin that mandate a rational and systematic evaluation of the many forces determining its impact on society. Only when they are put in proper perspective can we hope for effective and meaningful policy intervention.

Some background on the heroin problem helps to form such a perspective. First, the trend in heroin use continues upward; recent studies by the Drug Abuse Council and individual researchers attest to this. The "official" number of addicts has been set at around 600,000 by government agencies, which are known to be notoriously conservative. Other estimates have ranged upwards of 725,000 addicts and as many as 4.5 million active users.[2] Whatever the precise numbers involved, use of heroin has pushed beyond the urban ghetto and slum into suburbia, has permeated the entire socioeconomic spectrum, crossed racial and sex lines, and is now beginning to move into medium- and even small-sized cities.

Second, the "dollars and cents" nuances are even more striking. While at one time in the early 1900s a "hard-core" addict (to opium, usually, at that time) could support a habit on pennies a day, the average daily cost of a heroin habit today, as reported by the Drug Enforcement Agency, exceeds $60. Some simple arithmetic defines the size of the "heroin industry's" take as being in the billions of dollars per year [(600,000 addicts)(365 days)($60 per day)]—this using the most conservative figures only for addicts and their daily outlays and excluding occasional users, experimenters, and the like. In financial terms, the illicit heroin enterprise has assumed the stature of a corporate giant, rivaling firms at the top of Fortune's list of the 500 largest industrials.

Third, on the other (licit) side of the heroin problem are the activities of a variety of public and private organizations that attempt to deal with drug abuse and its nexus of related phenomena. At the federal level nearly three quarters of a billion dollars were earmarked directly for drug programs in fiscal year 1976. Untold hundreds of millions are also spent by state and local governments to match federal funds; to support supplementary social, health, and educational services; and to deal with legal consequences of heroin such as crime. In addition to these public funds there are private resources expended by businesses and households. There is little evidence to confirm a downward trend in the commitment of resources in the forseeable future. Drug abuse has become big, profitable business for both the licit and the illicit entrepreneur.

The situation as it exists is the result of a curious series of events worthy of further comment. Just a few decades ago neither heroin nor opiates elicited any social concern that even remotely resembles that exhibited today. However, over a relatively short span of years the situation has shifted radically, to the point where billions of dollars now change hands annually on one side of the heroin problem or the other, and yet the problem worsens. What, one might reasonably inquire, has been the outcome from the billions of dollars poured into the drug problem? What is to be done about the societal disruption that ranges from a vague urban miasma to theft, violence, murder, and support for a variety of illegal operations? What alternatives are open for dealing with the heroin "plague" and how effective are those policies that currently occupy a most favored status?

At the crux of each of these concerns lies one central issue: when and how should society intervene and exactly what conditions provide a legitimate milieu for the subjugation of private behavior to a broader collective welfare? An informed response must begin with some understanding of the evolution of the contemporary heroin problem.

The Evolution of Opiate Use as a Social Concern

Figure 8-1 outlines the major factors contributing to the current status of heroin (opiates) as an issue of social concern and an object of public policy. Society's concern has actually evolved rather gradually over the past several decades. Its inception, however, can clearly be placed at 1914, with the enactment of the

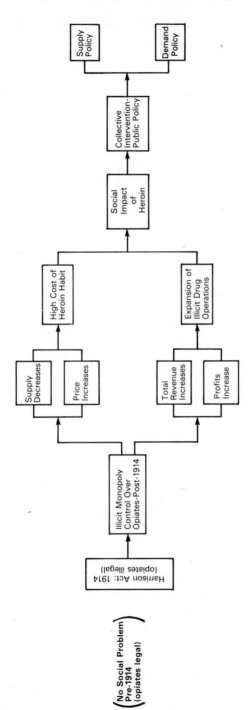

Figure 8-1. Evolution of the Heroin Problem

Harrison Act. Prior to this time a plethora of opiate mixtures were readily available and widely used for various physical and psychological ills. Relatively little use was associated with hard-core addiction, as we know it today, and the typical user tended to be older, white, female, middle to upper class, and not a criminal. The financial burden of opiate use was minimal, literally pennies a day. One could obtain at little expense all that was needed, and therefore there was virtually no resultant social disruption.[3] The decision to use opiates or not rested entirely with the individual, since society (qua government) had not yet chosen to intervene.

Out of this rather placid environment emerged legislaton in the form of the Harrison Act, which classified all addicts—and likewise any physician who attempted to treat them with opiates—as criminals. Strangely, the impetus for this precipitous change in legal status was not any widespread social malaise over the impact of opiates. Rather, pressure had emerged from within an already existing bureaucracy to "tighten up" on drug use and thus bring the U.S. position into closer conformance with existing international treaty provision. The new stance on opiates truly arose from innocuous beginnings.[4]

The impact of the Harrison Act and its subsequent legal refinements was far from inconsequential. To classify as illegal a substance that is in great demand places tremendous strain on enforcement even in the best of circumstances. Prohibition has aptly demonstrated this with alcohol, as have laws against prostitution and gambling with other "vices." Such laws are very difficult and costly to enforce. When the product in question has the peculiar attributes of heroin, meaningful enforcement becomes virtually impossible. Addiction, tolerance, and withdrawal make the opiate user infinitely less willing to forego consumption. The end result, as was true with alcohol and is true with sex and gambling, is that criminal entrepreneurs jump in to fill the vacuum created by the absence of a legal option.

An established clientele combined with virtual monopoly control attracted people willing to supply drugs, despite nominally severe legal sanctions. Criminal enterprise filled the void that had been created by the Harrison Act and supplied opiates. Of prime significance is the fact that the shift in legal status granted, de facto, a virtual monopoly over the importation, sale, and distribution of opiates. "Illegal" drugs became quite literally the only game in town.

Illicit control then worked in two primary ways to aggravate the heroin dilemma and generate a concatenation of unexpected outcomes for society. First, opiates became harder and harder to obtain. The competetive distribution that characterized pre-1914 gave way to an extremely limited supply. This inexorably forced up the price. What happened is that the new legal status served to produce scarcity out of what previously had been a state of abundance—end result: reduced supply and higher price. Tighter supply, rising price, and monopolistic control led to a steady increase in the cost of dependence. What previously claimed pennies a day now required larger and larger daily expenditures.

The second outcome of giving birth to an illicit drug monopoly was a fantastic growth in revenue and profit for drug entrepreneurs. The economic attractiveness of heroin, combined with a natural growth in demand (due to increasing tolerance), offered an ideal economic incentive to expand operations. A single kilo of 80 percent pure heroin can result in a "street value" of several hundred thousand dollars and generate nearly a million dollars in total income flow. When the tax-free status of this income is accounted for, drugs become a compellingly attractive form of enterprise. As the illegal drug industry expanded—and thus its clientele, revenue, and profits—another set of of forces came into play.

Exclusive criminal control of drugs led to a set of consequences totally unexpected in the original design of the Harrison Act or its legal progeny. The expense of a heroin habit could not be met out of an individual's own resources. This forced addicts to coerce needed funds from the rest of society. With an average habit costing nearly $60 per day there is very little opportunity for most to meet this expenditure legally. Much of the burden of an expensive heroin habit, therefore, was shifted from the addict. Theft, prostitution, "dealing," and other illicit activities became prime sources of funds, and the financial burden was increasingly imposed on the "rest of society." What began almost exclusively as an individual problem became rife with social implications.

All of this has produced an interesting anomaly. Prior to the 1914 legislation there was virtually no social malaise associated with opiate use. After enactment of legislation, society was forced to bear the cost of heroin dependence in the form of more prevalent drug-related crime. In addition, it was also asked to pay for a variety of public programs to "deal with the drug problem." The net effect has been a squeeze from two directions—more extensive and costly social ramifications from the illicit use of drugs and a rising pressure for expensive, tax-supported programs.

Curiously, the collective impact of heroin use—such as crime, law-enforcement and criminal justice expenditures, illness and death, and the like—now provides a mandate for governmental activity. Harmful individual behavior defines a rationale for government, acting as an agent for society, to intervene. The need for policy arises out of the consequences that surround drug use. Individuals qua individuals impose costs on others through their behavior; these persons have no immediate recourse and must turn to society qua government to effectuate a solution.

The key to the economic vitality of heroin lies in the incredible profits to be derived at every stage, from the opium field to an addict's arm. What starts out as ten kilos of raw opium, costing about $250 in the illicit opium market, is refined into one kilo of morphine base, worth at least $5,000. The morphine is processed further to obtain a kilo of dicetylmorphine (heroin), which sells for $10,000 to $20,000 a kilo. Once inside the U.S. border this single kilo of 80 percent pure heroin is cut to produce at least twelve kilos of 6 to 7 percent pure heroin that can ultimately sell for $400,000 and generate a cumulative income flow of $800,000. The return at every stage of distribution is high, from several hundred percent at the importation stage to enough to support one's own habit at the street level.

The illegality of heroin enables all participants in the black market to reap large returns, whether financial or in-kind. Perverse as it may seem, it is its legal status that has made heroin such a profitable enterprise. To understand this one must be aware of the peculiar demand for the drug.

The Demand for Heroin: Addiction, Tolerance, Withdrawal

Critical to understanding heroin's impact and, thus, to the structuring of public policy is an awareness of the unusual nature of the demand for heroin. For new and casual users and experimenters the quantity demanded will be very responsive to any variation in price. When heroin is less expensive, experimentation or casual use might occur, but as the price rises use is curtailed or foregone entirely. The demand curve for these users is quite elastic, since addiction has not yet set in, and would resemble the curve DD in figure 8-2a.

At the onset of addiction demand undergoes a fundamental change; price responsiveness shifts from high elasticity to high inelasticity. Addiction is manifest as an extremely powerful physiological and psychological dependence that produces a desperation when drugs cannot be obtained. If price rises, consumption does not fall; rather, the burden of a more expensive habit is simply assumed. Quantity demanded becomes extremely unresponsive to any change in price, and over a relatively wide range it could even be totally unresponsive.[5] This situation is shown by curve DD in figure 8-2b.

An aggregate demand curve for heroin would take the form of curve DD in figure 8-3. To the left of the "kink" point (p_1, q_1) is the inelastic portion comprised of addict demand; to the right is the demand by casual users and addict consumption beyond a maintenance level. The quantity at the kink point is the minimum amount needed by addicts to stave off withdrawal symptoms.

Extreme inelasticity is but one peculiar attribute of heroin demand. Associated with addiction is a derivative phenomenon known as the tolerance syndrome. Once addicted, the body develops an increasing tolerance to the drug. To avoid withdrawal or attain a constant state of euphoria, one's daily intake must grow; this means that demand increases simply with the passage of time. This is shown by the increase in demand from D_{t_2} to D_{t_4} in figure 8-4.

Underlying the inelasticity of demand is a lack of viable substitutes. Addiction to and tolerance for heroin preclude an addict from substituting the consumption of less expensive drugs. There is little advantage in using alcohol, barbiturates, or other less expensive drugs since they provide little in the way of long-run relief from opiate withdrawal. Also, addicts generally view the psychological effect of other drugs as grossly inferior to that of heroin. This produces a demand curve that is extremely inelastic, unlike what would prevail if an effective, cheap substitute could be obtained. Any increase in the price of heroin forces an addict to meet the added cost due to both higher price and the increased consumption associated with a rising tolerance. This produces a constant upward trend for daily drug expenditures and larger adverse consequences for society.

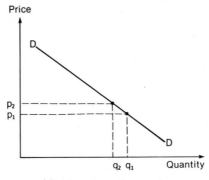

(a) Nonaddict Demand

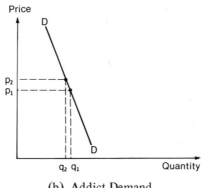

(b) Addict Demand

Figure 8-2. The Demand Curve for Heroin

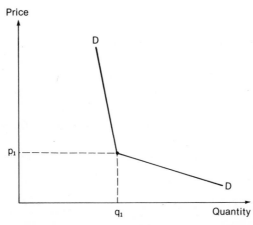

Note: This curve is a composite of the curves shown in figures 8-2a and 8-2b.

Figure 8-3. The Kinked Demand Curve: Aggregate Demand Curve for Heroin—
Occasional Users, Experimenters, and Addicts

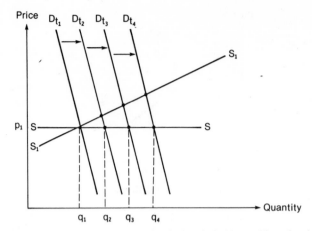

Note: With all other factors constant, the cost of a heroin habit would tend to increase from $(p_1 \cdot q_1)$ to $(p_1 \cdot q_2)$ to $(p_1 \cdot q_3)$ to $(p_1 \cdot q_4)$ assuming a perfectly elastic supply curve (S) at level p_1. A supply curve with any inelasticity would raise the cost even further, as suggested by supply curve S_1.

Figure 8-4. Demand Curve for Heroin Addict with Passage of Time (t):
The Tolerance Syndrome

Structuring Public Policy: A Simple Economic Framework

Many of the outcomes associated with the heroin problem are of direct economic interest. Factors such as price, monopoly control of a market, profit, and the externalities associated with drug use are all quite susceptible to economic analysis. Thus the formulation of public policy to cope with a black market activity can benefit from a simple supply/demand analysis of the influence of various strategies. From this one can infer at least the direction of change in some key variables such as price, profits, and revenue. It also suggests how the social disruption will be influenced through various policy options. For analytical convenience these policies can be categorized as primarily affecting supply or demand:

Supply[a]	*Demand*[a]
decrease:	*decrease:*
law enforcement	treatment/rehabilitation
customs operations	prevention/cure
opium crop control	isolation/removal
international cooperation	
increase:[b]	*increase:*
"legalization"	not relevant

---

[a]These policies are meant to be suggestive, not exhaustive.

[b]Increase to be read here as lessening restrictions on availability, not literally promoting an expansion in supply.

Needless to say, each of these broad categories is comprised of a collection of more specific policies.[6] If collective action is intended to ameliorate the perverse outcomes of heroin abuse a simple supply/demand framework can provide useful background for most effectively expending limited resources.

Looking first at a demand-reducing strategy we can refer to figure 8-5. Assuming a constant supply curve at SS and a kinked demand curve (DD), a reduction in demand (say, due to methadone) from D_1 to D_2 to D_3 has the effect of lowering price (from p_1 to p_2 to p_3) and also quantity (from q_1 to q_2 to q_3). As a result total revenue declines [from $(p_1 \cdot q_1)$ to $(p_2 \cdot q_2)$ to $(p_3 \cdot q_3)$], as do profits.[c] Thus a demand-reducing strategy will influence all of the key economic variables in a desirable direction. Lower price and quantity, and therefore profit and revenue, mean less need for an addict to resort to criminal behavior to obtain needed funds. This lessens social costs. Lower revenue and profits also tend to decrease the economic attractiveness of heroin distribution as a business.

On the supply side we can examine the impact of a policy (such as law enforcement) which concentrates on restricting availability. This is shown in figure 8-6. Assuming a kinked demand curve (held constant at DD), an initial reduction in supply—say, from S_1 to S_2—reduces quantity from q_1 to q_2 and increases price from p_1 to p_2. Since the drop in quantity is proportionately larger than the rise in price, total revenue will fall [from $(p_1 \cdot q_1)$ to $(p_2 \cdot q_2)$]. This will be the case as long as supply policy continues to act on the elastic (primarily nonaddict) portion of the demand curve, that is, that segment to the right of the kink point. Continued pressure from law enforcement, however, will eventually begin to have an impact on the inelastic portion of DD that represents hard-core addict demand. Once this occurs quantity continues to fall but price now begins to go

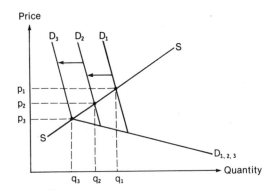

Figure 8-5. Impact of a Demand Reducing Policy: Assuming a "Kinked" Demand Curve for Heroin

---

[c]It should be kept in mind that total revenue to the heroin industry is equal to the expenditures made by addicts and users on drugs. These expenditures are in large part financed through illegal activities.

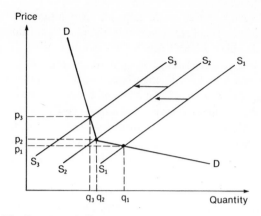

Figure 8-6. The Impact of a Supply Reducing Policy: Assuming a "Kinked" Demand Curve for Heroin

up more rapidly. With a drop in supply from S_2 to S_3, quantity falls from q_2 to q_3, while price rises from p_2 to p_3. Total revenue in this instance increases from $(p_2 \cdot q_2)$ to $(p_3 \cdot q_3)$ due to the inelasticity of demand—end result: higher revenue and profit which are associated with more perverse social consequences and a greater attractiveness for the heroin industry.

Just the opposite prevails with a strategy that lessens restrictions on availability, such as "legalization." The artificial scarcity created by legislation would be eliminated and in effect we would simply return to a contemporary variant of the pre-1914 competetive market situation. Price would plummet, illicit monopoly control would vanish, and the large profits and revenues to be gained from drug sales would dissipate. Last, but by no means least, the social costs associated with heroin would be lessened dramatically. Much of the drug-related crime and also the law-enforcement and criminal justice expenditures we now endure would be eliminated.

Considering all the options open, there seems to be much to favor a policy stance that lessens restrictions on heroin's availability. Legalization, in one of the many possible forms,[d] would break the criminal monopoly, thereby lowering illicit revenue and profit. If the intent of collective action is to lower the disruption that society is forced to endure from drugs, much can be said for recognizing and accepting the perverse economic outcomes of restricting supply and the lack of effectiveness of our existing demand-oriented programs such as methadone.[7] The immediate benefits to society from "legalization" are potentially large. There

---

[d]When we speak of "legalization" it must be noted that heroin is not currently legally available for *any* purpose. Legalization does not necessarily imply free market distribution. Rather, it opens the possibility, for example, of heroin maintenance as a treatment mode, something which cannot now be put into effect.

seems no more effective way to deal with heroin than to erode its economic *raison d'être*—profit.

Notes

1. Thomas Szasz makes this point very emphatically in *Ceremonial Chemistry* (Garden City, N.Y.: Anchor Press, 1974), most particularly as he ends the book, pp. 180-181.

2. See Leon Gibson Hunt, *Recent Spread of Heroin Use in the United States* (Washington, D.C.: Drug Abuse Council, MS-10, 7/74), and Leon Gibson Hunt and Carl D. Chambers, *The Heroin Epidemics* (New York: Spectrum Publications, Inc., 1976). The latter source provides separate estimates of addicts and users; see p. 112 particularly.

3. This point is documented in extensive detail by David F. Musto in *The American Disease* (New Haven: Yale University Press, 1973). James Harvey Young, *The Toadstool Millionaires* (Princeton, N.J.: Princeton University Press, 1961) provides a wealth of information on the patent medicines that were available in such incredible variety before federal regulations came into effect.

4. This is a point that Musto, *American Disease*, and others have emphasized.

5. Inelastic demand for heroin addicts is a fairly widely held view; see, for example, J. Dean Heller, "The Attempt to Prevent Illicit Drug Supply," *Drug Abuse in America: Problem in Perspective*, Vol. III in *The Legal System and Drug Control* (Washington, D.C.: GPO, 1973), pp. 387-390; or Roger D. Blair and Ronald J. Vogel, "Heroin Addiction and Urban Crime," *Public Finance Quarterly* 1 (October 1974): 457-459. Empirical estimates in Arthur D. Little, Inc., "Drug Abuse and Law Enforcement" (Cambridge, Mass.: submitted to the President's Commission on Law Enforcement and Administration of Justice, 1967), pp. D9-D12, lend support to this assumption.

6. For an elaboration on law enforcement see Mark Harrison Moore, *Buy and Bust* (Lexington, Mass.: Lexington Books, D.C. Heath, 1977).

7. Edward Jay Epstein in "Methadone: The Forlorn Hope," *Public Interest* (Summer 1974): 3-24, raises very serious doubts concerning methadone's capacity to deal with heroin addiction. Heller, "Attempt," is skeptical concerning the efficacy of policies designed to restrict supply; see p. 399.

Part IV
Effects of Police Training
on Police Policy

9

Police Professionalism: The Need for Clarity

Ralph Baker,
Fred A. Meyer, Jr., and
Dorothy Rudoni

Introduction

That the concept "police professionalism" lacks clarity is demonstrable by the differing connotations it produces. To some analysts, police professionalism is seen as the primary way of upgrading police personnel and police operations. Others view professionalism as a political strategy used by the police to further their own occupational and economic ends. Still others are unclear as to whether the term is a concept that applies to organizations or individuals. Robert W. Habenstein sees professionalism as an ideology:

> Certain groups, claiming special functions, have been able to arrogate to themselves, or command increased power over, the conditions of members' livelihood. . . . "Profession" is, basically, an ideology, a set of rationalizations about the worth and necessity of certain areas of work, which, when internalized, gives the practitioners a moral justification for privilege, if not license. . . .[1]

Since the 1930s there have been many efforts directed toward the improvement of the police. These efforts include the Wickersham Commission of 1931, the President's Commission on Law Enforcement and Administration of Justice of 1967, and the National Advisory Commission on Standards and Goals for the Police of 1973. For the most part, these studies were less concerned with defining police professionalism than with upgrading the American police in operational terms. Such an operational goal was when the President's Commission on Law Enforcement and Administration of Justice Task Force recommended that "the ultimate aim of all police departments should be that all personnel with general enforcement powers have baccalaureate degrees," and a central goal for police professionalization was identified and a major trend of the 1970s was launched (1967:279).

As in the Task Force Report, discussion about police professionalization has largely dealt with the goals to be achieved in order to establish professionalism. In addition to education, instrumental goals have included increased pay benefits, improved police-public relations, and enhanced status for police. It was assumed that the attainment of such goals would result in professional police performance. To date, the effectiveness of professionalization in generating optimum police performance has not been clearly established. Furthermore, there is a lack of clarity as to what police professionalism is and what its primary sources are. Despite the activity stimulated by the Task Force's call for baccalaureate degrees for police (LEAA funding, proliferation of police science and law-enforcement programs in colleges and universities), conclusive evidence of the relationship between education and police professionalism is lacking (Weiner, 1974).

Ambiguity about the substance and source of police professionalism stems from conflicting objectives associated with professionalization. Conflict is precipitated by several factors but is primarily the consequence of the nature of the police function and the political context in which police work.

Unlike medicine and law, policing as an occupation was well established before specified educational and training requirements were associated with its practice. With the exception of education, which did draw from norms established in private institutions, the traditional professions developed as their practitioners performed in the private sector. Professionals in law and medicine originally were essentially individual entrepreneurs.

Police, by contrast, have been publicly employed and controlled. Historically the major impetus toward police professionalization has been the desire to limit the political control of the police (Cooper and associates, 1975; Walker, 1977). A monopoly of force, paramilitary features of organization and function, and an unmistakable identity as "instrument of state" are characteristics associated with the police. These factors do not preclude professionalization; they do distinguish policing from the traditional professions.

Because the police provide a public service, are part of the public bureaucracy, and give effect to politically determined values, they are perceived primarily as public employees, not as professionals serving the public. Impressions of police performance are sometimes colored by political perceptions. So, too, of course, are the policy decisions which establish and regulate police programs. Lacking the autonomy which was partially a concomitant of "private" operation and the professional training enjoyed by those in established professions, the police have been more exposed and more vulnerable to control by political motive. This truism was never more evident that in the 1960s.

That the police are perceived to be involved in politics really could not be otherwise. The criminal law that the police enforce is a product of the political system. Regardless of the degree of immorality or reprehensibility of an act, it is not a crime unless it is prohibited by political authorities through the criminal law. In a sense, political leaders create crime. Edwin H. Sutherland and Donald R. Cressey have stated the political conflict thesis for the origin of the criminal law as follows:

> When an interest group secures the enactment of a law, it secures the assistance of the state in a conflict with a rival interest group; the opposition of the rival group thus becomes criminal. According to this theory, wrongful acts are characteristic of all clases in present-day society; the upper classes are subtle in their wrongdoing, the underprivileged classes are direct. The upper classes are politically important, and they prohibit the wrongful acts of the underprivileged classes, but the laws are defined

and implemented in such manner that many of the wrongful acts of the upper classes do not come within their scope. In this theory, the criminal law originates in the conflict of groups and in the inconsistency of the mores (1974:11).

The criminal law is a product not only of politics but also of the way the police enforce it. The police cannot fully enforce every criminal statute. They exercise a great deal of discretion. A variety of police practices have sensitized many to the importance of these discretionary practices. For example, the gathering of intelligence on political activists has been of concern in many cities. The police have regularly monitored the activities of groups that they perceive to be outside the mainstream of American political ideology. Their training appears to lead them to behave in this fashion. Another practice that has been of concern is the handling of the mass demonstrations of the 1960s. The choice of tactics to deal with demonstrators again indicates the great leeway open to the police. They have been criticized in those situations where they chose to use very forceful tactics to deal with nonviolent protesters, as in some of the demonstrations at the 1968 Democratic National Convention in Chicago.

Another indication of the discretionary power of the police is the complaints that come from minority groups regarding the unequal enforcement practices experienced in their communities. It has been alleged that racial prejudice has an impact on the enforcement policies used. In minority communities the police have been known to arrest individuals on petty charges as a means of controlling their behavior. Demonstrators have also experienced this treatment.

Peter K. Manning discusses the direct effects of this political nature of the police officer's job. "One is that many policemen become alienated; they lose interest in their role as enforcers and in the law as a believable criterion. The pressure of politics also erodes loyalty to the police organization and not infrequently leads to collusion with criminal and organized crime" (1974:103-104).

The relationship between the political nature of policing and the calls for police professionalism is unclear. It is difficult to ascertain whether those calling for more professionalization envisage the changes under the present political context of police work or whether such proponents perceive the political system in different terms.

Professionalism as a Strategy

In the 1970s professionalization emerged as a major police strategy. Those involved in policing were concerned with "upgrading" their salary and status. Critical observers of the police saw professionalization as a key for resolving societal problems. The latter included racism, excessive use of force, violation of defendants' rights, alienation, and antagonism between youth and police. Magali Sarfatti Larson observed, "Professionalization makes the use of discretion predictable" (1977:198).

That critics would call for upgrading the police is logical. That the police would come to adopt professionalism as a strategy is equally logical and predict-able. As Manning observes, the two primary goals of most bureaucracies, includ-ing the police bureaucracy, are to maintain their organizational autonomy and the security of their members. "To accomplish these aims, they adopt a pattern of institutional action that can best be described as 'professionalism.'" Manning believes that the concept of "police professionalism" cloaks the many kinds of activities carried on by the police, saying:

> The guise of professionalism embodied in a bureaucratic organization is the most important strategy employed by the police to defend their mandate and thereby to build self-esteem, organizational autonomy, and occupational solidarity or cohesiveness. The professionalization drives of the police are no more suspect than the campaigns of other striving, upwardly mobile occupational groups. However, since the police have a monopoly on legal violence, since they are active enforcers of the public will, serving theoretically in the best interests of the public, the consequences of their yearnings for prestige and power are imbued with far greater social ramifications than the relatively harmless attempts of florists, funeral directors, and accountants to attain public stature.[2]

Manning and others question the use of professionalism as strategy only "if in striving for the heights of prestige they fail to serve the altruistic values of pro-fessionalism." The strategy is also questioned if it means that a "faulty portrait of the social reality of crime is being painted, if their professionalism conceals more than it reveals about the true nature of their operations" (1974:107).

Modern police departments in turn use a variety of tactics to manage their public appearance of professionalism. Among these are the styles of patrol that attempt to reconcile the police department's preoccupation with bureaucratic procedures with the community's desire for public order, secrecy which controls public response to their activities, and the utilization of crime statistics and tech-nology.

James Q. Wilson identified three different styles of policing or patrol: the watchman style, the legalistic style, and the service style (1976:62).

The watchman style of policing is found in a department in which the pri-mary concern is maintaining order. There is not an overriding concern with en-forcing all laws. Officers are encouraged to ignore minor traffic and juvenile offenses. A certain amount of vice is tolerated. There exist different expectations for the behavior of different groups. Juveniles are expected to break minor laws and will generally be ignored when so doing. Blacks are generally left alone be-cause they are perceived to have a different level of morality. However, when a black person offends a white, the police will intervene because whites are seen as expecting this.

In the legalistic style of policing the stress is on law enforcement as opposed to order maintenance. The police officer is expected to enforce the letter of the law. Traffic tickets are issued at a high rate. A considerable number of juvenile offenders are arrested. A large number of misdemeanor arrests will be made. The police do not appear to apply different standards to blacks or juveniles. This style of policing has the potential of producing greater numbers of disgruntled citizens in a community—especially when citizens feel the police are being unreasonable or dogmatic about enforcing laws.

The service style of policing has generally been found in cities that are free of divisive racial and class cleavages. In such places the police attempt to discover the market demand that exists for their services. The police are expected to be courteous in their work. Generally, arrests are not made for minor infractions of the law. Rather, informal sanctions such as warnings are used. The police are seen as an agency that provides services.

To a large extent police patrolling appears to be symbolic in nature, whichever style is practiced. In the Kansas City study reported by Kelling and associates (1974) three approaches to patrol were taken. In some beats reactive patrol was practiced. That is, response was only made to incoming calls for assistance, with no other patrolling being done. In some beats proactive patrol was exercised. In these areas preventive patrol was intensified, with as much as three times the normal level of preventive patrol taking place. In a third area normal levels of patrol were maintained. The three types of patrol were found to make little difference in terms of the measures of the impact of patrol techniques. Citizens did not notice any difference among the areas. This finding would suggest that police patrol serves the symbolic function of assuring the public of protection. However, it does not appear to have a significant impact on victimization. Also, patrol does not appear to deter the incidence of crime to any marked extent.

The real utility of the different styles of policing, according to Manning, is that they "allow the police administrator a certain leeway in trying to control his men in line with the demands of the most powerful interests in the community. . . . "

Great numbers of complaints levied against the police would certainly be a blow to their professional status. Thus secrecy becomes an important tactic in keeping the public uninformed. As William A. Westley described this aspect of the police culture,

> Secrecy among the police stands as a shield against the attacks of the outside world; against bad newspaper publicity, which would make the police lose respect; against public criticism, from which they feel they suffer too much; against the criminal, who is eager to know the moves of the police; against the law, which they too frequently abrogate. Secrecy is loyalty, for it represents sticking with the group, and its maintenance carries with it a profound sense of participation. Secrecy is solidarity, for it represents a common front against the outside world and consensus in at least one goal (1970:111).

In a later work Jerome Skolnick discusses the working personality of the police role which results in police solidarity, social isolation from the public, and thus a preoccupation with secrecy (1967:chapter 3). The primary effect of the secrecy tactic is that it constrains many citizens from making complaints. No adequate records are kept regarding police misconduct. Police bureaucracies prefer to keep all investigations of such misconduct to themselves. The debates regarding the institution of civilian review boards in the 1960s made this point very clear.

The police have also used the tactics of utilizing crime statistics and technology to promote the public appearance of professionalism. The police have long been suspected of manipulating the clearance rate and the crime index to project an impression of efficiency. Skolnick has defined clearance rate as "the percentage of crimes known to the police which the police believe have been solved" (1967:168). The problem with using the clearance rate to measure police efficiency is two-fold. First, crimes which have not been reported to the police and thus remain unsolved do not enter into the equation to reduce the police department's measure of efficiency. Second, the accuracy of the number of reported crimes thought to be solved by the police is questioned. The criminal who confesses to more crimes than he committed does the police a favor and in return may be promised a "break" during plea bargaining. As for the crime index, no mandatory, centralized crime-reporting system exists. As Manning has concluded, "Because there has been very little in the way of standard reporting and investigating practices, the police have been able to control the crime rate to a large degree by controlling aspects of enforcement" (1975:109). The police bureaucracy also places great emphasis on the use of technology in the "war against crime," just as the military brass take great pride in weaponry innovations. To them, the purchase of new equipment is seen as an important step in the gaining of professional status.

To what degree police professionalism is only a strategy employed by the police is not an easy question to resolve. This lack of clarity, however, has not seemed to impede public recognition of the concept. During the 1970s public commitment to increased police professionalism was signaled both by rhetoric and by appropriations. Police education and efforts to improve the professional image of police were funded by LEAA. Law-enforcement and criminal justice courses and programs multiplied. So did expectations of those who were attentive to police policies. Priorities for spending were debated (more and better hardware versus increased personnel training and service functions); better community-police relations were demanded and sought; the increased representation of blacks, Spanish-Americans, and women on police forces generated claims, counter-claims, and controversy; so too did the issues of collective bargaining and unionization.

Obstacles to Professionalism

It is easier to chart the progress of police professionalism than it is to clarify its meaning. Richard A. Staufenberger assessed the progress in police professionalization by 1977: "... Selection procedures are more job related, training and conduct standards have been tightened, and higher education for police officers is much more the rule than the exception. Research . . . is currently being conducted on every aspect of policing. . . . At least two new professional organizations have been established for the purpose of upgrading the police" (1977:684).

There exist, however, some very real obstacles in the path to greater police profesionalism. A number of police scholars believe the greatest impediment to professionalism is the highly organized military rank structure that is an essential feature of most police departments. According to Staufenberger such a military rank structure "(1) admits few civilians to policy-making positions in police agencies; (2) discourages lateral entry into the departments; and (3) severely restricts discretion and initiative in the basic police officer" (1977:679). This lack of lateral entry, combined with the few promotional opportunities afforded by the rank structure, offers limited incentives for the career development of individual officers.

Policing as an occupation is associated with a number of professional organizations. None, however, has the same role within the occupation as the American Bar Association and the American Medical Association have in their professions. The police have no national association that enforces universal standards for its members. One of the best-known national organizations is the International Association of Chiefs of Police. The IACP was founded in 1893 and has a membership of approximately 10,000. As an organization comprised of heads of law-enforcement agencies it is not as association representative of the basic police officer. The IACP, then, is extremely limited in its role to serve as a professional organization capable of setting standards for all those who are concerned with the occupation of policing. A more recent professional association is the American Academy for Professional Law Enforcement, which was established in 1974. It is a small but national association that was formed to meet the needs of college-educated police officers. However, neither the AAPL nor any other police association has the prestige or clout commonly associated with occupations that have attained professional status.

The formation of police labor unions is viewed by many as a possible obstacle to professionalism. Staufenberger has observed:

> While certainly the so-called professional associations have, and will continue to have, a profound effect on the movement toward police professionalism, a convincing argument can be made that their effect will be completely overshadowed by the burgeoning police union movement. This movement is still in its infancy, but its growth and impact are being felt on all aspects of police policy.[3]

The growth of police unions is characterized by both its rapid growth and its fragmentation. The International Conference of Police Associations, the Fraternal Order of Police, the ICPA, the International Brotherhood of Police, the American Federation of State, County and Municipal Employees, and the Teamsters are all competing for members. Such growth of union activity raises such questions as to whether unionism and professionalism are antithetical. More specifically, union stances on such issues as lateral entry and a higher education requirement for promotion are not known. Thus unionism stands as a possible obstacle to professionalism.

Individual versus Organizational Professionalism

As we have seen above, officer education does not in itself change the conditions which most often appear to impede professionalization: these include paramilitary, hierarchial organization; political control; institutional ambivalence toward education. It is widely agreed that police work requires independent judgment and adjustment of police department practices to complex and changing circumstances, yet organizational constraints tend to inhibit the autonomy of individual officers.

Does professionalism inhere in the individual officer or in the organizational context in which the officer works? Neiderhoffer specified the following elements in an occupational field as being indicative of professionalism: (1) high standards of admission; (2) a special body of knowledge and theory; (3) altruism and dedication to the service ideal; (4) a lengthy period of training for candidates; (5) a code of ethics; (6) licensing of members; (7) autonomous control; (8) pride of the members in their profession; (9) publicly recognized status and prestige. These entail both individual capacities and organizational practices (1967:18-19).

Erika Fairchild has observed that there are two models of professionalism in policing: organizational or management professionalism and individual or subject matter professionalism. Fairchild describes the two thusly: organizational professionalism

> has certain attributes; merit hiring, well trained personnel, technical competence and capacity efficiency of operations . . . [and] owes much to the rational-legal bureaucratic model of Max Weber and has been exemplified in police operations by the work and writings of the late Orlando Wilson. . . . Individual or subject-area professionalism, on the other hand, is a concept which has varied connotations, but which often implies an occupational identity which stresses expertise or the acquisition of a systematic body of knowledge, self-regulation according to a set of ethics or principles, wide discretion in dealing with clients, and recognition by, and trust from the public in regard to professional status (1978:1).

George Ritzer's cogent discussion of "Professionalism and the Individual" provides a theoretical basis for distinguishing individual and organizational professionalism. Ritzer predicted that "by differentiating the individual and occupational levels of professionalism we can clarify . . . controversy . . . in the literature on professionals" (1971:72).

For the most part, occupational sociologists have generally ignored the subject of professionalism. Ritzer, however, has identified six characteristics of individual professionalism:[4]

a. general, systematic knowledge;
b. authority over clients;
c. community rather than self-interest which is related to an emphasis on symbolic rather than monetary rewards;
d. membership in occupational associations, training in occupational schools, and existence of a sponsor;
e. recognition by the public that he is a professional;
f. involvement in the occupational culture.

Ritzer goes on to describe how these various characteristics can be operationalized. He operationalizes general, systematic knowledge in the following way:[5]

1. How much job-related education and/or training has the individual had? What was the quality of the school attended or the training program completed?
2. Where did the individual rank in his graduating class?
3. Did the individual receive any honors while in training?
4. How do clients or customers evaluate the individual in terms of his job-related knowledge?
5. How do peers evaluate the individual in terms of his job-related knowledge?

It is possible, of course, for some individuals to be more professional on some dimensions than others.

The individual model most clearly projects the elements Neiderhoffer held were indicative of professionalism. "Individual professionalism" has been less frequently discussed by commentators on the police model than on the management model. References in the literature to "structural problems" and the constraints of bureaucracy" within which the police function have frequently implied that the bureaucratic organization of police is a major obstacle to individual professionalism. Skolnick wrote: ". . . The professional department which emphasizes rationality, efficiency, and impersonality, envisages the professional as bureaucrat, almost as a machine calculating alternative action by a stated program of rules, and possessing the technical ability to carry out decision irrespective of personal feelings" (1967:236).

Proceeding from that conventional view of police bureaucracy, some argue that professionalization is an organizational responsibility. Intradepartmental communication and overall organizational climate were cited by Robert M. Mendoza, Jr., as facilitating factors in the growth of police professionalism (1978).

It appears that much could be accomplished in diminishing the lack of clarity regarding police professionalism if only organizational and individual police professionalism would be consistently differentiated and operationalized. If such a conceptual difference were attained, then such questions could be raised regarding the congruence or discrepancy between the two levels of professionalism. In other words, will we find some nonprofessional officers in more professional departments, and, conversely, will we find some professional officers in relatively nonprofessional departments? According to Ritzer, whether the two levels of professionalism are congruent or discrepant in a particular case depends on three factors—individual, organizational, and occupational. The key question with regard to police professionalism is whether police organizations and policing as an occupation foster or impede the professionalism of the individual police officer.

Police View of Professionalism

Exploratory discussions with police officers concerning the meaning and source of professionalism indicate that officers distinguish between organizational and individual professionalism.[6] They acknowledge the impact of the department (rules, leadership) on performance but allege that the foundation of professional behavior is inherent in the individual officers. One policeman observed, "A department may frustrate a highly motivated, professional officer with guidelines and arbitrary decisions, but the department cannot make a *real* police officer out of an individual 'who isn't right for police work.' " When officers were asked to specify what made one "right for police work," the answer was, "*Not* formal education!" Neither was the answer specialized training schools such as the police academy. Academy training was seen as an aid in developing previously demonstrated ability.

Officers believe the greatest difference between experienced members of the force and new recruits is the "greater weight of the badge and gun" for recruits. They further believe this is true regardless of the educational background of the recruit.

An idea frequently expressed by officers is that "common sense" is the root of individual, professional police performance. Several times those who detailed how college training might contribute to officer effectiveness (given the requisite common sense) went on to comment bitterly, "The judges haven't helped the cause of police professionalism." Officers note that courts have ordered departments to recruit a specified number of persons from particular categories of applicants. Experienced officers appear to be somewhat resentful of "outside groups" monitoring police recruitment and promotion policy. "Affirmative Action" programs tend to be seen as contradictory rather than complementary to professional development.

More so than for most occupational groups, police attitudes toward women are deeply rooted in the past practices and continuing mystique of their job. Ironically, the absence of a tradition of professional education prior to recruitment onto the force could facilitate a much more rapid influx of minorities and women into police work than into the traditional professions.

Although a nexus between higher education and policing has not been established, the proliferation of academic departments and institutes of criminal justice and law enforcement may be indicative of long-range changes. Students at the Southern Police Academy Institute, University of Louisville, are advised that the following criteria are germane to the achievement of professional excellence: (1) mandatory educational standards; (2) lateral transfer; (3) transferability of retirement credits; (4) ethical standards; (5) career development program; (6) Certification of eligible professionals; (7) specialized literature; (8) continuous research (1976:4). With the exception of the absent "autonomy," this list is virtually the same as Niederhoffer's. The emphasis upon educational standards, certification, specialized literature, and research suggests a strong academic dimension to professionalism.

However, the relationship between police behavior and higher education is not certain. Barbara Raffle Price reported that ". . . more information is needed on the relationship between college education and police performance. Studies to date have shown any college education is associated with reduced complaints for graduate officers, but much more information is needed, including the effect, if any, of specific curricula" (1977:9). Price's general view of professionalism among police is that it is more a matter of rhetoric than of substance.

Interviews with officers reveal that police supervisors tend to distinguish between professionalism and unionization; however, it is not clear that rank-and-file patrolmen do so. An assumption of some police supervisory personnel that professionalization will offset a movement toward unionization may not square with the perceptions of rank-and-file patrolmen. Much will depend upon the extent to which general economic conditions and political decisions diminish or generate militancy among officers.

Conclusion

Samuel Walker examined the "origins, development, and fruition of the idea of police professionalization" and concluded that professionalization had left "an ambiguous legacy." In his view, professionalization was "not an unqualified triumph" (1977:167). Walker was focusing on what Fairchild and Ritzer termed "organizational professionalism." Why did the growth of professionalism (chronicled by Walker) fail to establish "policing as a profession" (as stated by Price)? Walker's answer is: "Little attention was given to the needs and perceptions of the rank-and-file patrolman" (111).

On the surface (in articles, speeches, and press releases) police professionalization has been a dominant trend in the 1970s. The consequent impact on policing is difficult to assess because of divergent views on the substance and source of professionalism. For an "idea whose time has come," the concept of police professionalism is encumbered with a heavy gloss of uncertainty, ambivalence, and controversy. Reappraisal of rhetoric about professionalism is well underway: examination of officer attitudes across ranks, years of experience, and educational background may help to clarify what values underlie the often announced goals for achieving professionalization.

Notes

1. Habenstein, Robert W. "Critique of 'Profession' as a Social Category," *The Sociological Quarterly* (November 4, 1963): 297. Reprinted with permission.

2. Manning, Peter. "The Policeman as Hero" in Isadore Silver, ed. *The Crime Control Establishment.* Englewood Cliffs, N.J.: Prentice-Hall, 1974. Reprinted with permission.

3. Staufenberger, R.A. "The Professionalization of Police: Efforts and Obstacles," *Public Administration Review* 37 (November/December 1977), p. 680. Reprinted with permission.

4. Reprinted from "Professionalism and the Individual" by George Ritzer in *The Professions and their Prospects,* Eliot Friedson, Editor, © 1971, 1973 pp. 62-63, by permission of the Publisher, Sage Publications, Inc. Beverly Hills/London.

5. Ibid., p. 64. Reprinted by permission of the Publisher, Sage Publications, Inc. Beverly Hills/London.

6. Explanatory interviews were conducted with police officers during June 1978 as an initial step in constructing a questionnaire on professionalism.

References

Cooper, Lynn, and associates. *The Iron Fist and the Velvet Glove.* Staff of the Center for Research on Criminal Justice, Berkeley, Calif.: 1975.

Fairchild, Erika S. "Professionalism in Corrections Administration," Paper presented at the 1978 National Institute on Crime and Delinquency Meeting, Bal Harbour, Florida, June 19, 1978.

Habenstein, Robert W. "Critique of 'Profession' as a Social Category." *Sociological Quarterly* 4 (November 1963).

Kelling, George L., and associates. *The Kansas City Preventive Patrol Experiment: A Summary Report* Washington, D.C.: The Police Foundation, 1974.

Larson, Magali Sarfatti. *The Rise of Professionalism: A Sociological Analysis. Berkeley:* University of California Press, 1977.

Manning, Peter K. "The Policeman As Hero," in Isidore Silver, ed. *The Crime Control Establishment*. Englewood Cliffs, N.J.: Prentice-Hall, 1974.

Mendoza, Robert Hernandez, Jr. Comments made on the panel "Professionalism in Criminal Justice," 1978 National Institute on Crime and Delinquency Meeting, Bal Harbour, Fla. June 19, 1978.

Niederhoffer, Arthur. *Behind the Shield*, New York: Doubleday, 1967.

President's Commission on Law Enforcement and Administration of Justice. *Task Force Report: The Police.* Washington, D.C. GPO, 1967.

Price, Barbara Raffle. *Police Professionalism.* Lexington, Mass.: Lexington Books: D.C. Heath, 1977.

"Professionalization, What Do You Think?" Handout distributed to students at the Southern Police Institute, University of Louisville, 1976.

Ritzer, George. "Professionalism and the Individual," in Eliot Friedson, ed. *The Professions and Their Prospects*. Beverly Hills, Calif.: Sage Publications, 1971.

Skolnick, Jerome. *Justice Without Trial*. New York: John Wiley, 1967.

Staufenberger, Richard A. "The Professionalization of Police: Efforts and Obstacles," *Public Administration Review* 37:6 (November/December 1977): 678-685.

Sutherland, Edwin H., and Donald R. Cressey. *Criminology*. Philadelphia: J.B. Lippincott, 1974.

Walker, Samuel. *A Critical History of Police Reform.* Lexington, Mass.: Lexington Books, D.C. Heath, 1977.

Weiner, Norman L. "The Effect of Education on Police Attitudes," *Journal of Criminal Justice* 2 (1974): 317-328.

Westley, William A. *Violence and the Police: A Sociological Study of Law, Custom, and Morality.* Cambridge, Mass.: MIT Press, 1970.

Wilson, James Q. *Varieties of Police Behavior*. New York: Atheneum, 1976.

10 Police Training about Criminal Procedure: Infrequent and Inadequate

Stephen L. Wasby

The policeman is supposed to protect your life, rights, and property in that order; in fact, he protects life and property, and doesn't know your rights.

— (police training officer)

That law-enforcement officers know about the requirements courts impose on them is by no means certain. Police complaints about the Warren Court's "revolution" in criminal procedure might suggest they do. Yet, without adequate training, are police likely to know about rulings seldom understood even by well-educated laypersons? Police can hardly implement the Constitution's procedural guarantees if they do not learn about them during their training, their formal socialization to their work. Those whose policy concern is implementation know that in some form the law *must* get into the hands of those who are expected to enforce it. Regardless of the accuracy of the assumption that police trained in the law will behave more in accord with legal rules, limited training can have only limited effects. Inadequate investment of effort in training means that we have no adequate test of the effects of training on police behavior.

Training is important because, beyond the transmission of specific skills, it is thought to reduce discretion. It thus helps to serve as a necessary, if perhaps not a sufficient, condition for the "rule of law." The Warren Court's criminal procedure decisions provided a set of rules to limit and guide police officers' discretion, yet that discretion remained "uninformed" and thus unchecked if the rules were not communicated. Training also contributes to "professionalization." Although there is not substantial agreement on the meaning of "professionalism," the ideal seems to be individuals following more than the rules of the organization of which they are a part; adherence to external norms is necessary (White, 1972:62). However, professionalism may be only rule-following without discretion, a form of bureaucratization (Henderson, 1975:111). Thus "rule-applier" police officers enforce rules universalistically not because they believe that rules should be used impartially on all persons but because they are command oriented and because they have found they can work within the Supreme Court's constraints, that is, that the rules do not decrease efficiency. If not fully "professional," these officers are at least different from "crime-fighters" who resent any limitations on the police or "tough cops" who feel threatened by professional standards such as college training (White, 1972:74-75). It is thus important to put the requisite information about the law into the "rule-appliers'" hands.

113

Communicating the Law

The amount of effort devoted to communicating the law has increased noticeably since the Supreme Court's ruling in *Mapp* v. *Ohio* (1961), excluding improperly seized evidence from state trials. Although it did not affect the overall means of communicating legal information to the police (Milner, 1971a:226), the *Miranda* decision (1966) produced another important increment in training. Because pre-1960 training had been quite skimpy, except perhaps in the very largest cities and some state police agencies, the post-1961 increase in communicating the law left training for officers generally inadequate. Passage of the 1968 Safe Streets Act, with its infusion of Law Enforcement Assistance Act (LEAA) funds, led to an improvement, but training deficiencies are still quite evident, with some states adopting mandatory training for new officers only within the last two years. Those who became officers after *Miranda* are not as likely to evidence the hostility to due process requirements shown by those who were experienced when the Warren Court acted. However, they are seldom informed of changes in the law, even those Burger Court rulings favorable to law-enforcement interests. All in all, the training picture in the late 1970s remains a woeful one.

"With the highly fragmented police system of the United States, the seemingly simple matter of transmitting new court rulings in a form usable by departments and individuals is a difficult job" (Bordua, 1966:ix). There are multiple information channels, but at the heart of the problem is a lack of *systematic* transmission of information. Training is only one way of transmitting legal rules to the police. Among others are the court system, in which local judges play a particularly important part, and both the mass and specialized media.

Government lawyers—attorneys general and local prosecutors— can play a significant role in transmitting information about legal rulings and deserve special attention. Some attorneys general publish, specifically for law-enforcement officials, bulletins in which Supreme Court decisions are related to state law and to officers' practical concerns. They may also hold informational meetings on major "impact decisions." Local prosecutors, while potentially a major means of communicating legal rules, rarely shoulder that task, not defining it as part of their role. Even when they are willing to teach the police, they often lack a regular link with police agencies through which information could be transmitted. Their lack of assistance has led some departments, not wishing to rely on random means of obtaining legal information, to hire police legal advisers. These lawyers, whom only the larger departments can afford to hire, interpret Supreme Court decisions, develop teaching materials, and help teach the new rules (Caplan, 1967:304; Carrington, 1970).

Milner's study of the impact of *Miranda* in four medium-sized Wisconsin cities is one of the few to tell us something about the communication of legal rules to police officers (Milner, 1971a). Both initially and overall, the officers heard about the decision from a wide variety of sources; conference-and-training sessions (rated the best source) and superior officers were major sources. The greater a department's professionalism, the more sources officers had and the more likely they were to have received information from training sessions. However, professionalization did not bring greater contact with sources of information outside the department unless those sources reinforced departmental ideology. (Although those approving of *Miranda* were more likely to have received information at training sessions, ratings of sources did not depend on approval of the decision.)

Following up Milner's study, Berkson (1970) found that small-town Wisconsin officers also gave high ratings to conference-and-training sessions, but that they lacked the contact with the state attorney general's office, which served as a regular source of information for larger departments. In a later study (Berkson, 1978:73-75), he found that Florida police officers claimed to have obtained reliable information about Supreme Court decisions from superiors, with coworkers another important source of information. He also found "no significant difference in levels of awareness [about Supreme Court decisions] between superiors and subordinates," with the latter more often correct about the decisions and the superiors more "unsure."

Wasby's study of small southern Illinois and western Massachusetts police departments revealed that they had no single primary source of information about Supreme Court decisions (Wasby, 1976). Little material about the cases was provided to the officers and many were confused about where such material—or the cases themselves—might be available. (Even when materials were available, time to read and absorb them often was not.) Bulletins, although criticized by some for not arriving fast enough, and training sessions were generally ranked as the most effective means of communication, and personal friends, newspapers, and radio and television as least effective. Massachusetts officers, with a more positive orientation to legal matters and to the Court itself, were more likely to consider the Court's published decisions helpful, and some had even arranged for subscriptions to the *Supreme Court Reporter*. The attorney general and prosecutors were frequently mentioned in both states, although Massachusetts officers, who had more of a statewide orientation, emphasized the attorney general while Illinois officers focused more on the state's attorney (prosecutor). Officers in both states overwhelmingly agreed that written communication about Supreme Court decisions was more effective than oral communication, but a combination of the two was preferred by some officers.

Training Programs

It is in training programs that oral communication reinforces written materials. Training takes a variety of forms. (For a general discussion, see Saunders, 1970.) Prerecruit training, which had its genesis in California's two-year community college programs, is of growing significance. Increasingly the route to a law-enforce-ment career includes some college work, either in such two-year programs or in four-year Criminal (or Administration of Justice) degree programs. Almost half of all police officers now have one or more years of college education, up from one-fifth in 1960 and one-third in 1970 (NILECJ, 1978:10). However, despite recommendations that police officers have a college degree, as of 1975 only 5 percent of departments required completion of one or more years of college (NILECJ, 1978:9). More than $40 million per year has been expended through the Law Enforcement Education Program (LEEP). LEEP funding was intended to assist preservice students, with tuition for in-service officers to come from other LEAA funding. Yet Hoover (1975:21) reported that only 16 percent of LEEP aid recipients were preservice students; the remaining 84 percent were in-service students.

Such federal funding has been based on the premise "that higher education for law enforcement and other line personnel is a necessary condition for upgrading their performance and for improving the responsiveness of the system" (NILECJ, 1978:9). Yet such premises are challenged by the recent finding that

> Occupational analysis studies, based on ratings of skill and knowledge needs for specific police officer tasks, failed to identify any major task of the basic patrol officer which necessitated a college-level educational background. . . .

Moreover,

> A review of available research findings designed to relate education—and other attributes—to police performance or police attitudes, similarly pro-vided limited evidence of superior performance by college-educated offi-cers (NILECJ, 1978:9).

There are also other difficulties. While the basic law-enforcement curriculum of the American Association of Junior Colleges (AAJC) includes three courses (nine hours of sixty-four) with law-based content (Criminal Law, Criminal Evi-dence and Procedure, and Criminal Investigation), such guidelines do not neces-sarily result in uniformity in actual programs, and there is a scarcity of qualified instructors knowledgeable about the law. Moreover, some of the materials used in these and other types of training programs are outdated at the time of their initial use. Many LEEP programs are also said to be of low quality, with many labeled "narrowly training-oriented" and called "seriously deficient . . . even when related to LEAA's own modest standards" (NILECJ, 1978:10).

Far more police pass through police academies than through prerecruit pro-grams. Larger departments have their own academies and extensive programs of fifteen weeks or more—up to more than thirty weeks in some locations—which all recruits must attend. Elsewhere, however, recruit programs may be as short as 240 hours, falling well below the National Advisory Commission's recommended 400-hour minimum. Indeed, departments accounting for roughly two-fifths of all those employed in law enforcement fail to meet the 400-hour standard. (By comparison, it takes approximately 3,500 hours to become a beautician and 5,500 hours to become a mortician, perhaps a monument to the cosmetologists' and morticians' lobbies.) The problem is particularly severe in small police agencies. Of those units with fewer than twenty-five employees, 31 percent of police departments and 22 percent of sheriffs' agencies "still provided no formal entry training to their line staff" as of 1975 (NILECJ, 1978:11-12). In addition, only one-fourth of those agencies met minimum duration standards for their programs.

Recruit training is sadly lacking in criminal procedure content. Most 240-hour programs contain at most thirty hours of law-related material. Little time, perhaps six hours, is left for instruction about criminal procedure after substantive criminal law (the definitions of crimes) is covered. As recently noted, there is also "very limited coverage of procedural and institutional aspects of criminal law practice" (NILECJ,1978:15), namely, how to apply general principles as officers, in the words of one FBI agent, "round the corner to the sound of tinkling glass." However, some of the most useful specialized media for communicating the law are found in connection with training. Of particular note are International Association of Chiefs of Police (IACP) publications such as *Legal Points* and *Training Keys*, the latter providing clear explanations of legal matters and applications to hypothetical situations. They are a welcome relief from discussions of relevant case law apparently written more for the lawyer than for the average officer—perhaps a result of the "dumb cop" stereotype: after all, police can't understand legal material, so why should we even try to write for them?

The picture concerning in-service training is, if anything, worse than that for prerecruit and recruit training. In-service training programs, which seem to cover everything *but* criminal procedure, range from the traditional method of reading bulletins at roll call, where "little time is actually available for training after administrative matters have been disposed of, and where those who conduct the roll-call sessions are not necessarily trained instructors" (Wisconsin Coordinating Council, 1968:19), to occasional night meetings and longer programs in which officers are detached from regular duties for two or three days or, rarely, several weeks. Despite this flexibility, few officers attend in-service training. During 1975, more than 90 percent of police and sheriffs' departments indicated that less than one-fourth of the officers in those departments had attended an in-service course. Indeed, only somewhat over one-third of all officers had *ever* taken a course beyond recruit training (NILECJ, 1978:12). In-service training could be used to follow up preservice and recruit training, but this opportunity to provide current information is often lost.

Effects of Training in Illinois and Massachusetts

What effects might training have in a particular area? Small-town southern Illinois and western Massachusetts officers in the early 1970s had had little training either before becoming officers or subsequently. More recent arrivals had, however, received more training, both initially and through in-service programs, and an increasing number were attending college classes, particularly under the Massachusetts incentive pay plans. However, precious little about the Supreme Court's rulings had been or was being transmitted to the men through training. Most chiefs said that, during their training, they had learned something about the Supreme Court's criminal procedure decisions, although this was affected by the timing of that training. Because of the Supreme Court's relative inactivity in criminal procedure prior to 1961, Massachusetts officers who received training prior to *Mapp* had been told little. Illinois officers with some training were more likely to have been informed of relevant decisions because they were more likely to have received their training later. Thus a slightly higher percentage of Illinois than Massachusetts officers had been given instruction about the exclusionary rule and about what constituted illegal searches and seizures.

Neither officers' length of service nor their formal education were related to their level of knowledge about Supreme Court criminal procedure doctrine in Massachusetts, but Illinois officers who had not completed high school or who had the longest police service (older officers with little education or training) showed less knowledge of the Court's rulings than those with more education. Those officers without in-service training were more likely to have higher knowledge scores than those with such training, probably a result of the fact that little in-service training dealt with the law.

The officers' formal education showed no relationship to their general view of the Supreme Court in either state. Those with some prerecruit law-enforcement education were, however, somewhat more likely to have a positive view of the Court. However, a contemporaneous study of officers in twenty-nine St. Louis area police departments showed relationships between training and attitudes—for example, toward Supreme Court decisions and toward protection of civil liberties, even those of people suspected of criminal acts—to be quite weak, even running in a direction opposite to the hypothesized positive effect (Smith and Ostrom, 1973:11). Neither the amount of police training nor the length of recruit training had a positive effect on attitudes toward "probable cause" limits on searches or toward interrogations—the subject of *Miranda*. About half the St. Louis area police viewed the Court's decisions as harmful or very harmful, while only 5 percent saw them as very helpful. However, college-educated officers were somewhat less likely to see the rulings as harmful.

The Limited Effects of Training

Why might training, particularly about the law, have such apparently limited effects? Part of the answer is to be found in the way in which legal rulings are communicated during training. Seldom is the rationale underlying a decision conveyed. The spirit and tone of communication about the law, particularly when the law is favorable to defendants' rights, is often negative, with the need for compliance stressed only infrequently. Training instructors, ambivalent about the rules they must communicate, often make only a perfunctory recitation or emphasize adhering to the letter of the rules. Like the instructors, many training materials engage in "negative advocacy," with stress placed on how to "live with"—if not avoid—Supreme Court standards.

The size and location of police departments also affect training. Large departments can spare more officers from duty to receive training and can commit more resources to training. Because of greater specialization, they can designate a "training officer." Small departments, however, have insufficient division of labor and specialization for one person to have the responsibility to monitor legal decisions and to transmit information about them to other officers. However, face-to-face communication may be greater in small departments than in large ones, where distance between headquarters and the field may hinder effective communication.

An agency's geographic location interacts with its size. Small-town departments outside metropolitan areas are unable to share resources with other units, unlike the situation in suburbia, where several departments can jointly support a training academy. Officials in small towns may also limit training in order to avoid having to pay higher salaries or having their officers, once trained, leave for higher-paying jobs. The traditionalism of small-town officials also limits resources committed to training: "Our officers weren't trained before and they did a good job. Why is it necessary now?"

Officers' "work situation," including the "milieu in which the police officer operates," "the characteristics of the police decision-making process, and . . . the relationship police have with their reference groups" (Milner, 1971b:467), perhaps is the most substantial factor limiting the effects of police training. The basic uncertainty characteristic of police work, including contradictory role expectations, drives officers to depend on other officers both on and off the job. The reinforcement of views from that source increases potential conflict with external authority like the Supreme Court and limits receptivity to communication about the law. This tendency is considerably reinforced when the police subculture coalesces into formal groups; their militance about police values is unlikely to lead to higher adherence to protection of defendants' rights.

A department's reward structure, usually keyed to arrest, traffic tickets, or the "clearance rate" for robberies, not to the implementation of legal rules, also has crucial effects on an officer's work. Moreover, police are seldom disciplined for failing to follow search and seizure limitations and are seldom rewarded, other than through limited incentive pay, for availing themselves of further training. Indeed, "the norms within the police organization, particularly the attitudes of superior officers and the emphasis on solving crime, are more important determinants of police behavior than judicial rules" (Landynski, 1972:49). If superior officers' commitment to legal rules leads to departmental training based on that commitment, officers' behavior may be affected. However, the many police executives who do not share the values embodied in appellate court decisions are instead likely to see training, particularly that outside the department, as a way in which their own control is reduced. Even when superior officers do have a positive attitude toward training, the commitment of resources is usually insufficient to overcome more deep-seated pressures from the job situation. As an astute observer recently remarked, "Police recruits are much like other young men of a similar background; it is police mores and the police role that make them adopt police behavior" (Chevigny, 1969:137).

Conclusions

Although not many officers engage in "search behavior" to inform themselves about the law, many officers—and particularly the younger ones—at least *say* they want to learn about the law. Massachusetts and Illinois chiefs were unanimous in saying it was important for police to know about Supreme Court decisions, and big-city departments Canon studied felt that police ought to be "very familiar" with Supreme Court decisions affecting law-enforcement officers (Wasby, 1976: 96). Can anything be done to communicate information about criminal procedure rules more effectively to those officers? The developing consensus in the law-enforcement community as to the most and least useful modes of communicating the law indicates that one would not have to develop completely new means of communication. Substantially better communication could be provided by developing more effective adaptations of available basic forms. Nor does one need to reach very far for suggestions on how to provide a better flow of legal information. Officers in both Illinois and Massachusetts, who sought more information more effectively presented, wanted more training, wanted it more up-to-date, and wanted it made more practical, with more emphasis given to problems of small-town police; these are hardly radical suggestions. Officers' expectations would be met by increases in the frequency of training sessions and of bulletins and by greater effort on the part of prosecutors or state attorneys general.

  Those officers who are willing to assume the responsibility for finding out the law need to be assisted by providing them with a threshold level of familiarity with the law, making legal materials more accessible, and providing someone to whom they can turn for further explanation. Because such officers consttute only a small proportion of the police, relatively aggressive "outreach" work will be required to bring materials to other officers, particularly in rural communities. One reasonable suggestion is that circuit-riding training officers could hold one-evening or one-day "update" programs on the Supreme Court's decisions and other relevant rules in every rural county seat on a rotating basis. That, at least, would be a start in the right direction; much more needs to be done.

References

Berkson, Larry. 1970. "The United States Supreme Court and Small-Town Police Officers: A Study in Communication." Unpublished ms.

——. 1978. *The Supreme Court and Its Publics: The Communication of Policy Decisions.* Lexington, Mass.: Lexington Books, D.C. Heath.

Bordua, David J., ed. 1966. *The Police: Six Sociological Essays.* New York: John Wiley.

Caplan, Gerald. 1967. "The Police Legal Adviser," *Journal of Criminal Law, Criminology, and Police Science* 58 (September): 303-309.

Carrington, Frank. 1970. "Speaking for the Police," *Journal of Criminal Law, Criminology, and Police Science* 61 (June): 244-279.

Chevigny, Paul. 1969. *Police Power.* New York: Vintage.

Henderson, Thomas. 1975. "The Relative Effects of Community Complexity and of Sheriffs upon Professionalism of Sheriff Departments," *American Journal of Political Science* 19 (February): 107-132.

Hoover, Larry T. 1975. *Police Educational Characteristics and Curricula.* Washington, D.C.: National Institute of Law Enforcement and Criminal Justice.

Landynski, Jacob. 1972. "Search and Seizure," in *The Rights of the Accused,* ed. S. Nagel. Beverly Hills, Calif.: Sage Publications, pp. 27-58.

Milner, Neal. 1971a. *The Court and Local Law Enforcement: The Impact of Miranda.* Beverly Hills, Calif.: Sage Publications.

——. 1971b. "Supreme Court Effectiveness and Police Organization," *Law and Contemporary Problems* 36 (Autumn): 267-487.

The National Manpower Survey of the Criminal Justice System: Executive Summary. Washington, D.C.: GPO. This project was supported by a grant from the National Institute of Law Enforcement and Criminal Justice, Law Enforcement Assistance Administration, U.S. Department of Justice, 1978.

Saunders, Charles B., Jr. 1970. *Upgrading the American Police: Education and Training for Better Law Enforcement.* Washington, D.C.: The Brookings Institution.

Smith, Dennis C., and Elinor Ostrom. 1973. "The Effects of Training and Education on Police Attitudes and Performance," in *The Potential for Reform of Criminal Justice,* ed. Herbert Jacah. Beverly Hills, Calif.: Sage Publications, 1974, pp. 45-82.

Wasby, Stephen L. 1976. *Small Town Police and the Supreme Court: Hearing the Word* (Lexington, Mass.: Lexington Books, D.C. Heath.

White, Susan. 1972. "A Perspective on Police Professionalization," *Law and Society Review* 7 (Fall): 61-86.

Wisconsin Coordinating Council for Higher Education. 1968. *Law Enforcement Education in Wisconsin: A Coordinated Approach.* Madison.

Cases Cited

Mapp v. *Ohio*, 367 U.S. 643 (1961).
Miranda v. *Arizona*, 384 U.S. 436 (1966).

Part V
Patterns of Police-Community Transactions

11 Citizen Coproduction of Community Safety

Stephen L. Percy

Studies of police agency structure, operation, and performance have abounded in recent years largely as a result of concern about increasing crime rates and growing citizen fear of being victimized. Traditionally, we have looked to the police to handle problems of crime and public safety. Most studies have examined (or speculated on) the impact of particular police strategies and arrangements on community conditions. Noticeably absent from most studies is recognition of the significant role that citizens perform in affecting community security and safety. Citizens are not simply "clients" of the police. They are instead active participants in the production as well as the consumption of community security and safety. Through a wide variety of actions citizens are coproducers with law-enforcement agencies of safe and secure community conditions.[1]

Exemplifying the realization of the importance of citizen coproductive functions is the following statement made by the National Institute of Law Enforcement and Criminal Justice:

> In study after study, the picture that emerges shows the citizen—both individually and collectively—as the linchpin of the crime control apparatus. Unless citizens report crimes promptly, unless they come forward with information to help police make arrests, unless they testify in court, and unless they actively support crime prevention efforts, the criminal justice system operates under severe handicaps.[2]

The National Advisory Committee on Criminal Justice Standards and Goals similarly concluded that "if the country is to reduce crime, there must be a willingness on the part of every citizen to give of himself, his time, his energy, and his imagination."[3]

This chapter examines the conceptual dimensions of citizen inputs into the production of community security and safety. Some data on coproduction from a recent study of policing in three metropolitan areas will be presented to demonstrate the current magnitude of citizen involvement in producing community security and safety. The final section of the article briefly considers measuring and assessing the impact of coproduction.

The research for this chapter was funded by the National Science Foundation (Applied Science and Research Applications) under Grant NSF GI-43949. The author gratefully acknowledges this support. Any findings, inferences, views, or opinions expressed herein are, however, those of the author and do not necessarily reflect those of the National Science Foundation. The author also acknowledges the valuable assistance of Frances P. Bish, John McIver, Elinor Ostrom, Roger B. Parks, and Eric J. Scott who commented on earlier drafts of this article.

Modes of Citizen Involvement in Producing Community Security

Citizen activities related to the production of community security may be classified according to a number of characteristics. Schneider and Eagle suggest that citizen activities may be classified as private action programs and collective action programs.[4] Bish and Neubert consider three types of citizen activities: (1) individual citizen activities, (2) group or joint activities, and (3) activities undertaken by citizens in direct cooperation with police.[5]

Inherent in the Bish and Neubert conception are two distinct but related production dimensions: (1) level of cooperation of citizens with other citizens and (2) level of citizen cooperation with police agencies. Simplified, these production dimensions can be arrayed in a 2 by 2 matrix as shown in figure 11-1. Little cooperation with police and direct cooperation with police represent the row categories. Individual/household activity and group activity categories are arrayed on the columns. Examples of the four types of citizen coproduction are listed in figure cells.

Citizens are undertaking activities to increase protection from crime at an increasing rate. The benefits of such activities accrue largely to the individuals, families, and businesses that undertake them. Individual/household activities undertaken with little or no cooperation with police agencies are listed in cell 1 of figure 11-1. These activities include installing home protection devices (for example, alarms, extra locks, and outdoor lighting) and self-protective activities (for example, learning self-defense skills, carrying a weapon, and avoiding dangerous areas).

Individual citizens and households in direct cooperation with police also affect the production of community security and safety (cell 2). One of the most fundamental coproductive roles of citizens is the reporting of criminal activity— both real and suspected—to the police. Citizen provision of crime-related information to police and testifying in court are other basic citizen activities long recognized as important.[6] Without these types of coproductive activity, police agencies can do little to apprehend criminals and control crime.

In recent years individual citizens have begun to undertake other functions in direct cooperation with police agencies. One example is citizens riding with patrol officers as auxiliary officers or as ordinary citizens. The City of Rochester, New York, uses a system of foot patrol with one sworn officer and one citizen walking beats together in downtown areas. Citizens are not expected to act as, nor are they trained to be, police officers; instead they aid in improving police interaction with citizens and business persons. Reporting suspicious circumstances to police and requesting vacation checks are further examples of individual citizen coproductive activities undertaken in direct cooperation with police agencies.

Citizen groups also perform important roles in the provision of community security and satisfaction (cells 3 and 4). Among these groups are block groups, mobile patrols, lobbying groups, and police-community councils. Block clubs are

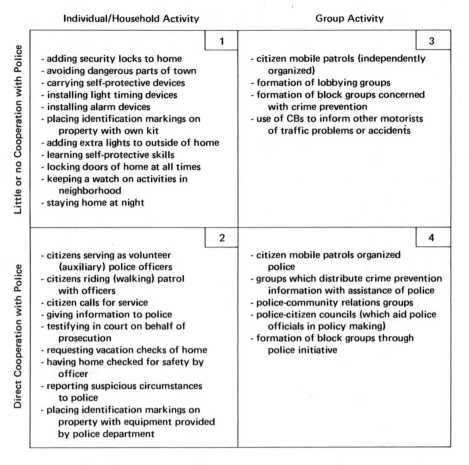

Figure 11-1. Dimensions of Citizen Coproductive Activity

generally created in response to some major and common problem affecting citizens in a geographic area. Club activities are related to combating or solving the common problem. Often this problem has been a sharp increase in a particular type of crime such as robbery, burglary, or sexual assault. Activities in response to these crime problems include providing crime prevention information, increasing citizen awareness of the problem, urging citizens to undertake surveillance, improving neighborhood lighting, and working with police to make police services more responsive. One illustration is the West Philadelphia (Penna.) block association that was formed following a rash of crimes in 1971; this group organized block meetings, reviewed home protection techniques, increased citizen surveillance, and organized citizen walks.[7]

Citizen patrols have been initiated in several urban areas. One form of citizen patrols involves citizen volunteers patrolling in their own cars, which are equipped with two-way radios but not with sirens or light bars. Citizens on patrol are instructed to notify the police in cases of crime or suspicious circumstances and *not* to become involved individually. These citizen complements to police patrol greatly enhance the surveillance in the community and have proven effective in reducing crime rates in some areas.[8] These patrols have thus far demonstrated little evidence of degenerating into citizen vigilante groups.

Another citizen group activity is the formation of a committee that (1) lobbies in state and local arenas for crime-related policies, (2) combines with police officials to form policy recommending bodies, and/or (3) distributes crime prevention information. The structures and activities of these groups are varied, although almost all reflect renewed interest in police, crime, and the criminal justice system. Police-community councils have been instrumental in conveying public wisdom and concern to police officials while simultaneously transmitting information on police activities to citizens. Originally viewed by officials as obstacles to police agency functioning, these police-community councils have been useful in enhancing police-community relations and police effectiveness in dealing with crime. Citizen groups concerned with crime prevention (some closely related to police agencies, others not) have aided in increasing public awareness of crime prevention methods, and thus have increased citizen involvement in the production of community security and safety.

It is difficult to separate some types of group activities in terms of their jointness of production with police agencies. Some block groups, for example, were formed largely through police initiative. In other cases the police were among the last to recognize the existence and importance of these groups. Mobile patrols are generally more closely related to police agencies, while citizen lobbying groups tend to be less closely connected. Because the degree of cooperation with police agencies varies among particular groups, some types of groups appear in both cells in the group activity column of figure 11-1.

Citizen Coproduction in Three Metropolitan Areas

Examination of empirical data on citizen coproductive activity demonstrates the magnitude of citizen involvement in the production of community security and safety. Let us examine individual/household self-protective activities to illustrate the current level of citizen coproduction. A survey of citizens residing in sixty neighborhoods located in three metropolitan areas—Rochester, New York; Tampa-St. Petersburg, Florida; and St. Louis, Missouri—was conducted during the summer of 1977. Approximately 12,000 citizens in these neighborhoods were interviewed by telephone on such topics as their perceptions of, experiences with, and evaluation of local police agencies, as well as the types of coproductive activities that they and their families have undertaken.

Table 11-1
Protective Activities Undertaken by Individuals/Households
(N = 12,054)

Some people nowadays are taking precautions to protect their homes and families from crime. For the next few questions please tell me whether you or any member of your household have done the following things to increase your safety from crime. Have you:

Activity Type	Number Stating Yes	Percent Stating Yes
Put extra locks on doors	6,252	52
Placed identification markings on property	3,525	29
Purchased a watchdog	2,644	22
Bought a light-timing device	2,600	22
Purchased gun or other weapon	1,615	13
Put bars on windows	912	8
Installed a burglar alarm	849	7
	Number Stating Always	Number Stating Sometimes
Do you lock your doors when you are at home *during the day*?	7,096 (59%)	2,475 (20%)
Do you stay home *at night* because you are afraid to go out?	1,295 (11%)	1,402 (12%)
Do you carry a weapon or something else to protect yourself from crime?	879 (7%)	916 (8%)

Table 11-1 presents data on activities undertaken by citizens and households. The data indicate that citizens are involved to a significant extent in every type of coproduction examined. A rather startling finding is the number of households that have added extra security locks to their homes. Over half of the respondents reported that extra locks had been added to their homes to increase security from crime. About 30 percent of respondents claimed to have placed identification markings on household property, 22 percent purchased a watchdog, and 22 percent bought light-timing devices. Thirteen percent of those interviewed stated that they had purchased some weapon for self-protection. To a lesser extent respondents reported undertaking more costly crime prevention activities, such as installing window bars and burglar alarm systems.

Approximately 60 percent of respondents reported always locking their doors when at home during the day, while 20 percent reported sometimes doing this. Eleven percent of those interviewed stated that they always stayed home at night because they were afraid to go out, while 7 percent reported always carrying a weapon or other self-protection device.

Table 11-2 presents data on self-protective activities of individuals/households in several income groups. There is variation in the types of coproduction under-

Table 11-2
Protective Activities Undertaken by Individuals/Households, by Family Income
(figures in percent; N = 10,159)

Activity Undertaken	Below $5,000	$5,000-$10,000	$10,001-$15,000	$15,001-$20,000	$20,001-$25,000	$25,001-$30,000	Above $30,000
	Reported Income of Respondent's Family						
Put extra locks on doors	49	54	53	51	50	55	51
Placed identification markings on property	18	24	31	37	37	42	43
Purchased a watchdog	18	22	24	24	24	24	20
Bought a light-timing device	12	18	22	26	33	38	34
Purchased gun or other weapon	10	13	15	16	15	18	18
Put bars on windows	9	9	6	6	5	6	6
Installed burglar alarm	4	5	8	8	8	10	14
Always lock doors when at home *during the day*	71	63	56	52	48	47	43
Always stay at home *at night* because afraid to go out	26	12	6	3	4	3	2
Always carry a weapon or self-protection device	7	8	8	7	6	6	7
Number of respondents:	2,137	2,374	2,140	1,632	903	459	514

taken by individuals/households in the income groups, although all groups are very active in coproduction. Individuals in wealthier households placed identification markings on property, bought light-timing devices, purchased weapons, and installed burglar alarm systems more often than individuals in less wealthy households. Less affluent individuals/households were more inclined to put bars in windows, to lock doors when at home during the day, and to stay home at night because of fear of crime. The propensities of citizens to put extra locks on doors and to carry self-protective devices were roughly equal across income groups.

Table 11-3 describes these same coproductive activities for whites and non-whites. There appears to be less variation between racial groups than income groups in undertaking self-protective activities. Nonwhites tended to install extra locks, purchase watchdogs, buy weapons, and install burglar alarms more often than whites, although the variation between racial groups is small in all cases. Whites purchased light-timing devices about twice as frequently as nonwhites, while nonwhites put bars on windows over three times as often as whites. Non-whites also claimed to stay home at night and lock doors during the day more often than whites.

Table 11-3
Protective Activities Undertaken by Individuals/Households, by Respondent's Race
(figures in percent; N = 11,971)

Activity Undertaken	Respondent's Race	
	White	*Nonwhite*
Put extra locks on doors	51	54
Placed identification markings on property	30	27
Purchased a watchdog	21	24
Bought a light-timing device	26	11
Purchased gun or other weapon	13	15
Put bars on windows	4	15
Installed a burglar alarm	6	9
Always lock doors when at home *during the day*	57	64
Always stay at home *at night* because afraid to go out	10	13
Always carry a weapon or self-protective device	7	7
Number of respondents:	8,439	3,532

Measuring and Evaluating Citizen Coproduction

To utilize citizen coproduction most effectively, the impact of types of coproduction on community security and safety must be examined. The first step in this assessment is to identify and measure coproduction; the next step is to assess coproduction's effects on safety and security in the community. A variety of research methods can be used in this context: citizen surveys, business surveys, examination of police agency records, elite interviewing, and observation of police activity. Particular research methods are better suited for examining some types of coproduction than others.

Survey research has been the most frequently used research mode in relation to analysis of coproduction. In addition to the study reported above, several other studies based on survey research have examined crime, fear, and citizen actions taken in response.[9] Survey research is well suited to measuring the types and levels of individual/household and business investment in protection devices and activity taken to reduce the risk of victimization. Surveys can also be used to measure citizen/household involvement with police and/or community groups related to the production of security and safety.

Surveys of business establishments might be utilized to measure the level of consumer purchases or expenditures on self-protective devices such as weapons, alarm systems, property-marking kits, door locks, and light-timing devices. Since it is impossible to establish that all purchases are made to increase individual or household safety, business surveys may tend to overstate the level of coproduction.[10] For example, some guns are purchased for hunting, and timing devices used for purposes such as the lighting of house plants.

Police agency records may contain useful data on various types of coproductive activities. Police departments may record the number of volunteer patrol officers or the number of citizens involved in police-sponsored crime control programs. Interviewing police officials, community leaders, and citizen group leaders can provide useful information on the levels (and perhaps effectiveness) of various types of coproductive activity, such as block groups and citizen mobile patrols. Citizen groups leaders are likely to have data on membership, types of activities undertaken by the group, and possibly the level of participation by members (for example, number of hours contributed).[11]

Finally, observation of police activity is another potential source of data on coproduction. Observation of patrol officers for entire shifts was one research strategy used in an evaluation of a police organization project of which this author is a part.[12] Observers took notes in the field and later completed detailed coding forms on encounters between patrol officers and citizens. Citizen actions during the encounter are recorded on the form. Analysis of observation data allows the measurement of coproduction in encounters with police (for example, describing and naming suspects, signing complaints).

Linking citizen coproductive activities to community security and safety is the final step in evaluating the impact of coproduction. Determining the unique effects of coproduction on community conditions is difficult in that many other factors including police agency activities, other public agency activities, and service conditions simultaneously influence community security and safety.[13] For example, one community condition related to safety and security is the victimization rate. A wide set of variables can potentially affect the victimization rate: amount of street lighting, age distribution of population, housing age and density, socioeconomic characteristics of citizens (service conditions); level of patrol activity, effectiveness of investigative activity (police agency activities); number of school dropouts, rate of locating jobs for unemployed (other public agency activities); citizen reporting of crime, level of surveillance, block group activities, investment in extra locks, outdoor lighting, and alarm systems (citizen coproduction). To determine the unique impact of coproduction on community conditions, such as the victimization rate, the influence of these other factors must be controlled.

It is also useful to examine the factors that affect the types and level of coproduction undertaken by citizens. Do wealthier citizens with extensive resources undertake coproduction, or is it poorer citizens who reside in high crime areas, or is it both? The data presented above suggest that coproductive activities are being undertaken by citizens in all income and racial groups. Other factors, such as the organizational arrangements of police agencies and the level of community organization, may also affect the types and levels of coproduction undertaken by citizens. With information on the determinants of coproduction we can better understand which factors stimulate coproduction and predict what types of coproduction will be undertaken in various situations.

Conclusion

The purpose of this chapter has been to present a conceptual model for classifying coproductive activities; to suggest the importance of citizen coproduction in the production of community security and safety; and to outline means of measuring and evaluating the impact of coproduction. In a brief format it is impossible to describe all types of coproduction and adequately discuss measurement and evaluation. Hopefully this chapter has been suggestive in these areas. Conceptual analysis of, and empirical research on, citizen coproduction is crucial to increasing our understanding of how to improve community security and safety.

Notes

1. Viewing citizens as coproducers of police (and other social) service is a rather novel and important aspect of colleagues associated with the Workshop in Political Theory and Policy Analysis, Indiana University. This concept has been discussed in several works, including Vincent Ostrom and Elinor Ostrom, "Public Goods and Public Choices," in E.S. Savas, ed., *Alternatives for Delivering Public Services: Toward Improved Performance* (Boulder, Colo.: Westview Press, 1977), pp. 7-49; Gordon P. Whitaker, "Size and Effectiveness in the Delivery of Human Services," *Journal of Human Services* (1977); Frances P. Bish and Nancy M. Neubert, "Citizen Contributions to the Production of Community Safety and Security," in Mark S. Rosentraub, ed., *Financing Local Government: New Approaches to Old Problems* (Ft. Collins, Colo.: Western Social Science Association, 1977); Richard C. Rich, "The Roles of Neighborhood Organizations in Urban Service Delivery," Working Paper W77-17 (Bloomington, Ind.: Indiana University, Workshop in Political Theory and Policy Analysis, 1977). Frances P. Bish will explore this concept in some depth in her dissertation, "Citizen Roles in the Production of Safety and Security" (1978).

2. "Community Crime Prevention, Research Brief" (Fall 1977), p. 7. This project was supported by a grant from the National Institute of Law Enforcement and Criminal Justice, Law Enforcement Assistance Administration, U.S. Department of Justice.

3. National Advisory Committee on Criminal Justice Standards and Goals, *Community Crime Prevention* (Washington, D.C.: GPO, 1973), pp. 1-2.

4. Anne L. Schneider and Jerry Eagle, "The Effectiveness of Citizen Participation in Crime Prevention: A Random Outlaw Model" (Eugene, Oreg.: Oregon Research Institute, 1975).

5. Frances P. Bish and Nancy M. Nuebert, "Ctizen Contributions to the Production of Community Safety and Security," in Mark S. Rosentraub, ed., *Financing Local Government: New Approaches to Old Problems* (Ft. Collins, Colo.: Western Social Science Association, 1977).

6. For a discussion of citizen cooperation and criminal clearance see Peter W. Greenwood and Joan Petersilia, *The Criminal Investigation Process Volume 1: Summary and Policy Implications* (Santa Monica, Calif.: Rand Corporation, 1976).

7. George J. Washnis, *Citizen Involvement in Crime Prevention* (Lexington, Mass.: Lexington Books, D.C. Heath, 1976), p. 16.

8. Ibid., p. 57. See also Gary T. Marx and Dane Archer, *Community Police Patrols: An Exploratory Inquiry* (Springfield, Va.: National Technical Information Service, 1972).

· 9. See, for example, Jiri Hehnevajsa, "Crime in the Neighborhood" (Pittsburgh: University of Pittsburgh, University Center for Urban Research, 1977). This volume reviews sixty studies on crime, many of which are based on citizen surveys. This volume is an excellent reference source and provides advice on the construction of surveys to examine citizen experiences with, and reactions to, crime. See also Paul Cirel and associates, *Community Crime Prevention Program–Seattle, Washington* (Washington, D.C.: National Institute on Law Enforcement and Criminal Justice, 1977); Anne L. Schneider, Janie Burcart, and L.A. Wilson, "The Role of Attitudes in Decisions to Report Crimes to the Police" (Eu (Eugene, Oreg.: Oregon Research Institute, 1975); Robert Yin and associates, *Patrolling the Neighborhood Beat: Residents and Residential Security* (Santa Monica, Calif.: Rand Corporation, 1976); and Roger B. Parks, "The Citizen Survey," Police Services Study Methods Report MR-1 (Bloomington, Ind.: Indiana University, Workshop in Political Theory and Policy Analysis, (1978). For a study that looks at business investment in self-protection see Ann P. Bartel, "An Analysis of Firm Demand for Protection against Crime," *Journal of Legal Studies* 4:2 (June 1975): 443-478.

10. Citizen surveys also may tend to overstate the level of coproduction if questions are not worded so as to stress that information is wanted on actions taken to increase self-protection and/or improve community security and safety.

11. See, for example, Annalee Moore, "The Citizen Organization Interview Form," Police Services Study Methods Report MR-13 (Bloomington, Ind.: Indiana University, Workshop in Political Theory and Policy Analysis, (1978).

12. See Edward Caldwell, "Patrol Observation Methods," Police Services Study Methods Report MR-2 (Bloomington, Ind.: Indiana University, Workshop in Political Theory and Policy Analysis, forthcoming, 1978). Reiss also discusses patrol observation with some reference to the roles of citizens in encounters; Albert J. Reiss, Jr., *The Police and the Public* (New Haven: Yale University Press, 1971).

13. For a more detailed discussion of the factors that affect community security and safety and the relationship of coproduction to these factors see Elinor Ostrom and associates, "The Public Service Production Process: A Framework for Analyzing Police Services," included in this volume.

12

Police Community Outreach and the Reduction of Crime: Evidence of the Effectiveness of Police-Community Relations Training and Affirmative Action from a Study of 161 U.S. Cities

Nicholas P. Lovrich, Jr.

Testing the Assumptions of a Criminal Justice Program: Reducing Crime through Police-Community Relations Training

The urban disorders of the 1964-1967 period gave rise to a number of studies, both governmental and academic, of police-community relations in American cities.[1] A uniform finding from these various reports and studies was that in many American cities the level of public hostility toward the police was quite high, particularly among minority and/or poorer citizens. Various reasons for the existence of this state of affairs were hypothesized, such as: contacts between police and poverty communities tend, by virtue of the oppressive socioeconomic conditions of declining urban neighborhoods, to place the police in the role of callous agent of oppression;[2] police officers too often are personally hostile to and/or ignorant of the communities and community residents they serve;[3] the absence of nonhostile communications and contacts between the police and the community creates the impression of distance and insensitivity on the part of law enforcement;[4] the predominately white city police forces are increasingly unrepresentative of the heavily minority populated communities they are to serve.[5]

The McCone Commission discovered that participation in the Watts riot was far more widespread than was at first suspected, and that a significant relationship could be shown between negative attitudes toward the police and participation in the rioting.[6] Concerning community attitudes toward the police elsewhere, the Kerner Commission wrote: "In 1967, an Urban League study of the Detroit riot area found that 82% believed there was some form of police brutality."[7] In reporting on the types of grievances expressed by citizens in fifteen major U.S. cities the Kerner Commission showed police practices to be the highest ranking grievance.[8]

The Crime Commission added findings from a study of police officers in Boston and Chicago which served to justify somewhat these negative perceptions of city police by blacks. Of 510 white policemen studied in these two cities the commission's study group classified 38 percent as "highly prejudiced, extremely anti-Negro," and 34 percent as "prejudiced, anti-Negro."[9]

In the area of crime control and effective police action regarding crimes against persons and property, the Crime Commission reported the startling findings of the National Opinion Research Center. In a nationwide survey of Americans (N = 2,072) in 1965-1966, it was found that fewer than half of all crimes experienced by citizens are reported to the police, and that the most frequent reason (55 percent) for failure to report crimes is the belief that the police would not be effective in handling the problem in question.[10]

It was the passage of the Omnibus Crime Control and Safe Streets Act of 1968, and the creation of the Law Enforcement Assistance Administration (LEEA), which served to provide federal monies for the creation of police-community relations (PCR) training programs in many American cities. The assumptions which advocates of police-community relations made regarding the advisability of public expenditures on this problem might be summarized as follows: PCR training of sworn officers would result in less offensive policing practices; less offensive policing practices would reduce community hostility toward the police; lower hostility would allow greater cooperative effort between the police and the community to achieve the mutual goal of crime reduction.

Although the LEAA was established in part to provide the funding necessary for local police authorities to carry out programs which would give substance to a national effort to preserve order in urban areas through improving police-community understanding, American cities differed widely in the degree to which they chose to make use of their now enhanced resources in this fashion. It is this differential degree of adoption of PCR training which allows the assessment of the effects of such training upon crime rates in American cities. If the assumptions of the advocates of PCR training are correct we should find that cities which have committed their resources to such purposes have experienced a lower rate of reported crime than cities which have not done so.

A Review of the Evidence: The Exploratory Comparison of Urban Crime Rate Trends among High and Low PCR Cities

Reflecting the widely shared interest of urban leaders and scholars of local government in the subject of PCR the International City Management Association conducted a survey (in late 1969) of 2,072 cities over 10,000 population on the question of PCR training and related programs in existence in those cities.[11] A total of 667 cities responded, with a response rate of approximately 70 percent for cities over 25,000 population. This survey provides information on such matters as the percentage of sworn officers receiving PCR training, the number of hours of PCR training new recruits received, the number of hours of in-service training received per officer, the size of PCR units and rank of officer in charge, and so on. This study utilizes the findings of the ICMA survey to categorize the 161 cities of over 25,000 population as to their degree of commitment to PCR training.

Any comparison of high and low PCR commitment cities for the analysis of the effects of PCR training on rates of reported crime would be futile if the groupings of high and low PCR cities were dissimilar in some important respects. The results of a comparison of high PCR cities (wherein a third or more of the sworn officer force had received or was receiving PCR training) and low PCR cities with regard to a composite indicator of "quality of life"—an indicator reflecting basic economic, social, educational, and related indexes extracted from the 1970 Census—reveal that the two groups of cities are not dissimilar with respect to overall quality of life.[12]

High PCR cities are neither distinctively better nor worse places to live in comparison to low PCR cities. Whereas 41 percent of the high PCR cities merit A or B ratings, a similar 43 percent of the low PCR cities were awarded such designations. The pattern of A through E ratings of cities employed by the EPA for measuring the overall quality of life is characteristic of the patterns of rating distribution which could be reported for each of the component indexes which make up that indicator. Whether the measures be those of economic condition (for example, personal income, employment, labor productivity, income equality between central city and suburbs), political condition (for example, voting turnout, per capita local government expenditures, range of local public services provided), environmental quality (for example, level of suspended particulates, volume of solid waste produced, parks per 1,000 population), health and education condition (for example, infant mortality, median school years completed, number of doctors and dentists per 1,000 population), or social condition (for exam-

Table 12-1
Comparability of High and Low PCR Cities: A Comparison of "Quality of Life" Indicators
(N = 152[a])

	High PCR Cities		Low PCR Cities	
A-rated	12	16%	16	21%
B-rated	18	24%	18	23%
C-rated	18	24%	17	22%
D-rated	18	24%	18	23%
E-rated	8	11%	9	12%

Statistical Summary: Chi square = .55
p > .95 [No significant difference]

[a]Nine of the 161 sampled cities are located outside of Standard Metropolitan Statistical Areas included in the EPA analysis.

ple, degree of equality of education and income distribution between white and nonwhite citizens, population density, percent of owner-occupied dwellings) the results are the same—high and low PCR cities are very similar in nature.

Figure 12-1 displays the results of the comparison of rates of reported crime for high and low PCR commitment cities. It is not suggested here that the Uniform Crime Report should be viewed as an impeccable source of information on crime; it is quite widely known that reporting practices often vary from police department to police department, that powerful motives for misreporting exist from time to time, that several important categories of crime are not tabulated in the FBI's crime index, and so on.[13] It is wise, however, to avoid the impulse to reject UCR statistics entirely. Although cross-sectional comparisons between cities are difficult to interpret and are hence of somewhat limited value, longitudinal comparisons of rates of change are of considerable utility. Whatever the reasons for varying crime reporting practices found in different cities, it is clear from the several victimization surveys now available for interpretation that the rates of change in reported crime are very closely reflective of the rate of change in survey-reported victimization.[14]

Figure 12-1 plots time-series graphs for the period 1960-1975 for the means rates of reported crime per thousand population (UCR index crimes) for both high PCR and low PCR cities. The periods both previous and subsequent to the inauguration of LEAA funding are of considerable interest. The time-series graphs previous to the 1969 point indicate the degree to which the high and low PCR city groupings are equivalent comparison groups. The graphs subsequent to 1969 indicate the degree of effect of factors unique to each subgrouping—that is, PCR training; the logic implicit in this latter comparison is that factors other than the variable under study affect the comparison groups in the same manner from the initial to the final time point.[15]

Results: The Positive Effect of PCR Training

A careful look at figure 12-1 will reveal that PCR training is related to the rate of reported crime; cities with high PCR commitment in 1969 have experienced a lower rate of crime than those which did not invest as fully in PCR training. A review of the period before 1969 shows that high PCR cities tended to report either slightly higher or nearly indentical rates of reported crimes as those reported by low PCR cities, a fact which further substantiates our confidence in the underlying similarity of the high and low PCR city groupings. The period subsequent to 1969 shows that the differential between high and low PCR cities is small but persistent, and of slowly increasing size. It is difficult to attach a degree of statistical meaning to the differences observed, but one reasonable way to interpret them is to make a simple comparison of the average differences in mean scores before and after the 1969 time-series intervention.

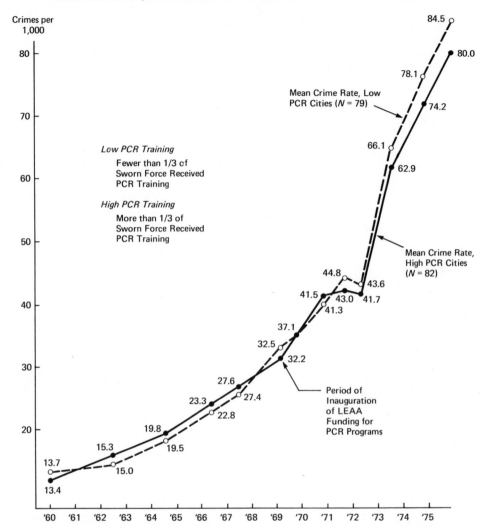

Figure 12-1. Comparison of Rates of Reported Crime for Cities with High and Low Police-Community Relations Commitment *(Means of UCR Index Crimes/1,000)*

It is very important to note that figure 12-1 seriously underestimates the degree of effect which PCR training might have upon rates of reported crime. One factor of underestimation stems from the fact that subsequent to the 1969 ICMA survey some significant number of low PCR cities did also become active in PCR training. Throughout the post-1970 period, then, the degree of difference between the high and the low PCR cities is reduced by the rate of subsequent adoption of PCR programs by cities classified as low PCR cities.

A second factor of underestimation is equally important to consider. It would seem reasonable to assume that a commitment to PCR programs would, if it were successful in building community confidence in the police, result in a higher rate of reporting of crime to the police. Table 12-2 presents evidence from LEAA victimization studies which directly relates to this question of differential rates of reporting of crime to the police in groupings of high and low PCR commitment cities.

Table 12-2 demonstrates that high PCR cities do elicit a higher rate of reporting of crime than do low PCR cities. This finding is most important for the proper interpretation of figure 12-1; the fact that high PCR cities experience *both* a higher rate of reporting of crime and a somewhat lower rate of reported crime as compared to low PCR cities would indicate that the overall effect of PCR training is considerably more dramatic than the parallel time-series graphs in figure 12-1 would indicate.[16]

Affirmative Action and Police Community Outreach: Demographic Representativeness and the Effectiveness of Police Services

Much attention has been devoted to the discussion of the justice and equity of public and private programs designed to promote the equality of employment opportunity for the victims of historical discrimination. Affirmative action has been defended as representing just, due compensation for past denial of equal opportunity,[17] and it has been condemned as a gross expression of inequity and "reverse discrimination" which does not stand the test of the Fourteenth Amendment's requirement of color-blind justice.[18] The question of the ultimate virtue of the affirmative action doctrine as the proper administrative reflection of the Civil Rights Act of 1964 is not the issue here; for better or worse President Johnson's Executive Order 11246, the creation of the Equal Employment Opportunity Commission, and the subsequent related legislative enactments and court decisions, have for the most part (Bakke notwithstanding) established a governmental commitment to promote equity through affirmative action.[19]

A question which has received far less attention, and which is most germane to our concern here, is that of the assessment of effects—that is, what impact upon program performance does affirmative action demonstrate? In the case of police community outreach the pursuit of better police community relations can often include emphasis upon minority recruitment. However, as with most other sectors of American society, American urban police departments have responded to the call for affirmative action with greatly varying degrees of effort and commitment.[20] Some police agencies have made very good progress toward the achievement of more fully representative officer corps while others have made little improvement in this area. The interesting question which arises here is

Table 12-2

Comparison of Survey-Estimated Robberies (Victimization) and Uniform Crime Report Robbery Statistics: A Comparison of High and Low PCR Statistics

City	High PCR Cities UCR as % of Survey Reported Robberies	City	Low PCR Cities UCR as % of Survey Reported Robberies
Newark	115.0	Los Angeles	71.0
Washington	97.6	New York	68.7
St. Louis	95.2	Boston	60.6
Cleveland	73.5	Pittsburgh	59.8
Detroit	72.6	Portland	58.8
Baltimore	71.0	Oakland	55.4
Miami	64.3	New Orleans	50.7
Chicago	63.8	San Francisco	50.6
Buffalo	58.8	Denver	49.2
Dallas	56.5	Atlanta	46.3
Houston	54.9	Cincinnati	39.4
Minneapolis	44.2	Milwaukee	19.1
San Diego	39.6	*Mean = 52.5%*	
Philadelphia	37.5		
Mean = 67.5%			

Source: Reprinted with permission from *Sample Surveys of Victims of Crime*, Copyright 1976, Ballinger Publishing Company and reproduced from *Surveying Crime* (1976), pp. 136-137, with the permission of the National Academy of Sciences, Washington, D.C.

whether affirmative action outreach activities, in combination with police community relations training, have a salutary effect upon crime reduction and crime control programs.

The would-be researcher is confronted with an important difficulty in this area of study. Information on minority employment—by municipality—is not publicly available, and such information is not covered by the provisions of the Freedom of Information Act. In order to assess the effect of affirmative action for this study it was necessary to resurvey those chiefs of police who reported the state of their minority employment in the 1969 ICMA survey. Of the original 161 cities some ninety-four both submitted their minority employment statistics to the earlier survey and responded to the author's survey inquiring after contemporary minority employment information. In addition to generously supplying affirmative action data, the responding chiefs of police also indicated their attitudes on a number of items relating to their PCR programs. Table 12-3 displays the results of this survey. Three areas of official attitude are of particular interest to this analysis. The responses to this survey—collected during the months of July, August, and September 1978—allow the investigation of the perception of value ascribed to PCR programs on the part of those who have to make decisions about the use of local police resources. In addition, the degree of sentiment

Table 12-3
Results of Update Survey of Chiefs of Police: Assessment of PCR Programs and Reported Programs and Reported Progress in Affirmative Action for the Period 1968 to 1978

Value of PCR Program

Item: How would you characterize the value of your PCR program?

Responses	High PCR Cities N = 48		Low PCR Cities N = 46		Totals N = 94	
Highly valuable	38	79%	32	70%	70	74%
Somewhat valuable	7	15%	6	13%	13	14%
Uncertain	1	2%	1	2%	2	2%
Not very valuable	0	–	1	2%	1	1%
A waste of resources	0	–	0	–	0	–
No answer	2	4%	6	13%	8	9%

Changes in PCR Programs

Item: How would you characterize the changes which have taken place in your PCR program since 1969? Has your program. . .

Responses	High PCR Cities		Low PCR Cities		Totals	
Grown in scale	24	50%	27	59%	51	54%
Remained relatively same in scale	15	31%	4	9%	19	20%
Been reduced in scale	7	15%	9	19%	16	17%
No answer	2	4%	6	13%	8	9%

Affirmative Action Program (For cities with 10%+ Minority population)

Mean Representativeness Ratios
% Minority Police Officers/% Minority Population

	High PCR Cities N = 40	Low PCR Cities N = 36	Totals N = 76
1968 Ratio	27.2%	28.4%	27.8%
1978 Ratio	52.4%	50.9%	51.7%
Change, 1968-1978	+25.2%	+22.5%	+23.9%

for expansion, maintenance, or reduction of PCR programs can be judged. Finally, the degree of progress registered in the area of affirmative action can be gauged for each city replying to the survey.

It can be seen that chiefs of police are overwhelmingly supportive of PCR programs. Those city representatives who demonstrated an early commitment to PCR activities remain committed to a belief in the worth of police community outreach efforts—a meaningful testament to the capacity of such programs to generate internal support. It is interesting to note as well that police chiefs from cities which did not take an early fancy to PCR training and related police activities also demonstrate a belief in the value of community relations programs. It is instructive to note that more than seven of ten chiefs of police relate that their programs have stabilized or grown since their inception, and more than half of the total sample report growth. From these responses it is evident that the belief in the value of PCR has spread and been imbedded within the police management fraternity. Perhaps the following quotation by a survey respondent will serve the purpose of highlighting this impression:

> The resistance to Community Relations programs from 1954 to the present has been remarkable. From a communist conspiracy in '54 to an inbuilt understanding by the last few recruit classes.

> Of course the program and needs differ from one community to another, one geographical area to another. We find general acceptance by the career officers who recognize PCR as a tool and a means of improving the patrol officer's role.

> The acceptance has been gradual and I believe if any patrolman was to be appointed as a Chief today he would first ascertain the quality and effectiveness of his PCR unit and encourage the effort.

The responses of police officials to the request for affirmative action information also provide some interesting insights. It can be seen that progress, though slow in coming and uneven in distribution (from a high of full representation to a total lack of minority representation), has occurred in the period under study. It appears that with an average attainment of only about 50 percent of parity in minority representation there remains much more to do in this field. From the responses registered by the survey respondents it would seem that affirmative action efforts will likely continue to reflect uneven progress, with some cities doing much and others doing relatively little to hasten minority representation.

The likelihood of the continuation of differences in police department action in affirmative action raises the interesting question of probable effects—that is, what impact will such strong or weak efforts have upon crime reduction programs? The answer to this question can only be discovered with the passage of an appropriate amount of time, but a hint as to probable results can be inferred from the historical record. What impact if any has the combination of affirmative action and PCR programs had upon crime reduction efforts since these areas began to receive special emphasis? Figure 12-2 presents some useful evidence on this question. The two time-series graphs displayed represent the mean rates of reported crime per thousand population (UCR index crimes) for two groups of cities of 10 percent-plus minority composition: (1) those twenty-six cities which have shown both a high commitment to PCR training and a higher than average minority representativeness ratio; and (2) those seventeen cities which have shown neither a high PCR commitment nor manifested a marked degree of progress toward minority recruitment. This comparison of opposites should afford a fair view of the overall effect of this combination of police community outreach programs.

It would seem reasonable to assume that effective community outreach programs—to the extent they achieved their primary goal of improved community

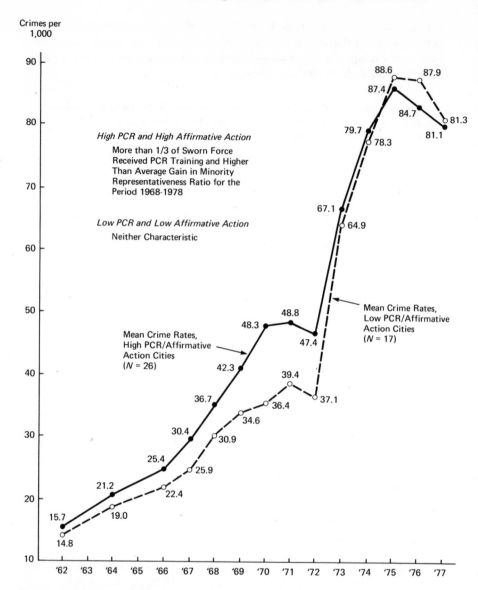

Figure 12-2. Comparison of Rates of Reported Crime for Cities with Both High PCR Commitment and Affirmative Action Progress versus Cities with Neither Characteristic *(Means of UCR Index Crimes/1,000)*

confidence and trust in the police—would initially generate a higher than normal level of citizen cooperation with the police, including the reporting of criminal activity; with time, however, as would-be violators of the law realized that the police could count on the cooperation of the community in their efforts to fight crime, they would be more fully deterred from engaging in unlawful behavior.

It must be pointed out that the meager evidence presented in figure 12-2 by no means proves the validity of the assumptions underlying the police community outreach paradigm. It is, nevertheless, most interesting to observe that these findings do coincide with predictions which can be derived from those paradigmatic assumptions.

Results: Further Evidence of the Effectiveness of Police Community Outreach Programs

The time-series graphs in figure 12-2 provide suggestive indications of two major effects of the combination of PCR training and progress in affirmative action. First, high PCR/affirmative action cities demonstrate a noteworthy jump in crime *vis-à-vis* the comparison group during the initial period of implementation. Such an increase in the rate of reported crime could be evidence of the impact of the higher rates of reporting caused by community outreach activities undertaken by high PCR/affirmative action police departments.. The second effect worthy of note is the later convergence and tentative reversal of positions of the comparison groups—that is, the high PCR/affirmative action cities begin with a higher mean rate of crime, experience a significant jump in crime, then as of 1977 end with a slightly lower mean crime figure. Of course, additional time is required for the identification of the stability of this trend, but as far as the information does allow, the impression left is one of noteworthy temporary change and important lag effects induced by the high PCR/affirmative action combination.[21]

The findings reported in figure 12-2 appear consistent with predictions one might make on the basis of the assumptions underlying the police—community relations as a crime deterrent concept. It will be recalled from the introduction to this essay that the logic of community outreach expenditures for crime reduction runs something like this: police outreach programs would . . .

> result in less offensive policing practices; less offensive policing practices would reduce community hostility toward the police; lower hostility would allow greater cooperative effort between the police and the community to achieve the mutual goal of crime reduction.

Conclusions: Police Community Outreach as an Effective Policy—Further Questions

The research reported here is far from complete; many questions remain unaddressed. It would be very useful to know which types of PCR training programs and affirmative action programs are most appropriate to which type of city; it could well be that the effect of such programs varies with certain characteristics of cities and their police departments (for example, city and department size, degree of professionalization, degree of centralization/decentralization, degree of commitment to specialization). These and other questions beg for further attention and study. The findings presented here, if they cannot be viewed as conclusive, can be seen as somewhat suggestive of the wisdom attending to the arguments of the early advocates of PCR programs; police-community relations training and related programs may be a means of both humanizing the provision of law-enforcement services and reducing the incidence of crime in American cities—a means "to maintain order in ways that preserve and advance democratic value."[22]

Notes

1. See the review of early literature on the major urban disorders in J. Boskin, "The Revolt of the Urban Ghettos, 1964-67," *ANNALS* 382 (March 1969): 1-14. The President's Commission on Law Enforcement and Administration of Justice, the National Advisory Commission on Civil Disorders, and the McCone Commission all stressed the key role of the police in the "causes" of urban disorder; on this point see G.A. Krebs and J.M. Waller, "The Police-Community Relations Movement: Conciliatory Responses to Violence," *American Behavorial Scientist* 16 (January-February 1973): 402-412.

2. See the empirical evidence reported in P.E. Smith and R.G. Hawkins, "Victimization, Types of Citizen-Police Contacts, and Attitudes toward the Police," *Law and Society Review* 8 (Fall 1973): 135-152.

3. For interesting studies of police attitudes see A.J. Reiss, "Police Brutality—Answers to Key Questions, " *Society* 5 (July-August 1968): 10-19; and M. Rokeach and associates, "The Value Gap between Police and Policies," *Journal of Social Issues* 27 (Spring 1971): 155-171.

4. Since the police constitute one of the most salient and pervasive contact points between minority and/or poverty citizens and governmental authority the degree of nonhostile contact existing between the police and these communities can have considerable importance for the whole political system. On this question see H.R. Rodgers and G. Taylor, "The Policeman as as Agent of Regime Legitimation," *American Journal of Political Science* XV (February 1971): 72-86.

5. On the question of racial and ethnic underrepresentation among law-enforcement officials and its effect upon public attitudes toward the police see P.H. Rossi, R.A. Berk, and B.K. Edison, *The Roots of Urban Discontent* (New York: John Wiley and Sons, 1974).

6. N. Cohen, ed., *The Los Angeles Riots: A Socio-Psychological Study* (New York: Praeger, 1970), p. 186.

7. National Advisory Commission on Civil Disorders, *Report of the Commission* (Washington, D.C.: GPO, 1968), p. 302.

8. Ibid., pp. 302-303.

9. D.J. Black and A.J. Reiss, "Patterns of Behavior in Police and Citizen Transactions," *Studies of Crime and Law Enforcement in Major Metropolitan Areas,* Vol. II, Section I, a report for the President's Commission on Law Enforcement and Administration of Justice (1967), p. 135.

10. P.H. Ennis, *Criminal Victimization in the U.S.: A Report of a National Survey* (NORC: May 1967), pp. 45-49.

11. *The Municipal Year Book, 1970* (Washington, D.C.: The International City Management Association, 1970), pp. 438-469.

12. For census-based quality of life indicators see U.S. Environmental Protection Agency, *Quality of Life Indicators in U.S. Metropolitan Areas, 1970: A Comprehensive Assessment* (Washington, D.C.: Washington Environmental Research Center, 1975).

13. For an excellent discussion of the many shortcomings of the FBI's Uniform Crime Reports as indicators of the incidence of crime see D. Seidman and M. Couzens, "Crime, Crime Statistics, and the Great American Anti-Crime Crusade: Police Misreporting of Crime and Political Pressures," paper presented at the Annual Meeting of the American Political Science Association, September 1972.

14. See the summary of findings generated from the National Crime Surveys in the National Research Council's *Surveying Crime* (Washington, D.C.: National Academy of Sciences, 1976), especially pp. 132-144. For direct sources of information on police-reported and victim-reported crime rates see: National Criminal Justice Information and Statistics Service, LEAA, *Criminal Victimization in the United States: A Comparison of 1973 and 1974 Findings* (Washington, D.C.: GPO, May 1976), and *Criminal Victimization Surveys in Eight American Cities: A Comparison of 1971/72 and 1974/75 Findings* (Washington, D.C.: GPO, November 1976).

15. Informative analyses of the possibilities and potential problems which are associated with multiple interrupted time-series designs can be found in T.J. Cook and F.P. Scioli, "Impact Analysis in Public Policy Research," in K.M. Dolbeare, ed., *Public Policy Evaluation* (Beverly Hills, Calif.: Sage, 1975), pp. 95-117, and V. Gray, "The Use of Time-Series Analysis in the Study of Public Policy," *Policy Studies Journal* 2 (Winter 1973): 97-102. The use of time-series analysis has received much attention in policy research as an especially useful component of quasi-experimental evaluation designs. On the application of such designs to the area of public policy research see: D.T. Campbell, "Reforms as Experiments," *American Psychologist* 24 (April 1969): 409-429; D.T. Campbell and J. Stanley, *Experimental and Quasi-Experimental Designs in Research* (Chicago: Rand McNally, 1963); and J.A. Caporaso and L.L. Roos, *Quasi-Experimental Approaches* (Evanston, Ill.: Northwestern University Press, 1973).

16. Some advances have been registered in recent years in the area of the development of statistical measures of the significance of pre- and postintervention differences in time-series analyses. Although the level of measurement prob-

lems, the confined number of time points, and the general problem of controlled effect do not allow the application of these models to this case, the interested reader may be wisely referred to L.A. Wilson, "A Review of Statistical Techniques Appropriate to the Analysis of Time-Series Quasi-Experiments," *Policy Studies Journal* 2 (Winter 1973): 118-122.

17. For many students and practitioners of public administration social equity understood as a compensatory conception represents the proper course correction" for contemporary society. A concise statement of this argument can be found in H.G. Frederickson, "Creating Tomorrow's Public Administration," *Public Management* 51 (November 1971): 1-13.

18. A rigorous critique of affirmative action—seen as a demeaning gift to the too often underqualified and unjust denial of opportunity to the most deserving—can be found in J.W. Foster, "Race and Truth at Harvard," *New Republic*, July 17, 1976, pp. 16-20.

19. A good source on the development of federal enactments and administrative law can be found in D. Rosenbloom, "The Civil Service Commission's Decision to Authorize the Use of Goals and Timetables in the federal Equal Employment Opportunity Program," *Western Political Quarterly* 26 (June 1973): 236-251.

20. For a good summary of strategies employed to recruit minority employees into the public service at the municipal level see F.J. Thompson, "Bureaucratic Responsiveness in the Cities: The Problem of Minority Hiring," *Urban Affairs Quarterly* 10 (September 1974): 40-68. On the question of representiveness in the public sector generally see Harry Kranz, "How Representative Is the Public Service?" *Public Personnel Management* 2 (July-August 1973): 242-255, and the Public Service Laboratory, *What Achieves Affirmative Action in Cities?* (Washington, D.C.: Georgetown University Press, 1975).

21. Evidence available on the impact of demographic representativeness upon public service agency performance indicates that the effects vary from area to area. There is considerable evidence that police services are especially sensitive to such effects. For an excellent review of the major findings in this area see Frank J. Thompson, "Types of Representative Bureaucracy and Their Linkage: The Case of Ethnicity"; R.T. Golembiewski and associates, *Public Administration: Readings in Institutions, Processes, Behavior and Policy,* 3rd ed. (Chicago: Rand McNally, 1976), pp. 576-601 (particularly pp. 585-588).

22. L.A. Radalet, "The Law and Order as They Pertain to Urban Unrest," in *Report of the Police-Community Relations Institute: Challenge of the Seventies* (Madison: University of Wisconsin, 1970) , p. 10.

13 Racial Prejudice and Police Treatment of Blacks

Robert Friedrich

In spite of all the attention lavished on the police in recent years, there remain many unanswered questions about their work and, particularly, about the causes and consequences of their actions. Among the most fundamental of these questions is this: To what extent do policemen's personal attitudes influence their official actions? A better understanding of the ways in which policemen's attitudes influence their exercise of discretion could lead to more effective policies regarding the recruitment, training, supervision, and deployment of police officers.

The conventional view, growing out of both common-sense notions and a long tradition in psychological research, is that police actions are very much the product of personal attitudes. Some state this view explicitly—Chwast, for example, writes that "the social and personal values of the law enforcement officer strongly condition the quality of service he delivers to different segments of the populace at large"[1]—but more often it is implicitly assumed. Underlying much of the by now extensive literature on police attitudes and personality is the oft unspoken assumption that such factors—authoritarianism, cynicism, and racial prejudice, to name a few—have an impact on what police do.[2] And implicit in the voluminous literature on police organization and discretion, where the focus is on structuring police work so that officers will do "the right thing," is the assumption that, without supervision and discipline, without controls on discretion, officers would follow their own inclinations rather than pursue organizational objectives.[3]

But some researchers have argued that policemen's attitudes are not in fact very important in determining what they do. Most often this is attributed to the effectiveness of the sorts of organizational constraints just mentioned. To illustrate, Bayley and Mendelsohn contend that

> the linkage between personal attitudes and occupational behavior is not clear-cut. Professional ethics and organizational norms can offset, often to a surprising extent, the basic attitudes and predispositions of people. This is especially true in organizations, such as the police, where discipline is tight and unrelenting.[4]

I would like to express my thanks to Albert J. Reiss, Jr., for granting me permission to use the data collected in his seminal police observation study for the President's Commission on Law Enforcement and Administration of Justice; to Donald J. Black for helping me to familiarize myself with the study and with the data and documentation which emanated from it; and to Elaine Ader Friedrich and D. Grier Stephenson for their encouragement and useful comments on this chapter.

This view is supported by a growing body of evidence, compiled by social scientists in many different disciplines studying many different kinds of people, which, as Wicker succinctly summarizes it, "taken as a whole . . . suggest[s] that it is considerably more likely that attitudes will be unrelated or only slightly related to overt behaviors than that attitudes will be closely related to actions."[5]

Nowhere is this clash in views about the ties between attitudes and actions more apparent than in the area of policemen's racial attitudes. Both popular and academic opinion commonly hold that racial prejudice influences the police's treatment of black citizens. Typifying this view is Mendelsohn's comment: ". . .Obviously an officer carrying around such a [negative] view is going to act on it at some points."[6] Presumably implicit in the great attention paid to the generally negative racial attitudes of the police is the assumption that such attitudes lead to unfavorable treatment. Advocates of police reform, in prescribing efforts to change policemen's racial views as a solution to police misconduct, have also implicitly endorsed such a view.[7] And there is, of course, a fair amount of anecdotal evidence suggesting that police mistreatment of blacks stems from racial prejudice.[8]

Confronting this view is a considerable body of evidence indicating that people do not, in many circumstances, manifest their racial feelings in their actions toward members of racial minorities.[9] More directly relevant, several observers of the police have concluded that policemen's racial views do not generally influence their actions toward citizens. For example, Skolnick finds that traffic warrant officers carry out their work "relatively evenhandedly" in spite of their antiblack feelings.[10] Similarly, Black and Reiss conclude that "while the proportion of white police officers who reveal anti-Negro attitudes is quite striking, . . . there is a general paucity of evidence of discriminatory or prejudiced behavior."[11] Most often the lack of relationship is attributed to the organizational constraints imposed on policemen.[12]

This clash in views stems from both an empirical source and a theoretical source. The empirical source is the seemingly conflicting evidence on whether attitudes do or do not make an important difference. To some extent this can be traced to the variable quality of the evidence, particularly that gathered unsystematically in very narrow contexts. Where this problem is not so serious, as in Reiss's systematic, large-scale observational study in three cities, problems of interpretation arise. Black and Reiss rest their conclusion on the disparity between the "striking" 70 percent of policemen who express prejudice and the mere 8 percent of blacks who are treated with any sign of prejudice and on their observers' reports of the "great disparity between the verbalized attitudes of officers in encounters with Negroes and members of other minority groups."[13] As Campbell has noted, such disparities do not demonstrate that attitudes do not affect behavior. They may simply reveal a threshold effect: expressing prejudice privately is much "easier" than acting it out publicly.[14] The more conclusive test—and the one to be employed in this chapter—is whether those who express prejudice verbally are more likely than those who do not to discriminate against blacks in their actions.

But the clash has a theoretical source as well. Too many researchers have sought a general answer to the question of whether attitudes affect behavior when there is good theoretical reason to expect that there may be no general answer. Clearly the police organization and other "significant others" in the police milieu promulgate norms which conflict with policemen's personal inclinations. Those who argue that attitudes powerfully influence behavior assume that, because "the police department has the special property that within it discretion increases as one moves down the hierarchy," these norms have little force to offset individual inclinations.[15] Those who argue that attitudes have little effect assume that organizational and other norms are strong or that, as Bayley and Mendelsohn put it, "discipline is tight and unrelenting." However, given the nature of police work, with the great diversity in the settings in which it occurs, it is possible that the force of such norms may be quite variable. If so, then so also may be the impact of attitudes. Therefore the best answer to the question of how much impact attitudes have on police actions may well be that it depends— it depends on the circumstances in which the action takes place.

Unfortunately, although the potentially contingent nature of the relationship between attitudes and actions has been recognized by many social scientists and by some of the most perceptive students of the police, it is a possibility that has as yet generated little systematic research in police settings.[16] The research described in the following pages is an attempt to redress that neglect. It examines the relationship between an attitude which has, as seen, been a major focus of interest in police research—racial prejudice—and two dimensions which are important "policies-in-effect" made by the police—their decisions to arrest suspected offenders and their interpersonal manner toward citizens. The basic hypothesis is that the more favorable a policeman's attitude toward blacks is, the more favorable will be his treatment of blacks.

The hypothesis that relationships between attitudes and actions may be contingent on the circumstances in which the action occurs is likewise tested with two factors that have been identified as important in the police milieu—the visibility of the action to the police organization and the visibility of the action to a partner. Here the expectation is that the relationship between policemen's racial attitudes and their treatment of blacks will be stronger in situations where visibility to the police organization or to a partner is low than in situations where visibility is high.

Data

The data used to test these hypotheses are drawn from the study conducted in 1966 by Albert J. Reiss, Jr., for the President's Commission on Law Enforcement and the Administration of Justice. For a period of six weeks in eight precincts in three major American cities—Boston, Chicago, and Washington, D.C.—observers were assigned to accompany police patrolmen as they went about their regular rounds. These observers had two basic tasks: (1) to interview the officers about their feelings toward their job and the people and problems they encountered in doing it; and (2) to observe and record in detail the characteristics of the situations and the citizens the patrolmen encountered and the actions taken by the patrolmen. Altogether, the thirty-six observers employed accompanied police on 840 patrols, in the course of which they watched nearly 600 policemen interact with over 11,000 citizens.[17]

The hypotheses advanced here require the measurement of three different classes of variables: the policemen's racial attitudes, their actions toward citizens, and the visibility of those actions to the organization and to their partners. Assessment of the policemen's racial views was based on the results of the observers' interviewing. The officers' statements about blacks were categorized as very negative, negative, neutral, or positive. Because each policeman could be observed on several different patrols by different observers—on average, in fact, each policeman was accompanied on about 2.5 patrols—the quality of the characterization of the policeman's attitude (specifically, its independence of the particular observer and the particular circumstances on each patrol) was improved by taking as the measurement of the attitude for each officer the mean of his opinion along the continuum across all the patrols on which he was observed.[18]

Assessment of the police's actions toward citizens on the two dimensions of behavior identified earlier—arrest and manner—relied on the observers' descriptions of each encounter. Following LaFave's definition of arrest as the taking of a suspect into custody, a suspected offender was regarded as having been arrested when he or she was taken to the station.[19] The manner of the policeman toward the citizen was measured by collapsing the six-category scheme used by Reiss's observers into a four-category ordinal continuum ranging from very negative (originally "hostile, nasty, provocative" and "openly ridiculing or belittling") to negative ("brusque, bossy, authoritarian" and "subtly ridiculing or belittling") to neutral ("businesslike, routinized, impersonal") to positive ("good-humored, playful, jovial") behavior.[20]

Assessment of the visibility of the encounter was similarly based on the observer's characterization. Following Black and Reiss, who argue that discretion is more limited in citizen-initiated encounters than in police-initiated ones because the organization has greater opportunity to monitor what goes on in the former than in the latter, encounters in which citizens initiate police intervention were treated as being of high visibility to the police organization, while encounters in which police intervene on their own were treated as being of low visibility.[21] Whether an encounter was characterized as being of low visibility to a peer or as being of high visibility depended on whether the policeman worked along or with a partner.

Each of these measurement procedures is fraught with the potential for error. Each of the judgments the observer had to make could be difficult enough in its own right—for example, was the policeman being good-humored or was he really subtly ridiculing the citizen; was peer visibility really high when the officer was working with a partner, but the partner briefly left to run a warrant check?— but observers were required to make many of them and to make them quickly. Further, observers were instructed to take only brief notes on the scene and to fill out the detailed report later in order to minimize the obtrusiveness of their observation. All these factors virtually dictate that the amount of measurement error in these data is considerable. Little can be done about this, especially after the fact, except to note that the problem exists and to recognize its probable effect, assuming the error is essentially random—the strength of the relationships observed is probably attenuated considerably from what it would have been were the measurements less contaminated by error.

Data Analysis

Under the basic hypothesis advanced here, the more favorable the attitude a policeman holds toward blacks the less likely he should be to arrest black people and the more friendly should be his manner toward black people.[22] In order to test these propositions most definitively, analysis was confined to only those encounters involving black citizens—for the obvious reason—and white policemen—since to include black policemen as well would run the risk of confounding the effects of race or any of its correlates with the effects of racial attitude. The net effect of these restrictions is to reduce the number of cases on which this analysis is based to about half the original total.[23]

Does a policeman's racial attitude influence his propensity to arrest black suspects? Figure 13-1 indicates that it does. The most prejudiced officers are substantially more likely to arrest than the favorably inclined. The relationship, which holds up even in the face of controls for a number of potentially confounding factors, runs counter to the view that personal attitudes have no impact on official police decisions.[24] However, those who have minimized the impact of such attitudes can certainly find some reassurance here, for, as the measure of association shows, the relationship is, by the usual statistical standards, clearly a meager one.[25] Personal prejudice, it seems fair to say, has some influence on the arrest decision, but it is far from decisive.

Even if the impact of racial attitudes on arrest is slight, it might be expected to be greater on the manner of the officer, since that is both a more spontaneous and a less visible (to the department) behavior.[26] The expectation does not, however, appear to be borne out at all by the evidence in Table 13-1. Indeed, the results there seem to run counter to any expectation. Neither the percentages nor the tau-b correlation reveals the expected tendency of more favorable attitudes

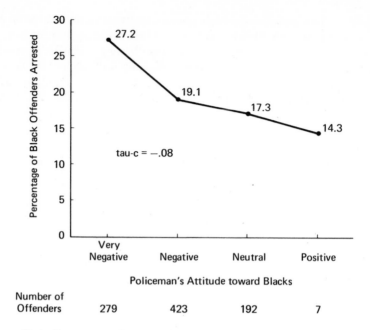

Figure 13-1. Percentage of Black Offenders Arrested by Policeman's Attitude
toward Blacks (in Encounters with White Policemen Only)

leading to more favorable treatment.[27] Rather, the trend is for more favorable
attitudes to lead to slightly more neutral, impersonal treatment. This stands as a
puzzling result until it is recognized that, in the context of police work, there
may be alternative definitions of "favorable" treatment. One is, of course, the
conventional view of favorable treatment as friendly and good-humored treatment and unfavorable treatment as hostile treatment. On the other hand, though,
in the bureaucratic context of the police and in light of the emphasis often placed
on police professionalism, an alternative view would be of favorable treatment as
neutral, impersonal treatment and unfavorable treatment as expressive, personal
(that is, hostile and/or friendly) treatment. The relationship observed here, then,
may result from the tendency of the less prejudiced officers to treat citizens
"better" and the more prejudiced officers to treat blacks "worse," not in the
conventional sense, but in the professional sense.[28]

Because this unexpected sort of relationship will figure prominently in the
rest of this analysis, it will be useful for comparative purposes to have a measure
of its strength. The measure adopted as most appropriate is gamma, calculated
on the table after manner has been rescaled to range from very personal (very
negative) to personal (negative or positive) to impersonal (neutral).[29] This rescaled
version of manner will be referred to as the impersonality dimension in order to

Table 13-1

Policeman's Manner toward Black Citizens by Policeman's Attitude toward Blacks (in Encounters with White Policemen Only)

Policeman's Manner	Policeman's Attitude toward Blacks				
	Very Negative	Negative	Neutral	Positive	Total
Very Negative	1.2%	.7%	.3%	0.0%	.8%
Negative	11.7	8.9	7.6	13.1	9.5
Neutral	73.9	77.8	80.2	82.0	77.3
Positive	13.2	12.5	11.8	4.9	12.5
Total	100.0	100.0	100.0	100.0	100.0
Number of Interactions	1,653	3,959	890	122	6,624
Tau-b with friendliness dimension = .02			Gamma with impersonality dimension = .11		

distinguish it from the original scaling, which will henceforth be referred to as the friendliness dimension. Thus the tau-b with the friendliness dimension of and the gamma with the impersonality dimension of .11 at the bottom of Table 13-1 indicate that there is hardly any tendency in this table for more favorable racial attitudes to lead to more friendly treatment, but a slight tendency for more favorable attitudes to lead to more impersonal treatment.

Even under this "alternative definition" explanation of the unexpected results in table 13-1, one anomaly remains unexplained—the irregularly high percentage of negative treatment of blacks by officers with positive attitudes. One possible explanation is that officers with problack attitudes may take a particularly dim view of black offenders, whom they may see as damaging and discrediting the black community. If so, this tendency should be more pronounced for offenders than for nonoffenders. Table 13-2 demonstrates this to be the case, though the very small number of interactions between black citizens and white policemen with favorable attitudes toward blacks dictates caution. While favorably disposed officers are most prone to treat black nonoffenders neutrally, they are also most prone to treat black offenders negatively.[30] A comparison of the percentages and measures of association for the two panels of table 13-2 further reveals the tendency toward impersonality to be more pronounced for nonoffenders than for offenders, while the tendency toward friendliness (particularly once the irregularity in the favorably disposed officers' treatment of black offenders is set aside) is more pronounced for offenders than for nonoffenders. This suggests that policemen may tend to follow organizational norms of impersonal behavior in dealing with nonoffenders, but their own norms of personal behavior in dealing with offenders.

These results make two important points. First, although deficiencies in the

Table 13-2
Policeman's Manner toward Black Nonoffenders and Offenders by Policeman's Attitude toward Blacks (in Encounters with White Policemen Only)

Policeman's Manner	Policeman's Attitude toward Blacks				
	Very Negative	Negative	Neutral	Positive	Total
	Nonoffenders				
Very Negative	.4%	.6%	0.0%	0.0%	.5%
Negative	7.3	3.8	2.6	3.8	4.5
Neutral	78.6	83.5	87.2	91.0	82.9
Positive	13.7	12.1	10.2	5.1	12.1
Total	100.0	100.0	100.0	100.0	100.0
Number of Interactions	1,084	2,654	577	78	4,393
Tau-b with friendliness dimension = .01		Gamma with impersonality dimension = .18			
	Offenders				
Very Negative	2.6%	1.3%	1.3%	0.0%	1.6%
Negative	26.9	23.1	18.9	44.8	23.8
Neutral	58.7	60.6	61.3	55.2	60.1
Positive	11.9	14.9	18.5	0.0	14.4
Total	100.0	100.0	100.0	100.0	100.0
Number of Interactions	387	891	238	29	1,545
Tau-b with friendliness dimension = .05		Gamma with impersonality dimension = .03			

measuring procedure are almost certainly partially responsible, the relationship between racial attitudes and police action is, in any absolute sense, a weak one. Second, the nature of the relationship between prejudice and behavior is, as the evidence for manner demonstrates, not always the simple one expected. The impact of attitude on action depends on other factors—in this case, the situational status of the citizen involved and perhaps the definition of appropriate behavior which the actor has in mind. Taken together, these results argue against making simplistic assumptions about either the magnitude or the character of the impact of racial prejudice on police actions.

Policemen's racial attitudes do, then, have some impact on their actions. The next question is whether the relationship between attitude and action depends on the visibility of the action to significant others in the police milieu—in particular, to the police organization and to partner. As noted earlier, the most straightforward expectation here would be that the conventional sort of relationships between the independent variable of prejudice and the dependent variables of arrest and friendliness of manner would be stronger in situations less visible to the department and to peers and weaker in situations more visible to department and peers. However, if the tendency of less prejudiced officers to treat black nonoffenders more impersonally does stem from the officers' adoption of an organizational norm of neutral behavior as "good" behavior, then it might also be expected that this tendency would be stronger in situations of greater visibility to the organization and weaker in situations of lesser visibility to the organization.

The observational data yield results that are in all respects consistent with these expectations (as table 13-3 shows). The relationship between prejudice and arrest is slightly stronger in situations less visible to the organization than in situations more visible. More clear-cut are the differences in the strength of the relationship between prejudice and friendliness of manner. When visibility is high, there is virtually no tendency whatsoever for more favorable attitudes to lead to friendlier behavior, but, when visibility is low, such a relationship definitely emerges. Increased visibility to the organization, both these results show, does tend to suppress conventional relationships between attitudes and actions. Further, increased visibility to the organization also seems to lead to stronger relationships between racial prejudice and impersonality of manner, though here the differences are very small. The pattern, though, is at least consistent with the idea that organizational norms are more salient to officers when they operate in situations where police organizations can more readily monitor their behavior.

The results in table 13-3 also provide an important clue to understanding why the conventional relationships between racial attitude and police bahavior observed in figure 13-1 and table 13-1 are, overall, as weak as they are. Attitudes have their greatest conventional effect in situations of low visibility to the police department, but, as the numbers of cases in table 13-3 show, most encounters

Table 13-3
Correlations between Various Dimensions of Police Behavior and Policeman's Attitude toward Blacks by Visibility to Police Organization

	Dimensions of Police Behavior				
		Tau-b with Friendliness of Manner to:		Gamma with Impersonality of Manner to:	
Visibility to Police Organization	Tau-c with Arrest of Offenders	Nonoffenders	Offenders	Nonoffenders	Offenders
Low	−.12	.20	.17	.14	.01
(Police-initiated) (N)	(187)	(219)	(321)	(219)	(312)
High	−.07	−.01	.02	.19	.05
Citizen-initiated) (N)	(713)	(4,174)	(1,224)	(4,174)	(1,224)

between police and citizens are of relatively high visibility to the department in terms of this dimension. This is because most police service is provided reactively—in response to citizen initiative—rather than proactively—as the result of police initiative. Attitudes can have a greater effect, in other words, but police work is currently structured, at least in terms of the balance between reactive and proactive encounters, so as to minimize the tendency of policemen's racial attitudes to carry over into their arrest decisions and the friendliness of their manner.

Just as the evidence supports the hypothesis about the effects of one important audience for a policeman's actions—the department—so also does it support the hypothesis about the effects of another—the partner. Because a policeman who works alone need not concern himself with what a partner thinks, it stands to reason that his attitudes will influence his behavior more than they would if he were working with a partner. Table 13-4 shows this to be true. Relationships between prejudice and arrest and between prejudice and friendliness of manner toward both offenders and nonoffenders are stronger when visibility to a partner is low than when it is high. Once again, increased visibility works to suppress the impact of attitude on arrest and friendliness of manner. And once again, the results help to account for the overall weakness of the conventional relationships between racial attitudes and police behavior. The *N*s in table 13-4 reveal a heavy reliance on two-man patrols in the departments studied. By deploying officers most often in a way that enhances peer visibility, these departments again structure the work environment so as to minimize the tendency of policemen's racial attitudes to influence their arrest decisions and the friendliness of their manner.

But what effect should the presence of a partner have on the relationship between prejudice and impersonality of manner? Here perhaps the key consideration is that the partner is also a member of the police organization and possibly is perceived as an extension of it. If so, then the presence of a partner might very

Table 13-4
Correlations between Various Dimensions of Police Behavior and Policeman's Attitude toward Blacks by Visibility to Partner

	Dimensions of Police Behavior				
	Tau-c with Arrest of Offenders	Tau-b with Friendliness of Manner to:		Gamma with Impersonality of Manner to:	
Visibility to Partner		Nonoffenders	Offenders	Nonoffenders	Offenders
Low (no partner present—one-man patrol)	−.11	.08	.14	−.03	.01
(N)	(129)	(391)	(127)	(391)	(127)
High (partner present—two-man patrol)	−.07	−.01	.03	.23	.05
(N)	(771)	(4,002)	(1,418)	(4,002)	(1,418)

well evoke organizational norms and thus enhance the relationship with impersonality in the same way that greater visibility to the organization does. As the correlations describing the relationship between racial attitude and impersonality in table 13-4 indicate, this is exactly what happens. In the case of both nonoffenders and offenders (but particularly in the former), greater visibility of an to a partner increases the magnitude of the relationship between prejudice and impersonality of manner.

Of course, it must be recognized that not all partners are equally likely to evoke organizational norms and, indeed, that some may evoke very different standards of behavior. Perhaps the most fruitful way of dealing with this possibility within the limits of the data gathered by Reiss is to regard as the norm of behavior evoked by the partner the racial attitude of the partner. The relationship between an officer's attitude and his action should then be stronger when his action is congruent with his partner's inclination than when it is not. In simpler terms, the relationship between an officer's racial attitude and his action should be stronger when his partner shares his racial views than when his partner does not.

Because, as noted earlier, the arrest decision cannot be attributed to a particular officer in a team, this part of the analysis must be confined to the manner of the policeman. The results presented in table 13-5 reveal that the partner's views have little impact on the relationship between prejudice and the friendliness dimension—to be specific, none for nonoffenders and only a slight one for offenders—but a more substantial one on the relationship between prejudice and impersonality. The uniformly weak relationships between prejudice and friendliness of manner may perhaps be attributed to the diminished force of the conventional norm of friendliness here, since all these encounters do involve teams of officers. The emergence of the slight difference in the case of the offenders is again consistent with the idea that officers adhere more to personal inclinations than to

Table 13-5
Correlations between Various Dimensions of Police Behavior and Policeman's Attitude toward Blacks by Similarity between Policeman's and Partner's Attitudes toward Blacks

| | Dimensions of Police Behavior | | | |
| Partner's Attitude toward Blacks | Tau-b with Friendliness of Manner to: | | Gamma with Impersonality of Manner to: | |
	Nonoffenders	Offenders	Nonoffenders	Offenders
Similar	.00	.07	.33	.31
(N)	(1,976)	(642)	(1,976)	(625)
Different	.00	−.02	.12	−.11
(N)	(1,608)	(625)	(1,608)	(625)

organizational norms in the case of offenders, compared to nonoffenders, and suggests that a supportive peer does indeed enhance the expression of personal attitudes in behavior. But more vivid evidence of the effect of social support is seen in the relationship between prejudice and impersonality—which is, of course, consistent with the greater force of the organizational norm of impersonality in the presence of a partner. Here, very clearly, officers are more likely to translate their favorable (or unfavorable) attitudes into impersonal (or personal) treatment when their partners hold similar racial views than when their partners hold differing racial views.

Although the strength of the relationship between racial attitude and police treatment of citizens never attains what could be considered even a moderately strong level, the results presented in tables 13-3, 13-4, and 13-5 do consistently reveal the impact of attitude on action to vary with the visibility of the action to significant others in the police environment. Clearly one of the central hypotheses of this study is borne out: the relationship between racial prejudice and police treatment of citizens does depend on the circumstances in which police action takes place.

Summary and Policy Implications

In general, a policeman's attitude toward blacks seems to exert only a limited influence on his behavior toward blacks. Further, the very nature of that influence depends on the type of behavior and the type of the citizen involved, with more favorable attitudes leading to fewer arrests of offenders, a slightly more friendly manner toward offenders (except among the most favorably disposed officers), and a more impersonal manner toward nonoffenders. The strength of the influence varies with the visibility of the police action to two significant others in the police milieu—the police organization and the policeman's partner. Greater visibilityto the organization and to the partner consistently diminishes relationships between the independent variable of racial prejudice and the dependent variables of arrest and friendliness of manner, but strengthens relationships between prejudice and impersonality of manner. The greater the similarity between an officers' racial attitude and his partner's racial attitude, the stronger the relationship between his own attitude and the friendliness of his manner toward offenders and between his own attitude and the impersonality of his manner toward all citizens.

These results suggest that, left alone, policemen tend to follow their own inclinations in dealing with black citizens, with officers holding antiblack attitudes treating black citizens antagonistically (in terms of both arrest and manner) and officers holding problack attitudes treating them amicably. However, when not left alone—when significant others such as the organization or the partner enter into the scene—then the expression of personal feelings is muted or deflected into different channels. In the case of arrest, increased exposure to the organization or to a partner mutes the effect which an officer's own racial views have on his decisions, probably because officers know that the organization expects them to keep their personal feelings out of their official decisions. In the case of manner, increased exposure seems to deflect the effects of prejudice on manner for nonoffenders and to mute the effects for offenders. This may be due to the bureaucratic nature of modern police organizations and to the recent emphasis on police professionalism, both of which establish as a norm for policemen's manner a neutral, impersonal demeanor, so that "good" behavior comes to be seen as neutral, impersonal treatment and "bad" behavior as expressive, personalized treatment.

The results of the data analysis do suggest, however, that policemen adopt this organizational definition more readily for nonoffenders than for offenders—toward whom the feeling may be more one of "anything goes" and more in situations where the presence of the organization is strongly felt—in higher-visibility, citizen-initiated encounters and encounters where a partner is present. In situations with two officers, where the norm of impersonality appears to be more salient, the presence of a like-minded partner is, as might be expected, more conducive to the expression of the attitude in behavior than the presence of a different minded one.

Discussion of the policy implications of conclusions based on such limited evidence and sometimes ambiguous results as these is obviously a tenuous enterprise. The data were gathered in just a few precincts in only three cities. Only patrolmen (as opposed to other types of policemen) were observed. The patrolmen may have behaved differently because they were being observed. The procedures used to measure racial prejudice were far from ideal. Perhaps more important, the observations were made at a time in American history when society in general, and both the police and black people in particular, were experiencing special strains—the 1960s. Finally, the relationships found in the data are generally weak and, though they vary in ways consistent with expectations, the differences are often not sharp.

All these things make generalizations from these results to "the police" in general in the United States today a risky enterprise indeed—and so, as a result, are any general prescriptions for policy. Nevertheless, a tentative effort seems justified—if for no other reason than that the enterprise here proceeds from a base of evidence stronger than the even narrower, less systematically gathered and anecdotal evidence that has underpinned most such discussions in the past.

The overall weakness of the relationship between racial prejudice and police actions suggests that efforts to change the racial attitudes of policemen will not result in sweeping changes in the police treatment of blacks. Racial attitudes are simply not all that decisive as determinants of police actions. Attempts to recruit officers with more positive views of blacks or to inculcate more favorable attitudes in recruits or veterans—even if they are successful in the first place and even if attitudes do not eventually turn negative as a result of exposure to the police environment—are, given the generally weak linkage between prejudice and performance, unlikely to effect great changes in police behavior. This is not, however, to say that such efforts would be completely wasted. One reason is that even slight improvements in the fairness and tone of police treatment are desirable. This is especially important when it is remembered that the effects of such improvements on public evaluations of the police are likely to be compounded over the years, just as the effects of undesirable treatment were compounded in the past. Another reason is that, as has been shown, racial prejudice can play a more important role in some situations than in others. Thus improvements in attitudes could lead to substantial behavioral change in some instances—particularly those where visibility to organization and partner is low.

Though these results suggest that attitudinal change will be relatively ineffective as a strategy for remaking police behavior toward blacks, they also suggest an alternative. Throughout this analysis, differences in visibility have been observed to affect relationships between prejudice and performance. One possibility is for police departments to manipulate levels of visibility in ways that promote their objectives.

To be specific, certainly one objective of a democratic police organization is to insure equal treatment for all citizens. When the treatment citizens receive varies from officer to officer because each officer acts on his own inclinations rather than on organizational directives, that objective is not served. These results suggest that police departments can reduce the dependence of policemen's actions on their own attitudes, and thus promote the important organizational objective of equal treatment, by influencing the visibility of police actions.

One way is to keep visibility to the organization high. This can be done by emphasizing reactive rather than proactive initiation of encounters—as is already generally the case in American police departments—and by employing the various other devices which have been developed to enhance visibility to the organization, such as radio checks, extensive log-keeping, and close supervision by sergeants in the field—as is increasingly the case in American police departments.

Another way is to keep visibility to partners high by deploying officers in teams rather than individually. There has been much controversy of late over the relative merits of one-man versus two-man patrols, with recent empirical evidence seeming to favor one-man deployment.[31] These results suggest that, from the standpoint of minimizing the effect of personal attitudes on police actions, officers might better be assigned to work in teams. And, the results on the effects of similarities and differences in partners' attitudes suggest, the constraining effect of the partner will be greatest if partners are assigned so that they differ rather than resemble one another in their racial attitudes.

All these strategies, the evidence suggests, should tend to reduce the dependence of arrest decisions and friendliness of manner on personal prejudices. However, two qualifications should be noted. One is that manipulating visibility so as to reduce the effects of prejudice on arrest and friendliness of manner would have the effect of enhancing the relationship between prejudice and impersonality. This seems a desirable result, though, since it is arguably better from the standpoint of professional policing to have antiblack officers treating black citizens personally (a mixture of antagonistic and friendly behavior) and problack officers treating them impersonally than to have antiblack officers treating black citizens antagonistically and problack officers treating them amicably.

The other qualification is that decisions intended to affect behavior through the manipulation of visibility can be taken rationally only after weighing their other costs and benefits. The desire to minimize the impact of racial attitudes on police behavior may justify emphasizing reactive service, deploying two-man patrols, and assigning dissimilarly inclined officers to work together, but such steps may also incur other costs—for example, the additional expense of two-man patrols and the psychological and social difficulties that paring up officers with conflicting racial views may create. Without weighing the trade-offs—which may be very difficult to do—police departments run the risk of purchasing limited benefits at high costs.

The analysis presented here, of course, addresses only the relationship between white policemen's racial attitudes and their treatment of black citizens. Generalization to other attitudes and behaviors would be unwarranted, especially since the data analyzed here were gathered at a time when the racial attitudes of policemen and their treatment of blacks were very salient issues to the policemen themselves, police organizations, and the public. Nevertheless, the results obtained here do suggest some considerations that should be kept in mind whenever the relationships between policemen's attitudes and their actions are addressed, whether explicitly or implicitly. Relationships between attitude and action may not be strong or of the form expected. The strength and the form of the relationship may vary, depending on the type of action and the type of citizen toward whom the action is taken. In addition, the strength and form of the relationship may be quite sensitive to the type of audience to which the action is visible.

Scholars and administrators alike prefer to think that the world is simple—that, to take the example explored here, how people act is determined by their personal attitudes. A simple world is easier to explain and easier to manage. The results of this study suggest that, at least with respect to the question of the relationship between policemen's attitudes and their actions, the world is more complicated than some have thought. Thus these results urge caution on both police scholars and police administrators and they issue a challenge—to develop a more sophisticated understanding of the complexities of police behavior and to develop policies that use that understanding to enhance the quality of police performance.

Notes

1. Jacob Chwast, "Value Conflicts in Law Enforcement," in *The Ambivalent Force*, eds. Arthur Niederhoffer and Abraham S. Blumberg (San Francisco: Rinehart Press, 1973), p. 113. Others who make this general assumption explicit include Helena Carlson, Robert E. Thayer, and A.C. Germann, "Social Attitudes and Personality Differences among Members of Two Kinds of Police Departments (Innovative vs. Traditional) and Students," *Journal of Criminal Law, Criminology, and Police Science* 62 (December 1971): 564; and Milton Rokeach, Martin G. Miller, and John A. Snyder, "The Value Gap between Police and Policed," *Journal of Social Issues* 27 (Spring 1971): 156.

2. The literature on police attitudes and personality is too vast to cite here. Besides, several excellent reviews already exist. See Rokeach, Miller, and Snyder, pp. 156-158; Robert W. Balch, "The Police Personality: Fact or Fiction," *Journal of Criminal Law, Criminology, and Police Science* 63 (March 1972): 106-119; and Joel Lefkowitz, "Psychological Attributes of Policemen: A Review of Research and Opinion," *Journal of Social Issues* 31 (Winter 1975): 3-26.

3. James Q. Wilson, *Varieties of Police Behavior* (Cambridge, Mass.: Harvard University Press, 1968), pp. 2-3.

4. David H. Bayley and Harold Mendelsohn, *Minorities and the Police* (New York: The Free Press, 1969), pp. 162-163. See also Jerome H. Skolnick, "The Police and the Urban Ghetto," in Niederhoffer and Blumberg, *The Ambivalent Force*, p. 225.

5. A.W. Wicker, "Attitudes versus Actions: The Relationship of Verbal and Overt Behavioral Responses to Attitude Objects," *Journal of Social Issues* 25 (1969): 65.

6. Robert A. Mendelsohn, "Police-Community Relations," in *Police in Urban Society*, ed. Harlan Hahn (Beverly Hills, Calif.: Sage Publications, 1970), p. 167.

7. U.S. President's Commission on Law Enforcement and Administration of Justice, *The Challenge of Crime in a Free Society* (Washington, D.C.: GPO, 1967), p. 100; Jesse Rubin, "Police Identity and the Police Role," in *The Police and the Community*, ed. Robert F. Steadman (Baltimore: Johns Hopkins University Press, 1972), p. 48.

8. See, for example, L.H. Wittemore, *Cop!* (Greenwich, Conn.: Fawcett Publications, 1969), pp. 278-279.

9. Wicker, pp. 52-59.

10. Jerome H. Skolnick, *Justice without Trial* (New York; John Wiley, 1966), pp. 83-86.

11. Donald J. Black and Albert J. Reiss, Jr., "Patterns of Behavior in Police and Citizen Transactions," in U.S. President's Commission on Law Enforcement and Administration of Justice, *Studies in Crime and Law Enforcement in Major Metropolitan Areas*, Field Surveys III, Vol. II, Section 1 (Washington, D.C.: GPO, 1967), pp. 137-139.

12. Black and Reiss, pp. 137-139; Bayley and Mendelsohn, pp. 162-163; Skolnick, "The Police," p. 225.

13. Black and Reiss, p. 138.

14. Donald T. Campbell, "Social Attitudes and Other Acquired Behavioral Dispositions," in *Psychology: A Study of a Science*, Vol. 6, ed. Sigmund Koch (New York: McGraw-Hill, 1963), pp. 159-162.

15. Wilson, p. 7.

16. For comments in the general social science literature, see Wicker, pp. 66-75; and Allen E. Liska, "Emergent Issues in the Attitude-Behavior Consistency Controversy," *American Sociological Review* 39 (April 1974): 261-272. For comments pertaining directly to the police, see Skolnick, "The Police," p. 225; and James Q. Wilson, "The Police in the Ghetto," in Steadman, *The Police and the Community*, pp. 64-65.

17. A more detailed description of the observational study and references to the materials on which the description is based are found in Robert J. Friedrich, "The Impact of Organizational, Individual, and Situational Factors on Police Behavior" (Ph.D. dissertation, University of Michigan, 1977), pp. 205-211.

18. Such a procedure assumes a stable underlying attitude—an assumption which, given the substantial cross-patrol variability found in these responses, is problematic. Nevertheless, given the circumstances in which they were gathered, the responses seem reasonably stable and thus this procedure seems the most defensible alternative. For a more detailed discussion, see Friedrich, pp. 347-349.

19. Wayne R. LaFave, *Arrest* (Boston: Little, Brown and Co., 1965), pp. 3-7. This, of course, begs the difficult question of what constitutes an offender. The definition employed here is that employed by Reiss ("Police Observation Report Instructions," unpublished document, p. 4): "the person(s) who is seen as 'out of line' or as a possible violator of some sort in the situation . . . a sociological, not a legal category for these purposes." Later on the data will be divided between offenders and nonoffenders—essentially offenders and everybody else. However, one group—what Reiss calls members of offender groups—will be excluded from these breakdowns because the group was defined to include both the "least active" offenders when there were several and some people who were not really offenders at all, but only "supported or stood with" the offenders.

20. The adjectives in quotation marks are taken directly from the observation schedules used by Reiss's observers.

21. Black and Reiss, pp. 6-7.

22. This assumes, of course, that arrest is a less favorable treatment than release and that a hostile manner is a less favorable treatment than a friendly manner. These seem to be reasonable assumptions, though it should be noted that release may have less favorable connotations than arrest if it stems, as Wilson suggests it sometimes does, from a perception by the police that blacks "want, and . . . deserve, less law enforcement because to the police their conduct suggests a low level of public and private morality, an unwillingness to cooperate with the police or offer information, and widespread criminality" (*Varieties*,

p. 141). Michael Banton makes a similar point in *The Policeman in the Community* (New York: Basic Books, 1964), p. 173. This sort of prejudice might lead to lower arrest rates by the more prejudiced officers. If it does, it would tend to weaken the negative relationship expected between racial attitude and arrest. A Similar reversal might occur between racial attitude and manner if more prejudiced officers take offenses by blacks less seriously than less prejudiced officers and therefore respond in a less harsh manner than less prejudiced officers. If so, it would similarly weaken the positive relationship expected between racial attitude and manner. Some slight evidence for this possibility will emerge in the data analysis.

23. A word about the number of cases is in order at this point. In assessing the hypotheses involving arrest, the number of cases is the number of black offenders confronted by white policemen (about 900). The unit of analysis here is the offender, whether he interacts with one or with two policemen. The offender is used as the unit of analysis rather than the individual policeman's decision to arrest because the original observation schedule did not have the observer identify which officer, in a two-man team, made the arrest decision. For the same reason, the measure of the policeman's racial attitude in tests relating it to arrest is, when two officers were involved, the average of the two officers' attitudes. In assessing the hypotheses involving manner, the number of cases is the number of dyadic interactions between black citizens and white police (about 8,300). The unit of analysis here is the interaction between two people so that, for example, a citizen meeting two officers would constitute two interactions. Because Reiss's schedule recorded the manner of each officer separately, each officer's manner can be related to his own racial attitude.

24. Factors controlled for an analyses not presented here included length of service, satisfaction with job, precinct, and city.

25. Kendall's tau-c is used throughout this analysis to describe the relationship between racial attitude and arrest because it is most appropriate for relationships between ordinal variables with unequal numbers of categories.

26. Jerome H. Skolnick and J. Richard Woodworth, "Bureaucracy, Information, and Social Control: A Study of a Morals Detail," in *The Police: Six Sociological Essays*, ed. David J. Bordua (New York: John Wiley, 1967), pp. 121-122.

27. Kendall's tau-b is used throughout this analysis to describe the relationship between racial attitude and the basic manner variable because it is most appropriate for relationships between ordinal variables with equal numbers of categories.

28. If such a redefinition of "good" behavior as impersonal behavior does take place, one would expect it to be more apparent in professionalized or "legalistic" departments than in traditional or "watchman" departments. A look at the

relationship within each of the three departments shows that it is indeed stronger in the ostensibly more professional departments and weaker in the more traditional department. See Friedrich, "The Impact," pp. 462-465.

29. Gamma is used here rather than either of the tau measures because it better captures the scalar quality of the relationship—greater prejudice does not necessitate an expressive manner, but it makes it more likely. Because gamma is a more liberal measure than the taus, it cannot be directly compared to them. Here, though, the emphasis is on comparing the strength of a relationship between a particular pair of variables across different situations, rather than comparing the strengths of relationships between different pairs of variables, so this poses no problem.

30. Note also that the high percentage of negative treatment for black offenders by the most favorably inclined policeman is consistent with the reversal possibility raised in note 22. The least prejudiced officers may be most inclined to hold the black community to the same standard of behavior as the white community and to respond negatively to those who violate that standard.

31. Linda Charlton, "One-Man Police Patrol Cars Are Safer, More Efficient, Foundation Report Says," *New York Times*, June 6, 1977, p.18.

14 Public Complaints against the Police

Gerald Caiden and
Harlan Hahn

Introduction

The public comes into frequent daily contact with law-enforcement officers. Inevitably, such frequent contact must give rise to complaint. Members of the public do not always understand or appreciate police actions and may misinterpret them. If they were more informed, they probably would uphold the police. However, there is a certain portion of the public that by disposition, socialization, or ideology is antipolice and is prejudiced against the police whatever they do. No amount of explaining or reasoning will overcome their dislike. They will remain persistent critics and habitual complainers who simply cannot accept a state of facts which does not coincide with their beliefs; they cannot be accommodated in this world. A small number of these achieve wide publicity and thereby have a lingering and detrimental effect on police image. On the other hand, they do often pursue questionable police actions that disturb the public generally and their fellow citizens who are reluctant to challenge the police openly. For in the thousands upon thousands of contacts between police and public, some police actions are irregular, even illegal, and by any measure constitute misconduct warranting at least disciplinary action and possibly criminal prosecution. After all, the police are only human; they do make mistakes, and among their number can be found law-enforcement officers who do not live up to their oath of office, or, for various reasons, are no longer fit to be entrusted with police duties. In short, among public complaints against the police, a certain percentage are justified, should be taken seriously, and point to police shortcomings which should be rectified.

This conclusion raises several key issues: Should the public be encouraged to complain against the police, even at the cost of larger number of complaints submitted by cranks and malicious folk? How should complaints be made and acknowledged formally? Who should do the preliminary sorting of complaints and investigate their validity? What should be done with the findings of investigations and how could they be used to prevent repetition?

The Public's Right to Complain

It is a premise of democratic society that citizens should have the right to complain against public officials in their official capacity in exercising the powers entrusted to them by the community. They should have this right as a fundamental expression of civil liberty, whether or not they exercise that right wisely. It is crucial to ensuring responsibility and accountability on the part of public authorities. It acts as a safety measure, a pressure valve on the body politic. It focuses on actions, decisions, and abuses of public power that give offense. It holds officials, both elected and appointed, in line and subordinate to the public will. It substantiates evidence of excessive sense of self-importance by officials, an indifference toward the feelings or the convenience of individual citizens, and obsession with the binding and inflexible authority of departmental decisions, precedents, arrangements, or forms, irrespective of how badly or with what injustice or hardship they may work, a mania for form and procedure, and preoccupation with administrative niceties and an inability to consider the meaning of government as as whole. It throws up, every so often, cases of such misuse of power and gross injustice by officialdom against defenseless citizens that offend the moral precepts of civilized mankind.

Citizens can and do complain to whoever will listen. They go to the mass media and hope that the embarrassing publicity that ensues will make officialdom react. But the mass media lack competence and ability to investigate the validity of complaints and to gain remedial action. Mass media also have their own axes to grind and often lack objectivity. Aggrieved citizens use political channels as best they can. But they deal with busy people who rarely have the resources to undertake any investigation for themselves and who cannot be bothered to deal with every case that comes to them, only those few where the charges are really serious or in which they have a close personal interest. The public seek legal advice, which is expensive and not always reliable, and find that few of their complaints are capable of legal redress, and those that are entail lengthy delays, heavy expense, and a stacked situation in which they are likely to be the loser, whatever the outcome. Complainants go straight to the source, to the very department or authorities which have given the offense, often to find that there are no means provided for handling complaints, that their complaints are handled by the very same officials whose conduct is being questioned, that they are victimized for being troublemakers and they experience retaliation, and that if their complaints are found, for whatever reason, unjustified, they may be liable for making false charges or perjuring themselves. Whichever way citizens turn, they may find that there is no easily accessible, cheap, reliable, objective system capable of instigating remedial action on justifiable complaints.

The Case of the Police

The lack of adequate remedial avenues is especially true in the case of public complaints against the police. Police tend to be cut off and to cut themselves off from the rest of the community. They tend to be a close-knit group in which professional loyalty is highly prized. They, and the bodies that represent them publicly, tend to resent any unnecessary outside interference in what they consider to be internal police affairs, and what constitutes an internal matter is widely interpreted, more extensively than in most other areas of government. They claim organizational independence to prevent politicization of police services and they support exceptional staff privileges by virtue of the peculiar conditions under which they operate. They also command considerable political and public support that makes anyone employing the usual channels for public redress of grievances wary of tackling the police. Mass media want to preserve their good relations with the police to gain ready access to newsworthy items, and reporters working alongside the police tend in time to become cop-buffs and protect the police from public criticism, except for the sensationalist press that seems to glory in disillusioning the public about law enforcement. Politicians fear the wrath of police sympathizers if they take a strong stand against police attitudes and views of public policy, or if they challenge police versions of events involving the police. The legal profession's relations with the police are similarly complicated. In many cases, lawyers advise clients to take their complaints directly to the police.

Like any other group of hard-working, devoted public servants who believe they are doing a good job under the circumstances, police do not welcome complaints and they are not particularly obliging to complaints. In the United States many police departments have no procedures at all for handling public complaints, or complaints are referred to the very person whose conduct is being questioned. In other departments, complainants are required to write their complaints on forms which specifically state that if the information provided is not substantiated, the complainant is liable for prosecution for making false statements. Except as otherwise provided, the police investigate themselves. They are not obligated to notify complainants or indeed anyone else of the results of their investigations or of the manner of the investigation. Rarely does anyone outside the police know what use, if any, is made of the evidence accumulated by internal investigations of public complaints.

Almost every American police department of any appreciable size has procedures for the processing of complaints lodged against police officers by the public or other officers. These in-house procedures are usually administered by a separate organizational unit whose primary responsibility is the investigation of complaints. These units, commonly titled "Internal Affairs," "Internal Investigation," or "Inspectional Services," are not usually viewed favorably by police officers. Their work is often carried on in an atmosphere of suspicion, hostility, and noncooperation, moreso in the case of public complaints than charges brought by officers and police administrators, which tend to be of a different nature, having more to do with rule infringement than abuses or misuse of public position. Almost universally, police oppose external investigation of public complaints, and militant police campaigns against them have killed many such proposals and succeeded in the abandonment of some external review procedures. Police consider their work already so difficult that they are reluctant to have any external agency established solely to scrutinize the way they have done their duty, thereby placing them in greater jeopardy than other public servants.

The Exceptional Nature of Police-Public Relations

While one may sympathize with the police for not wanting to be singled out, the present situation in general in regard to official handling of public complaints leaves much to be desired, and that of the police in particular is intolerable, for, in this case, the police are in a somewhat exceptional position. First, compared with other groups of public servants, police are given exceptional powers and they have exceptional opportunities for misusing them. They are armed and trained to use their arms. Much of their work is discretionary and involves the exercise of personal judgment: whether or not, for instance, to intervene when the peace is being disturbed or an offense has been committed, or when to hold someone responsible for breaches of the peace and infringements of the law. In some circumstances, they themselves are sorely tempted to take the law into their own hands or use their position to commit blue-coat crime. They cannot always under pressure and provocation maintain their dignity, and on such occasions their conduct may give offense—they may swear or provoke or use excessive force. Whatever the reason, they may contravene official rules and norms, forget instilled training and procedures, and violate civil rights, including the denial of an individual's civil rights by killing someone in the course of their work.

Second, because of the exceptional nature of police powers and opportunities, relations between police and public are highly sensitive, certainly tension-ridden and emotional, and potentially explosive. For many, police are the symbol less of public service than of governmental authority, less of public assistance than of the punitive powers of the state or the community. By upbringing or experience, dealing with the police under any circumstances, whether being directed, cautioned, or arrested, is a traumatic experience in which actions on both sides are likely to be misinterpreted and behavior is quite out of character. This is apart from sections of the community who cannot identify with the police at all and who may in fact consider the police as their enemy, and from sections of the police force who cannot identify with the public they supposedly serve and who may consider the public, or part of it, their enemy. It must also be recalled that police officers deal with people at their worst—when drunk or violent or doing something wrong—and in time they become cynical and jaundiced in outlook and often experience burn-out when overworked and hard pressed. Such circumstances are hardly conducive to exemplary conduct.

Third, public complaints are not taken seriously enough. On the whole, the public do not complain needlessly. They believe they have reason. They may be wrong or misinformed, but any misapprehensions they may have about the police as revealed in their complaints ought to be cleared up. Complaints are symptomatic of general unease that may be traceable to faulty administration, inadequate training, and misbehavior—things that could be corrected. Further, a certain proportion of the complaints, sometimes as many as one in every two, reveals that injustice has been done and ought to be righted. People are not just interested in what affects them personally. It is part of a good man's well-being and peace of mind to know that the society to which he belongs does justice to his fellow man also. Anything which helps people to obtain justice in their dealings with powerful authorities, like the police, has value for all, even those who do not need it for themselves. It is part of the everlasting struggle for moral advancement, not only in the individual soul but also in society at large.

Fourth, as far as can be ascertained, complaints against police have jumped appreciably in the United States over the last decade, although there has been some decline in recent years. A general unease with policing prevails and the belief persists that, despite assurances to the contrary, the police have not changed and their performance has not improved appreciably. More seriously, individuals feel that they are powerless against law-enforcement agencies; that protest is useless, as nobody listens, nobody cares; and that they cannot bring about changes in the nature of policing. Their inaction is mistaken for indifference or apathy. They are neither indifferent nor apathetic. Nevertheless mass media seem to believe that only by sensationalizing can they attract public attention to police deficiencies. The attendant distortion and exaggeration upset the police, who feel they need a public protector to shield them from blatant dishonesty and to present their side of the case. The police themselves are unhappy with the way they are treated in mass media and resent being placed on the defensive much of the time.

The Search for More Effective Complaint-Handling Machinery

Democratic regimes around the world have sought more effective complaint-handling machinery that would reassure both public and police. In recent years, the two most popular services have been the establishment of ombudsman offices and the introduction of police appeal boards. The Scandinavian countries, New Zealand, Canada, Australia, and Israel, for example, have opted for the ombudsman office, a special agency independent of the executive that investigates public complaints against public maladministration. Most of the ombudsman offices are empowered to investigate public complaints against law-enforcement bodies, and in some cases the national police have established their own ombudsman or public complaints offices in addition. In the United Kingdom, the Police Act of 1976 provided for regional Police Complaint Boards, composed of at least nine civilians, to superintend the investigation of complaints and disciplinary outcomes, and two members together with the relevant chief constable would consttute a disciplinary tribunal to review disciplinary action.

These two major devices have also been adopted in the United States. The ombudsman device has been adopted in four states (Alaska, Hawaii, Iowa, and Nebraska) and upwards of ten regional or local government bodies. The police department in Kansas City, Missouri, has established its own ombudsman office, an Office of Citizens' Complaints independent of the department and headed by a civilian who has his own expert investigatory staff. Appeal or investigatory boards have taken the form of review boards and are variously composed. Some have been solely composed of civilians (for example, Philadelphia, Chicago); others have been a mixture of civilians and sworn police officers (for example, New York). Both sets of institutions guarantee the public's rights to complain against police, conduct independent investigation of complaints, and publish annually statistical summaries of their work.

With the possible exception of Kansas City, the police have been highly resistant to external review of public complaints. They claim that

1.   Civilians cannot properly understand or appreciate the circumstances under which police work.
2.   External review encourages malicious complaints.
3.   Appointees are drawn from police antagonists.
4.   Investigations entail double jeopardy for police officers.
5.   External review is unnecessary inasmuch as internal review is superior.

An analysis of the actual operations of external review in the United States reveal that few civilians have been unable to appreciate police work. Indeed, they have tended to protect police organizations and to be more lenient with police offenders than internal reviews. Some review boards have run into legal problems over double jeopardy because they have conducted investigations themselves and recommended disciplinary action. Internal reviews have dealt with a large volume of complaints and have been much more severe with police offenders. They have been able to draw on the full resources of the police in conducting investigations and they have, on the whole, built up a reputation for honesty and fairness.

Against the police claims, it has been held that the police should not investigate themselves. Justice should not only be done, but it should be seen to be done. There should be "neutral territory" for the receipt of complaints against the police. Oral and anonymous complaints should not for that reason be rejected or ignored, as is usually the case in internal review. There should be a wide rather than narrow definition of "complaint" that would initiate independent investigation. An offense of "false report" or "false complaint" should be strictly circumscribed. In brief, an independent element should be infused into the process of receipt, handling, investigation, and determination of complaints against police to ensure adequate public scrutiny of complaints and increase public confidence in the complaint-handling system, hopefully without either undermining the responsibility of police administrators for discipline or exposing accused police officers to more than one judicial process on a single matter. Supporters of external review claim that

1. People are afraid to lodge a complaint about a police officer with a police department and do not trust the police to investigate themselves in the public interest.
2. Anonymous complaints, if properly scrutinized and filtered, are important in uncovering police malpractice.
3. Police are reluctant to reveal all they know and, for reasons of organizational loyalty and self-preservation, they suppress evidence.
4. Police deal severely with complaints brought by police officers and with relatively minor infringements of official regulations, but leniently with public complaints of serious import concerning police misconduct toward individuals.
5. Police are sloppy in investigating severe cases of police misconduct.

Again, available evidence seems to support most of these claims, but there seems agreement that independent police investigations are usually reliable, professional, economical, and objective, providing conflicts of interest are avoided. Investigators in internal affairs are jealous of the reputation of the police and zealous in the pursuit of possible misconduct. They are not at all lenient toward offenders and their justice often has to be tempered by the mercy exercised by police administrators and review panels.

A Recommended Solution

It is possible to reconcile both views by devising complaint-handling machinery that draws on the best features of the opposing sides. The public should not be precluded from lodging complaints against public officials in any way now open to them or available to them in the future. In addition a special office independent of police administration should be established to receive complaints against the pplice from both public and police officers, orally and anonymously if necessary. Such an office—a Police Ombudsman or an Office of Citizens' Complaints or a Police Complaints Board—should be able to call on the expertise of its own experienced staff or the internal affairs department for investigations of all prudent and serious complaints. The findings should be conveyed to the complainant and to the chief of police, and the office should be empowered to publish summaries of his findings and to review the subsequent actions he takes. The office would not conduct disciplinary hearings, nor would it be empowered to impose its recommendations. It would be strictly an onbudsmanlike institution. Executive action would be decided by the chief of police alone and it would be his prerogative whether to recommend to the attorney general's office that criminal proceedings might be instituted against police officers or what disciplinary proceedings should be followed or where administrative reforms might be made.

Our own preference is for a county ombudsman to be attached to the board of supervisors and empowered to receive, handle, investigate, and determine public complaints against the county's administration, including law-enforcement bodies. Failing that proposal, we suggest that an office of citizens' complaints, headed by a public figure of renown, independent mind, and judicious temperament, possibly with legal qualifications and knowledgeable about police matters, should be established in the attorney general's office to deal with public complaints about the whole system of justice administration in the county, that is, police, correctional institutions, and courts. As a third choice, we would advocate a similar office or police ombudsman in the sheriff's department to deal with complaints against county law-enforcement officers.

Police Shootings

Whenever police officers have to discharge their firearms in the course of their duties, the incident is considered by police departments as serious. Consequently, such incidents would automatically fall within the jurisdiction of our proposed complaint-handling machinery. Because the public has to be protected against possible use of excessive force by the police, the discharge of firearms should be subject to inquiry, and the head of the public complaints office would be an ex officio member of any inquiry. He would be specifically empowered (1) to see that all such inquiries were properly conducted, and (2) in the event of his disagreement with the inquiry's findings, to disclose publicly his minority report. His role would be to act as public protector, not inquisitor or advocate. His assets would be independence, objectivity, sensitivity, and concern with the public interest. He should not lay claim to powers of enforcement, for he neither creates standards with the authority of a legislative body nor restricts himself to the application of legally binding norms. He should not usurp exective responsibility, but neither should he be resigned to any lack of influence. The sanction of his disapproval should be sufficient to trigger effective response.

Part VI
Effects of the Media
on the Police

15

Evaluating Crime-Fighting Policies: Media Images and Public Perspective

Doris A. Graber

Crime has been a matter of major concern to the American public since the mid-1960s because of its high human and property costs. Gallup poll reports regarding the public's choices of the most important issues facing the United States show crime as receiving from 2 to 29 percent of the votes in the past ten years.[1] In October 1976, 6 percent of Gallup's sample rated crime as a crucial issue, as did 6 percent of the respondents in the study reported here. A further mark of concern with the crime problem is the fact that 64 percent of the respondents indicated that they were moderately or seriously worried about becoming crime victims, 19 percent were slightly worried, and only 15 percent said that they were not worried at all. Seventy-six percent reported taking precautions in line with their concern about victimization and were able to recall from one to four steps, such as new locks to protect property, avoiding certain areas of town, or traveling in groups, particularly at night.

Polling data also indicate that the public pays attention to news about crime-related matters and has definite ideas about causes of crime and measures that might prevent it.[2] Since the mass media, which are the chief sources for public information, feature many stories about crime and its aftermath, the public has more information readily available about this area of public policy than about most other areas. Judging by the comparatively small number of "don't know" replies in response to questions about crime and the criminal justice process, the public appears to feel relatively more competent in this area than in other areas of public concern.

The crime problem has received a good deal of attention from government officials as well because of its deleterious effects on American society and because of the pervasive public concern which it has elicited. A plethora of government-sponsored investigations have looked into all aspects of the problem and many recommendations springing from this research have been widely discussed.[3] Politicians take the public's views about crime and crime fighting seriously because these views measure public satisfaction, which is an important goal in public policymaking.[4] It is particularly important in a policy area like crime fighting, where public cooperation is required to achieve best results. Equally important for many

The research reported here was made possible through the financial support from the Center for Research in Criminal Justice, University of Illinois at Chicago Circle, Hans W. Mattick, Director. Computer services were made available through the Computer Center at the University. The support of these organizations is gratefully acknowledged.

politicians is the fact that public dissatisfaction with the government's capabilities to preserve law and order may lead to electoral sanctions. The 1972 presidential campaign is a recent example of the prominence which the "law and order" issue can assume in elections.

The Research Question

Despite the importance of the public's perspective on ways to cope with the crime problem and the successes and failures of current crime-fighting policies, researchers have paid comparatively little attention to this aspect of public attitudes. For the most part, they have failed to investigate what information is made available to the public about crime fighting, what the public learns from this information, and how it uses this information to form its evaluations about crime-fighting policies. The research reported in this chapter was undertaken to contribute to the closing of this knowledge gap.

To shed light on the public's perspective on crime-fighting policies, three major questions need to be raised and answered. First of all, we must ask how much and what kind of information is supplied to the public for judging the nature of the crime problem and governmental efforts to cope with it. Second, we need to know how much attention the public pays to this kind of information and what kind of knowledge it extracts from it. Finally, we must assess the kinds of perceptions of crime and crime fighting which people develop on the basis of this information and the types of evaluations to which these perceptions lead. After describing the public's perspective on crime and crime-fighting policies, we shall then speculate about their implications and consequences.

These questions need to be assessed in the context of the general information environment in which individuals operate. The inclusion of contextual considerations is important to avoid some of the distortions which inevitably occur when people's concerns in one area of public policy, such as crime, are examined in isolation, ignoring competing concerns. In this chapter, therefore, we will present comparative data on crime and noncrime information made available by the mass media to the public. To keep data about public information in a perspective which will capture differences in information levels and evaluations which may exist at various times, we have spaced our interviews over an entire year. Many questions were repeated in a variety of contextual settings within the interviews. Furthermore, we have attempted to increase the level of confidence in the reliability of our interview data by using multiple, heterogenous measuring techniques for probing perceptions about crime fighting.

The Data Base

The data base which we have used for this investigation has two major components: analysis of people's perceptions and analysis of mass media content. People's perceptions were gathered through a series of nine to ten interviews conducted from January 1976 to January 1977 with four small panels of voters. Media data come from matching content-analyses of four daily newspapers, one weekly paper, and nightly newscasts on three national and two local television stations.[5] Most of these media were content-analyzed on a daily basis to reflect as closely as possible the full information supply made available to our panels. Sampling of this information pool would have made the analysis vulnerable to the omission of key events and would have made it difficult to tell how many news stories are repeated with varying degrees of frequency.

The Panels and the Interviews

Members of the four panels were selected from a randomly drawn sample of voters in three locations.[6] These were Evanston, Illinois, a suburban community near Chicago; metropolitan Indianapolis, Indiana; and Lebanon, New Hampshire, a small New England town. Registered voters were used on the assumption that this somewhat select pool would tap the more politically alert elements of the population whose perceptions were likely to be the most informed in the three communities. The final sample was drawn to represent various levels of interest in politics among registered voters, availability of adequate time for media exposure, directly or through conversations with others, and different use patterns for print and electronic media. The sample was also structured to reflect a balance of demographic characteristics. Table 15-1 presents data on age, sex, education, and occupation of the sample.

All of the panels were small because we wanted to investigate knowledge and learning about public issues intensively and over an extended period of time. The high costs involved in this procedure made it mandatory to keep respondent

Table 15-1
Demographic Characteristics of the Four Panels
(in percentages; N = 164)

Age		Sex		Occupation		Education[a]	
Under 30	= 27%	Male	= 51%	Skilled workers	= 20%	Grade School	= 17%
30-40	= 24	Female	= 49	Sales and Service	= 15	High School	= 16
41-50	= 10			Professional	= 13	Trade School	= 24
51-60	= 20			Homemaker	= 12	College	= 43
61-70	= 10			Retired	= 9		
71-80	= 7			Business	= 8		
Over 80	= 1			Clerical	= 6		
				Unskilled	= 6		
				Students	= 4		
				Miscellaneous	= 4		
				Unemployed	= 3		

[a]Each grouping signifies graduates. The trade-school grouping includes people with partial college educations.

numbers small.[7] Three of the panels had forty-eight respondents each. Except for two personal interviews, these respondents were contacted by telephone. The fourth panel had twenty-one respondents and was used for more intensive analysis of the questions explored through the larger panels. We shall refer to it as the "core" panel. To provide additional information on factors which might explain particular information acquisition and use patterns, members of the core panel, prior to the regular interviews, were questioned in detail about past and current life experiences and information use behavior. Members of the core panel divided 43 percent-24 percent-33 percent in their attitudes regarding the handling of accused persons on a seven-point scale running from liberal, to middle-of-the-road, to conservative. On a general seven-point liberal, middle-of-the-road, conservative scale, the division was in even thirds.

Members of the core panel were interviewed in person and their interviews, averaging between one and two hours in length, were tape-recorded. While the interviews of all four panels contained many open-ended questions to permit respondents to formulate the major outlines of the subject areas as they perceived them, the core panel received the widest array of such questions. Broad questions were followed by more focused questions designed to elicit a common data base. To get as rich a response as possible, probes and follow-up questions were unlimited for the core panel. Respondents were routinely asked why they had given the answers they did.

Members of the core panel were also questioned during each interview about an array of twenty to thirty news stories which had been covered by the newspaper and/or television news programs to which they normally paid attention. Stories of all types, prominent in the news during the preceding month, were included. Out of a total of 285 news stories for which recall was tested, 25 percent dealt with matters relating to crime and crime-fighting policies.

In addition, subjects in the core panel completed daily diaries throughout the year in which they recorded the news stories which had come to their attention from the mass media or through personal contacts. They were instructed to enter any news story which they remembered at the time set aside for diary completion. Diary forms requested brief reports on the main theme of the story, its source and length, and the respondent's reasons for interest in the story and her or his reaction to it. A minimum of thirty minutes was to elapse between story exposure and diary entry, to allow forgetting processes to operate. In most instances, the actual interval was four hours or more. Respondents who were unable or disinclined to write their own diaries were contacted daily by a telephone interviewer who completed the diary forms for them.

To detect possible sensitization effects which might result from the repeated interviews and diary-keeping, several checks were run, using respondents who had not been included in the four panels. Recall of stories was scored on a four-point scale, ranging from one for "none" to four for "a lot." The latter rating was awarded whenever respondents could spontaneously relate three or more major aspects of a news story. Comparisons of the mean recall scores showed no significant differences between the panel members (mean recall = 2.3 points) and the control group (mean recall = 2.4 points) based on responses about knowledge of randomly selected, specific, recent news stories ($p < .05$).

The News Sources

The major daily newspapers used by our respondents were the *Chicago Tribune*, the *Indianapolic News*, the *Indianapolic Star*, and the *Lebanon Valley News*. The *Chicago Tribune* and *Lebanon Valley News* were content-analyzed on a daily basis for six days per week. For the Indiana papers, every fourth day was coded, including Sundays. The content analyses recorded various aspects of story prominence and format, as well as up to three main topics for each story. "Stories" were defined as including editorials, letters to the editor, features, and cartoons, along with ordinary news reports, but excluding advertisements, obituaries, puzzles, radio and television listings, and similar types of announcements.

In addition to the general analysis, crime stories in the *Chicago Tribune* were also coded on such features as the nature of the crimes that were covered, discussions of causes and motivations of crime, details revealed about particular crimes and apprehension, prosecution, conviction, and penalties, and content of stories dealing primarily with the police, the courts, and the correctional system. The purpose of the crime content analysis was to provide a fairly detailed picture of the images of crime which this particular newspaper presented to the two panels located in Evanston. To supplement the analysis of *Tribune* stories, the crime content of the weekly local newspaper read by the Evanston panels was also coded, though in a much more limited fashion. Additionally, a sample of crime stories from the *Chicago Daily News* and the *Chicago Sun-Times* was analyzed to determine how much variability there was in the treatment of crime stories by papers published in the same locality.

The content analysis of print media was complemented by analyses of the nightly early evenings newscasts of the three national television networks. Procedures were similar to those used for print media, but with adaptations required by the different medium. To get a fuller grasp of television fare used by the Evanston panels, the two mightly local newscasts which received the most attention from these panels were also content-analyzed on a daily basis.[8]

To keep this essay within reasonable limits, we are presenting detailed data for two news sources only: the *Chicago Tribune* and NBC local news. There are our amplest sources in terms of numbers of stories, as well as the major sources of news for the core panel which produced our richest data. Since the differences among various papers and various network and local channels were moderate, the *Tribune* and NBC data can be considered representative of general press and television coverage trends between mid-January 1976 and mid- January 1977.

Mass Media Crime Information Available to Panel Members

To answer our first question about the information supply made available to the public about crime and crime fighting, we coded 19,068 *Tribune* news stories of all kinds. Of these, 18.8 percent (3,592) dealt with matters relating to crime or the criminal justice system. We shall refer to them collectively as "crime" stories. Our content analysis scheme of coding up to three topics per story yielded a total of 33,197 topics. Of these, 21.1 percent (7,025) were crime topics. NBC local news covered 6,614 stories for the coding year. Nineteen percent (1,262) of these were crime stories. Of the 11,011 topics covered in these stories, 21.5 percent (2,371) related to crime.[9] Thus roughly one-fifth of print and television coverage dealt with matters of crime. Compared to other significant topics, crime information supply was quite ample, indeed.

Table 15-2 puts the data into a comparative framework. It lists *Tribune* and NBC local news data for the eight crime topics used for the media study and for eight noncrime topics selected for their substantive diversity and as a numerical match to the crime stories. Comparisons with the selected topics rather than the entire array of topics simulate news consumption behavior in which the individual generally pays attention to only a limited array of stories in a paper or newscast. The topics selected for comparison are examples and do not present the choice patterns of all panel members.

Table 15-2 shows that stories about individual crimes, the judiciary, and the police are given substantially more play than topics like Congress, city government, education, or energy policy. This preference bestows an importance on crime topics which many social scientists deem out of proportion to the impact of crime on the welfare of the American public. This type of distortion, it has been argued, deflects attention from noncrime issues and unduly enhances the public's fear of crime and the socially harmful consequences of that fear.[10]

Since amount of attention which news stories received is affected by the

Table 15-2
Distribution of Selected News Topics in Press and TV Local News
(in percentages; N = 12; 144 press news topics, 4,333 TV news topics)

Crime Topics	Press	TV	Noncrime Topics	Press	TV
Individual crimes	16.5%	16.2%	Education	7.3%	7.4%
Judiciary	15.5	12.1	Congress	6.9	3.1
Police/security	12.7	7.8	Disasters/accidents	5.9	12.5
Political terrorism	5.2	8.4	City government	5.2	8.5
Corrupt politics	4.0	4.6	Middle East	4.9	2.9
Drug crimes	1.8	1.7	State government	4.8	5.6
Business crimes	1.7	3.8	Political gossip	4.4	3.6
Gun control	0.5	0.2	Energy policy	2.7	1.8

prominence given to them within a news offering, such as one newspaper issue or one news broadcast, we examined relative placement of these stories within papers and newscasts, along with story length, pictorial emphasis, and other attention-arousing features. As table 15-3 indicates, crime stories are displayed slightly less prominently than other stories. But the difference is so slight, and not even consistent for all prominence features, that for all practical purposes the two types of topics receive similar coverage.[11] We can therefore conclude that crime-related subjects receive above-average amounts of coverage but do not receive preference in display.

Analysis of the substance of crime stories reveals that better than half of the total (51.3 percent) have as their major thrust either the court system, the correctional system, or the police (courts, 33.3 percent; police, 15.8 percent; correc-rections, 2.2 percent).[12] The bulk of these stories are descriptive; stories with ex-

Table 15-3
Comparative Prominence of Crime and Selected Noncrime Stories
(N = 3,592 crime and 3,531 noncrime press stories and 1,262 crime and 1,283 noncrime TV news stories; percent of stories in each category which share most prominent and least prominent position)

		Crime Stories		Noncrime Stories	
		Press	*TV*	*Press*	*TV*
Section[a]	most prominent	60.3%		62.3%	
	least prominent	19.0		16.4	
Page[b]	most prominent	18.4		16.3	
	least prominent	37.5		34.1	
Headline[c]	most prominent	4.8	40.8%	4.8	36.6%
	least prominent	57.6	59.2	57.5	43.6
Pictures[d]	presence	18.9	6.0	28.1	29.2
	absence	81.1	0.0	71.9	20.3
Story length[e]	most prominent	4.6	21.8	5.9	18.0
	least prominent	25.5	57.9	26.0	60.6

[a]Most prominent equals section 1, least prominent equals sections 3-15.

[b]Most prominent equals page 1; least prominent equals page 6 and beyond.

[c]For press, most prominent equals 7 or more comlumn inches, least prominent means 2 or less column inches, multiplying height by length in each case.
For TV. most prominent equals presence of verbal or written headline, least prominent equals absence of verbal or written headline.

[d]For press, presence means any size picture; absence means no picture.
For TV, presence means use or graphics or film for 75% more of stories in individual crime or noncrime subcategories; absence means graphics or film used for 50% or less of subcategory stories.

[e]For press, most prominent equals 20 column inches or more; least prominent equals 5 column inches or less.
For TV, most prominent equals 120 seconds or more; least prominent equals 60 seconds or less.

plicit evaluations are scarce. Barely over 1 percent of all crime stories contained explicit evaluations of either the courts, the correctional system, or the police (courts, 1.3 percent; police, 1.1 percent; corrections, 1.2 percent).

Taking a closer look at evaluation stories, we find that court system evaluations received the most prominent coverage among stories dealing with evaluation of the criminal justice system, with 54 percent appearing on the first three pages. This was slightly above the average 46 percent figure for crime stories in general. For correction system evaluations, the figure was just above average, 47 percent, and police stories trailed with 27 percent. In section placement, evaluation stories did considerably worse than other crime stories. Against an average of 61 percent of crime stories appearing in the first section, only 43 percent of the police evaluation stories, 34 percent of the correction system evaluations, and 26 percent of the court evaluation stories appeared in the front section. This yields an average of 34 percent, slightly over half the comparable overall figure.

Substantively, the evaluations were heavily negative, with the courts and the correctional system faring worst. The police fared reasonably well. Table 15-4 tells the story.

Thus far we have been discussing explicit evaluations only. But the media contain a series of implicit evaluations as well. The clearest example are stories which assess fluctuations in the crime rate. For most observers, increasing crime rates are equated with poor performance by the criminal justice system; stable or declining rates signify satisfactory or good performance. Sixty percent of the small number of stories which assessed crime rates (1.6 percent of the total) indicated that crime was increasing and the remainder depicted crime rates as stable or decreasing or a mixture of the three. Again, these stories were displayed less prominently than other crime stories. Only 28 percent appeared on the first three pages, compared to the average rate for crime stories of 45 percent; and 47 percent were covered in the first section of the paper, compared to 61 percent for other crime stories.

Another indicator by which the public evaluates police performance is the success of the police in apprehending criminals. Forty-six percent of the crime stories provided data about apprehension of suspects. Of these, 41 percent indi-

Table 15-4

Press Evaluations of the Police, the Courts, and the Correctional System
(percent of stories making various assessments; N = 30 police, 35 court, and 32 correctional system evaluation stories)

	Improving	Stable	Declining	Mixed
Police	23.3%	36.6%	20.0%	20.0%
Courts	2.8	14.2	40.0	42.8
Correctional system	0.0	15.6	25.0	59.3

cated that no arrests had been made. In the remaining cases, arrests were reported. In two-thirds of the arrest cases, all suspects had been apprehended. In the rest, some suspects remained at large. Judging by the criteria enunciated by our panel members and reported below, a 59 percent arrest rate is deemed good performance. This makes the media picture favorable.

Penalties are also an important indicator by which the effectiveness of the criminal justice process is judged. As reported later in this paper, our panel members were highly critical of this phase of criminal justice policy. This makes it important to look at media information abut penalties. Only 11 percent of the crime stories covered the topic explicitly. Of these, 12 percent of the murder cases reported the death penalty. Additionally, long prison sentences, in excess of 11 years, were reported for 75 percent of the kidnapping cases, 40 percent of the rape cases, 38 percent of the robbery cases, 29 percent of the murders and 17 percent of the manslaughter cases. All other reported penalties involved prison sentences of ten years or less. Table 15-5 provides data on sentencing reported in media crime stories.

The subject of penalties was discussed in other contexts as well. A fourth of the stories dealing with crime prevention (2.7 percent of the total) pointed to short-comings in sentencing and penalties as a factor in criminal activities. Likewise, nearly half of the general discussions of criminal justice policies (4.0 percent of total stories) dealt with penalties and the correctional system. This included discussion of the death penalty, sentencing in general, granting immunity, plea bargaining, continuances, parole, and decriminalization of various victimless offenses. When causes of crime were mentioned (4 percent of total stories), the largest single share of the blame for crime was placed on deficiencies in the criminal justice system. Better than one-third of the accounts (37.1 percent) indicated that the criminal justice system encourages crime by excessive leniency in dealing with criminals.

Four percent of the stories dealing with individual crimes also contained comments on criminal law changes and prison reform, gun control, and on per-

Table 15-5
Sentences in Crime Cases Reported in the Press
(in percentages; N = 309 mentions)

Prison	34.9%
Release without penalty	24.2
Further legal steps pending	21.6
Fine and prison	6.7
Death	4.2
Mental institution commitment	4.2
Fine only	3.8

missible media reporting of crimes. The impression left in most of these stories was that something was remiss with the court and correctional systems. In the stories in which civil rights violations by criminal justice agencies were discussed (2.7 percent of total stories), the preponderant tone was negative as well. Violations were alleged in 59 percent of the cases. In the remainder, the case was mixed and occasionally favorable, indicating that law-enforcement agencies had actually protected civil rights.

Summing the evidence on media evaluations, we see a mixed picture. Explicit evaluations of police, courts, and correctional institutions showed a mixture of positive and negative comments, with negative ones predominating for the correctional system and the courts. Implicit evaluations gave a predominantly negative picture for crime rate trends and provided some grist for the mills of those who believe that sentences are too light. On the other hand, the data on apprehension rates were favorable in light of the public's standards.

The Public's Images of Crime and the Criminal Justice Process

Our next question concerns the amount of attention people pay to crime information and the images of crime and criminals which they extract from the media information which is supplied to them directly or indirectly. To answer this question, we shall turn to data from the interviews with all four panels. Unless indicated otherwise, the data are based on the entire sample of 164 respondents. Percentages reported are based on the total number of respondents who answered each question. At times, this is somewhat less than the sample total.

Investigating attention patterns is important because media images are not automatically transferred to media audiences. Rather, transmission requires that the audience become aware of the media image and that audience members then internalize and/or transform it in full or in part. We investigated attention to media crime stories both directly and indirectly, asking for chief sources of information as well as for the amount of attention given to the information supply. Directly, we inquired on two occasions whether panel members learned about crime mostly from the mass media, personal knowledge, or conversation. Ninety-five percent of the answers rated the mass media as the primary source. However, 38 percent cited other sources as well. Only 14 percent of the panel members had had any personal involvement with crime through victimization of family members, self, or close friends. An even smaller percentage had ever known a person accused of crime.

While our respondents used the media as prime sources for factual data about crime and criminal justice matters, they used them less frequently as sources for evaluations. For instance, in questions assessing crime danger at various sites, 57 percent named the mass media as the source of their knowledge, while the rest cited word of mouth as their source. Reliance on media was even less for evaluation of crime-fighting activities. Only 24 percent of the panel members cited media as origins of these evaluations. Personal experience and personal evaluations were mentioned as chief sources by 57 percent. The remaining 19 percent named conversations or professional sources.

The fact that media are prime information sources does not mean that all media information is absorbed. To the contrary, when we asked our panel members repeatedly how much attention they paid to media information, fully half claimed that they paid little attention only, 48 percent claimed to give a lot of attention, and 2 percent claimed that they paid no attention at all. Inattention was largely due to competing claims on the respondents' time and not to distrust of the media. Between one-half to three-fourths of our respondents generally judged both press and television coverage of crime stories as accurate. Complaints about distortion of crime news were rare. However, there were complaints about sensationalism and lack of detail.

Data on story recall confirm that a large number of crime stories were ignored or quickly forgotten. Only 24 percent of the members of the core panel could recall most (85 percent of the crime stories to which they had been exposed during the four to six weeks preceding each interview. Nevertheless, the overall recall rate of crime stories was somewhat better than recall of other types of stories when we compared recall rates for selected crime and noncrime topics[12] People also reported more reactions to crime than to noncrime stories and they related crime stories more often to their past or current personal behavior. This indicated a higher degree of involvement with crime stories.

Examination of stories reported by core panel members in their diaries discloses that individual crimes represented the single largest category. Overall, crime topics constituted 16 percent of the 15,419 topics mentioned in the diaries. Table 15-6 rank orders diary stories according to the frequency of mention of eight crime and eight noncrime topics. Assigning point values to each story equal to its group ranking, crime stories come up with the winning low score, with 29 percent fewer points than noncrime stories. The matching data for press and television coverage are quite similar to the diary data. This is an interesting demonstration of the influence which mass media have on the array of topics to which media audiences pay attention.[14] In contrast to diary and specific story recall, spontaneous general recall of crime stories was low. During various interviews, an average of 35 percent of the panel could not spontaneously recall any crime stories when asked generally what stories they remembered, rather specifically whether they remembered story X or Y.

Despite inattention and extensive forgetting, our subjects developed a substantial knowledge base from the media information available to them. It consisted of a lot of specific information about particular crimes, such as the Patty Hearst case and the Chowchilla kidnapping case. Every respondent could give a reasonably complete brief account of the gist of events presented in the media about these crimes. People also acquired some general notions about trends in

Table 15-6

Rank Order of Frequency of Diary, Press and TV Mentions of Crime and Selected Noncrime Topics

(N = 4,287 for diary mentions, 12,144 for press mentions, and 4,333 for TV mentions)

Crime Topics	Noncrime Topics	Diaries	Press	TV
1. Individual crimes		18.4%	16.5%	16.2%
2. Judiciary		10.8	15.5	12.1
	3. Disasters/accidents	10.7	5.9	12.5
	4. Political gossip	8.4	4.4	3.6
	5. City government	7.3	5.2	8.5
6. Political terrorism		5.9	5.2	8.4
	7. Education	5.7	7.3	7.4
8. Corrupt politics		5.6	4.0	4.6
	9. Middle East	5.2	4.9	2.9
	10. Congress	5.1	6.9	3.1
11. Police/security		4.5	12.7	7.8
	12. State government	4.5	4.8	5.6
13. Business crimes		2.9	1.7	3.8
	14. Energy policy	2.5	2.7	1.8
15. Drug offenses		1.3	1.8	1.7
16. Gun control		.3	.5	.2

crime rates, specifics of crime commission, and general characteristics of criminals and victims.[15] Since the media supply few analytical stories about the crime problem, this indicates that respondents were able to make generalizations from the specific data on their own and to construct their own stereotypical images.

Beyond descriptive generalizations, our panel members were also able to speculate about causes of crime and possible ways to reduce the crime rate. Although media crime stories supply relatively little information about crime causes (only 5 percent of all stories discuss causes, and only 3 percent mention remedies), all panel members could cite at least one cause of crime; a majority could cite multiple causes. Most panel members could also suggest remedies to reduce crime and crime-related problems. Similar to public opinion poll data, the percentage of "no" and "not sure" answers was lower for these types of questions than for most other public policy questions.[16]

Knowledge about crimes was not limited to violent offenses. Our subjects were reasonably well versed about various types of white-collar crimes as well. When presented with a list of the most common white-collar crimes and asked for their comparative seriousness and frequency, 85 percent out of a total of 2,760 answers voiced judgments of various kinds. Most panel members likewise had opinions about the relative frequency of commission of white-collar crimes compared to violent offenses. A somewhat higher percentage gave don't-know answers when quizzed about likely criminals and victims for these types of crimes.

While information levels about various crimes, criminals, victims, and the law-enforcement system were high, information levels about public programs designed to help victims of crime were spotty and generally low. The potential boost which crime-fighting evaluations might receive from this knowledge was thus diminished. When asked, "Have you heard or read anything about programs which provide for (1) public compensation for crime victims; (2) protection of women who are beaten by their spouses; (3) protection of children who are physically abused by their parents; (4) assistance to people who have been cheated by merchants; and (5) assistance to people endangered or injured by environmental pollution?" 86 percent of our respondents knew one or more organizations which would assist them if they felt defrauded by business people. Sixty-two percent were aware of antipollution programs that might protect them from health and property hazards. But only 43 percent had heard of programs to compensate crime victims, only 14 percent knew where to turn for aid for abused children, and barely 10 percent had heard about protection for battered wives. It is interesting to note that the rank order of knowledge level parallels the rank order of frequency of the acts against which the average person might need protection.

Compared to the scanty knowledge about victim assistance programs, and the ample knowledge about details related to crime commission, how much did our panel members know about the police, the courts, and the correctional system? The answer is, "A substantial amount." We shall present the various facets of public knowledge in the context of the evaluations which people gave for these services and the proposals they made for service improvement. These evaluations and proposals indicate familiarity with the promptness and efficiency with which the police and courts generally operate, with recruiting and training policies for policemen and prison personnel, with custodial and rehabilitation policies in prisons, with court procedures like plea bargaining, immunity grants, and suspended sentences, with the bail and parole system, and with fluctuations in the crime rate and the rates of recidivism.

The Public's Evaluation of the Police, the Courts, and the Correctional System

To answer our third question, regarding public perceptions and evaluations of the criminal justice system, we asked panel members a series of general evaluation questions about the performance of the police, the courts, and the correctional system. General questions were followed by more specific ones about features of these systems which had been mentioned as matters of concern. We queried panel members most extensively about their evaluations of the police, since that is the criminal justice branch with which the average citizen has closest contact. Presumably, this makes the quality of policy activities of most immediate concern to him. It also is the area where public cooperation is most sorely needed.

Questioning about the police began with the query, "In general, would you say that the police are doing a good job, a fair job, or poor job in protecting the comunity?" After the initial judgment had been rendered, we probed for reasons behind it. To put the replies into a time perspective, subjects were then asked, "Compared to five years ago, are they doing a better or worse job, or just about the same?" Again, reasons for the answers were solicited.

Fifty-seven percent of the panel members gave the police a "good" rating; the rest rated it as "fair." There were no "poor" ratings. However, many respondents qualified their judgment by indicating that performance varied in different parts of the city and suburbs, and with respect to different crimes. Racial distinctions were also noted, with service to the white community rated superior. When asked for reasons for "fair" ratings, the difficulty of the problems facing the police, insufficient manpower, and lack of public cooperation were cited, along with lack of skills and dedication, and the poor caliber of police personnel. A typical comment often was prefaced by, "Considering the tough problems they face," or "Given community attitudes," followed by a favorable evaluation. This leaves the impression that a large proportion of those who give the police less than top ratings put the blame on the "system" rather than on the particular institution. A few respondents indicated that their judgment was based on media appraisals, but most claimed to have judged independently.

Since apprehending criminals is widely considered to be the most important function of the police, our subjects were requested to rate the success of the police in catching criminals. Forty-eight percent of the panel saw the police as very successful, 14 percent made the opposite judgment, and the remainder gave answers qualified according to various crimes. In general, the rate of solving murders was deemed much better than solution for other crimes.[17] Again, the bulk of reasons given for negative assessments were difficulty of catching criminals and insufficient manpower, rather than police deficiencies. In line with the notion that apprehending criminals is a difficult task, the standards which were used to make favorable ratings were relatively low. People who judged the apprehension success rate as good estimated it as ranging from less than 10 percent to a top level of 75 percent. Eighty percent of the group which considered apprehension rates as "good" had estimated them to be below 50 percent.

In view of the widely publicized images of police-hating publics in the late 1960s and early 1970s, the favorable ratings may seem surprising. However, they actually present a continuation of the approval rates registered in polls conducted in the late 1960s.[18] Since the publicized complaints had depicted public perceptions of the police as "pigs" who violated citizens' civil rights, we asked a direct question to test the status of that reputation. Only 29 percent of the panel members felt that the complaints of civil rights violations were justified and based on incidents of physical brutality, failure to inform accused persons of their rights, illegal searches, and insensitivity to the needs of crime victims. But the vast majority of our subjects did not voice the charges of yesteryear.

If these figures represent a change in appraisal by some panel members, it may spring from the view that police performance has improved. Thirty-one percent of the sample indicated that they believed that the police were doing a better job than they had done five years previously. Better training and better technology were given as reasons for the changes. However, 62 percent of the group thought that performance was about the same and the remaining 7 percent rated it as worse or could give no judgment. Lack of improvement or deterioration was blamed on increased difficulty of the job because of surging crime rates, rather than on personal or organizational deficiencies of the police.

While the police had received fairly favorable ratings, the correctional system did not. Sixty-five percent of the respondents rated its performance as "poor," 15 percent rated it as "good," and the remaining 20 percent gave it a "fair" rating. The reasons for the generally poor ratings were expressed in terms of three criteria: expected results, staff, and facilities. Over half of the sample expressed disappointment with the failure to rehabilitate criminals, as shown by high rates of recidivism. Twenty-five percent of the respondents also deemed prison staffs and mangement poor, 14 percent mentioned poor facilities, and 14 percent mentioned mixed-up purposes of the institution. As one respondent expressed it,

> If they are going to rehabilitate criminals, it's doing a lousy job. If it's merely a place to store them, to keep them off the street, they are doing a better than average job, as long as they keep them. If the purpose of the correctional system is to punish, revenge, they don't do as well as they used to because it's becoming more plush and convenient. The punishment isn't what it used to be. I think the correctional system is all mixed up as to its purposes.

Half of our respondents felt that the performance of the correctional system had remained unchanged during the past five years, 30 percent thought that it was worse, and 20 percent thought that it was better. Overcrowding, rather than personnel or organizational deficiencies, was given most frequently as the reason for failure to improve over the past five years. Overcrowding was also linked to complaints about unduly brief prison sentences, dismissals of cases without penalties, and leniency in granting paroles. In the words of one respondent,

> The jails are full to the brim. They can't let any more criminals in, and they've got to let some out. That's why really bad criminals are thrown back out on the street; psychotics, murderers, rapists, they all get out.

The court system received poor marks as well, though not quite as poor as the correctional system. Forty-two percent of our respondents evaluated it as "poor," 11 percent called it "good," and the remaining 47 percent gave it "fair" ratings. Table 15-7 provides comparative figures for the courts, the police, and the correctional system., as well as for crime-fighting efforts at various govern-

Table 15-7
Comparative Performance Ratings for Crime-Fighting Activities
(in percentages; N = 168 answers)

	Good	Fair	Poor
Police	57%	43%	0%
Courts	11	47	42
Correctional system	15	20	65
Federal government	29	5	66
State government[a]	24	10	66
City government[a]	29	19	52
Suburban government[a]	43	24	33
General public	10	5	85

[a]Figures are for Illinois state government, Chicago city government, and suburban government in Evanston, Illinois.

mental levels and by the general public. In each instance, individuals were only moderately consistent in casting mostly negative or mostly positive votes.

Poor ratings for the courts were based on the quantity and quality of the judges, on legal procedures, and on the inadequacy of penalties. Forty-eight percent of the complaints mentioned the corruptibility and laziness and insufficient number of judges, excessive judicial leniency, and abusive treatment of accused persons. Legal procedures, such as long delays or judgments based on technicalities, were scored by 15 percent and 37 percent of the panel members complained about inadequate sentencing and an overly lenient parole system. As one respondent put it somewhat extremely, "Society gets no protection at all from the courts. All the marbles are on the criminals' side." Another complained:

> There's something wrong with the sentencing. I don't go along with all the legal technicalities, guys getting off because of a legal technicality. They've still committed the crime. If they do apprehend a guy for mugging or raping or something like that, it's a two-time loser that's been in and out of jail on bail a couple of times. To me, I always want to say, "What's that guy doing out of jail?"

Comparing court performance in 1976 with that of the early 1970s, the sense of deterioration was great. Fifty-nine percent of the panel members felt that courts were performing worse than five years earlier; eighteen percent judged performance as better; the remaining 23 percent considered it stable. Overloading of the court system was perceived as the chief reason for failure to improve and for deterioration. As with the police and the correctional system, the major share of the blame was placed on circumstances beyond the control of the institution, rather than on personnel or organizational deficiencies. The idea that criminal justice institutions should be organized to cope with current workload levels is almost totally absent from the judgments recorded in our interviews.

Since panel members had frequently mentioned overly light penalties as one of the reasons for poor performance by the criminal justice system, we asked their views on the appropriateness of sentences, as well as standards by which judges might determine appropriateness. Sixty-five of our respondents deemed all sentences generally too light; 20 percent thought that some but not all, were too light; and 5 percent thought that sentences were too severe. Panel members had difficulty in articulating standards by which sentences might be applied or judged. Criteria for sentencing which were mentioned frequently were (1) the percentage of cases in which sentences were below the legal maximum for a given crime; (2) the percentage of cases in which sentences for repeaters were substantially harsher than sentences for first offenders; (3) comparisons of the severity of current sentences with sentences for similar offenses in the past. The idea was also expressed that (4) crimes with serious social consequences should receive far heavier penalties than crimes with lesser consequences; and (5) that the death penalty should be used more often for the most vicious crimes.

Answers to general questions about causes and remedies for crime corroborated the perceptual trends which we have outlined. Judicial leniency was mentioned prominently as a reason for spiraling crime rates, with the implication that stiffer sentences and greater certainty of punishment would reduce recidivism and discourage first offenders. Overall, 12 percent of all causes of crime ($N = 255$) were linked to failures of the criminal justice system.

Since the criminal justice system operates at various levels of government, we asked our respondents' perceptions of the adequacy of performance at each of these levels and possible corrective measures. Levels included were the federal, state, urban, and suburban. Except for the suburban level, "poor" performance levels were registered by over half of the answers (see table 15-7). Many of the answers explaining these ratings and indicating ways to improve performance provided additional confirmation that the criminal justice system is perceived as weak and that several areas are in particular need of reform. Table 15-8 presents a list.

Table 15-8
Frequency of Mention of Reforms to Improve Crime Fighting at Various Governmental Levels
(in percentages; N = 110 answers)

Harsher, more certain penalties, including death	33.6%
Correction of economic and educational deficiencies	20.9
Reform of the court system	19.0
Reform of police law enforcement	9.0
Decriminalization of drug use	5.4
Reform of prison system/rehabilitation efforts	4.5
Tighter gun control laws	4.5
Reduction in media emphasis on crime	2.7

The table shows that, along with the stress on the deficiencies of the criminal justice system, many respondents believe that economic and social causes produce crime and require reforms. This emphasis on the need to correct the social and economic causes of crime was strongest of all in response to a question regarding steps that citizens could take to aid the fight against crime. Eighty-six percent of the recommendations suggested that citizens should work for programs designed to reduce economic and educational deficiencies among the crime-prone population. Fourteen of the recommendations called for better crime reporting by citizens and for more participation in stopping illegal activities. One percent called for better home security measures. Overall, 85 percent of the panel members believed that citizens were lax in aiding the fight against crime.

Summary and Conclusions

What general observations and conclusions can we draw from our study? In the first place, it is worthy of note that the mass media, which are the public's major source of information, supply a large amount of data about specific crimes, but provide comparatively little analytical or evaluative information to help citizens put this information into a realistic perspective. Specific evaluations of the police, the courts, and the correctional system are particularly sparse. Nonetheless, the public manages to use the factual criteria supplied about individual crimes to develop its own generalizations.

The public's evaluations of the criminal justice system are largely negative. Eighty-one percent of our respondents see crime as rising, particularly in suburban areas, and deem the criminal justice system as incapable of coping adequately with these increased responsibilities. However, a major part of the blame for crime-fighting deficiencies is put on general socioeconomic conditions—such as population shifts, heavy unemployment, or alcoholism and drug abuse—beyond the control of the criminal justice system.

Although the criminal justice system does not receive a heavy burden of blame for the ongoing state of affairs, trust in the system appears to be eroding. When asked to compare levels of trust in various public institutions at the present time with levels remembered from five years ago, 43 percent of our subjects voiced less trust in the police, and 62 percent trusted the courts less. Since 57 percent also trusted politicians less, and 62 percent trusted Congress less, erosion of trust in the criminal justice system obviously is not unique, but that does not lessen the seriousness of this state of affairs in a democratic society.

Since evaluations are apparently based on the factual conditions reported in the media, and not on media evaluations, which tend to be ignored, any changes in public perceptions hinge on charges in factual reporting.[19] Evaluations of the criminal justice system might improve, for example, if there were fewer crime stories, reducing the impression that crime is rampant. The image of the system could also be improved by reporting higher rates of apprehension and conviction of criminals and by providing evidence that penalties are swift, certain, and substantial and that the number of repeaters have been sharply reduced. In part, changes in media policies could produce more favorable coverage of the criminal justice system by putting crime incidents and facts about the criminal justice system into a more realistic, less sensational perspective. But the major burden for improved evaluations of the criminal justice system will fall on the system itself. Major changes in institutional practices are required to alter the facts on which mass media reporting is based. These institutional changes will be infinitely more difficult to achieve than mass media reforms. Hence, for the foreseeable future, the public's esteem for the criminal justice system is likely to remain at a low ebb.

Notes

1. See *Gallup Opinion Index,* annual volumes, 1967-1976. Similar data can be found in the annual volumes of *The Harris Survey Yearbook of Public Opinion* and in the National Opinion Research Center's annual *Codebook for the Spring (Year) General Social Survey.*

2. The most complete review of public opinion data on crime is contained in four reports by Hazel Erskine in the spring, summer, fall, and winter issues of the *Public Opinion Quarterly* 38 (1974). The reports are entitled "Fear of Violence and Crime," pp. 131-145; "Causes of Crime," pp. 288-298; "Control of Crime and Violence," pp. 409-502; and "Politics and Law and Order," pp. 623-634. For polling data after 1973, see the sources cited in note 1. For suggestions on the limitations of polls, see Terry Baumer and Fred DuBow, "Fear of Crime. in *Polls:What They do and Do Not Tell Us,* American Association for Public Opinion Research paper, 1977. Also see Michael J. Hindelang, "Public Opinion Regarding crime, Criminal Justice , and Related Topics," *Journal of Research in Crime and Delinquency* 11 (July 1974): 101-116.

3. The reports of the Kerner and Eisenhower commissions and voluminous reports by the Surgeon General's office are examples.

4. Douglas Scott, "Measures of Citizen Evaluation of Local Government Services," in Terry Nichols Clark, ed., *Citizen Preferences and Urban Public Policy*, pp. 111-128. Also see Clark's introduction to the volume, pp. 5-11. And Daniel Katz and associates *Bureaucratic Encounters: A Pilot Study in the Evaluation of Government Services,* Ann Arbor, Michigan: SRC-ISR, 1975, pp. 1-3, 120-132.

5. The newspapers are the *Chicago Tribune,* the *Indianapolis News,* the *Indianapolis Star,* the *Lebanon Valley News,* and the *Evanston Review.* The television network newscasts come from ABC, CBS, and NBC. The local newscasts are from CBS and NBC. Collaborators for the content analyses as well as

the interview data were Professor Maxwell McCombs of Syracuse University and Professor David Weaver of Indiana University and their associates. Each investigator and associates were responsible for data collection in their geographical location.

6. More detailed data on sample selection, statistical correlations, reliability data, and so on are available on request from the author. For evidence that personal and social characteristics have little effect on crime perception see John E. Conklin, *The Impact of Crime* (New York: Macmillan, 1975), pp. 79-81. For some conflicting data see Glen Broach, "Dissonance Theory and Receptivity to Structural Perceptions of the Causes of Urban Crime." *Western Political Quarterly* 27 (September 1974): 491-499.

7. The argument that generalizable findings about human behavior can be made on the basis of intensive study of small numbers of individuals has been made persuasively by many scholars. Examples are Steven R. Brown, "Intensive Analysis in Political Research," *Political Methodology* 1 (1974): 1-25; Robert E. Lane, *Political Theory: Why the American Common Man Believes What He Does* (New York: The Free Press, 1962), pp. 1-11; and Karl A. Lamb, *As Orange Goes: Twelve California Families ane the Future of American Politics* (New York: Norton, 1975), pp. vii-xiii, 3-23.

8. The local broadcasts were coded directly from the actual broadcast event. The network newscasts were analyzed from written abstracts prepared by the staff of the Vanderbilt Television News Archives. Comparison of control-codings taken from the actual broadcast with abstract-codings showed no signicant differences for the type of coding relevant to this chapter. The reliability of coding for the content analyses was carefully checked and controlled. Since many different coders were involved in this project, it is difficult to report a single reliability figure. Our procedure was to have the same coding supervisor check each coder's work following the initial training period, and at various intervals thereafter. excluding simple identification categories like paper or station name and date, which would inflate reliability figures, intercoder reliability averaged 85 percent and intracoder reliability averaged 90 percent.

9. Comparable NBC network news figures are 10 percent of total stories and 12.8 percent of all topics relating to crime. CBS and ABC figures for local and network news, respectively, are quite similar.

10. See, for example, *Crime and Its Impact: An Assessment*. The President's Commission on Law Enforcement and Administration of Justice *Washington, D.C.: GPO, 1967), pp. 85-109, and sources cited there. Also David G. Clark and William B. Blankenburg, "Trends in Violent Content in Selected Mass Media," in George A. Comstock and Ali A. Rubinstein, eds., *Television and Social Behavior: Media Content and Control,* Vol. 1 (Washington, D.C.: U.S. Department of Health, Education and Welfare, 1972) pp. 188-243; and Jack B. Haskins, "The Effects of Violence in the Printed Media," in David Lange, Robert Baker, Sandra Ball, eds., *Mass Media and Violence* (Washington, D.C.: GPO, 1969), pp. 493-502. For a brief, lucid discussion of the effects of fear of crime, see Wesley G. Skogan, ed.,

"Public Policy and the Fear of Crime in Large American Cities," in John A. Gardiner, ed., *Law and Public Policy* (New York: Praeger, 1977), pp. 1-17.

11. For television, differences between crime and noncrime stories were significant (.01) only for the use of film. For the *Tribune,* the two types of stories differed significantly (.01) in section placement, headline size, and use of pictures. There were no significant differences in page placement and story length. However, there were substantial differences (.01) when media groups were compared to each other. Chi square statistics were used. For comparative data which show that crime subjects receive average display, see E. Terrence Jones, "The Press as Metropolitan Monitor," *Public Opinion Quarterly* 40 (1976): 239-255; Shari Cohen, "A Comparison of Crime Coverage in Detroit and Atlanta Newspapers, " *Journalism Quarterly* 52 (1975): 726-730; and John C. Meyer, Jr., "Newspaper Reporting of Crime and Justice: Analysis of an Assumed Difference." *Journalism Quarterly* 52 (1975) 731-734.

12. The intensive crime story analysis is based on 2,769 stories.

13. Exceptions were recall rates for political corruption and police stories, and recall rates for stories about energy, accidents, political gossip, and city government. We measured the recall rate for each panel member by scoring recall of 50 percent or more of the stories in a given category as "high" and recall of less than 50 pecent of the stories as "low." The overall recall rate of a given topic was judged by subtracting the low scores from the high scores.

14. The similarity should not be overemphasized. We computed the significance of relationships among diary and press and television coverage of particular topics, using chi square. Out of forty-eight relationships, twenty-six were significant at the .01 level, ten at the .05 level; but 12 were not significant.

15. The data are discussed fully in "The Impact of Crime News on the Public: A Case Study of Newspaper and Television Crime Coverage and Its Effects on Perceptions and Actions of Mass Media Audiences," a report prepared for the Center for Research in Criminal Justice, University of Illinois at Chicago Circle, 1978.

16. See the polls reported in the sources cited in note 2. For comparison, consult other reports in the *Polls* section of the *Public Opinion Quarterly.*

17. These perceptions accord with the facts reported by the FBI. For 1976, the following arrest rates were reported: murder: 79 percent; aggravated assault: 63 percent; forcible rape: 52 percent; robbery: 27 percent; burglary: 17 percent; larceny-theft: 19 percent; and motor vehicle theft: 14 percent.

18. See *Crime and Its Impact: An Assessment.*

19. For data indicating what mass media information is the basis for public reactions to crime problems, see James Garofalo, "Victimization and Fear of Crime in Major American Cities," American Association for Public Opinion Research paper, 1977; also see "Public Attitudes towards Crime and Law Enforcement," in *Crime and Its Impact: An Assessment,* pp. 85-95, especially pp. 86-87; Conklin, *The Impact of Crime,* p. 22 ff; and F. James Davis, "Crime News in Colorado Newspapers," *American Journal of Sociology* 57 (January 1962): 325-330.

16 Evaluating TV Impressions of Law-Enforcement Roles

John H. Culver and
Kenton L. Knight

As entertainment, TV police shows have done quite well. Replacing westerns as a dominant genre in the 1960s, the contemporary police shows focus on stories which have a "real world" orientation to hold viewer interest with their plots, characters, and situations. Television, of course, not only entertains but is also an educating medium. In this capacity, the TV portrayal of the police is woefully inaccurate and misleading, and as a result the gap between the public's perception of the policing and what the police can actually do is widened. Moreover, the "supercop" shows have fostered another problem: the police perceptions that he must be like a Kojak or Baretta in order to (1) be appreciated by the public, (2) advance within the department, and (3) be a successful cop in his own mind.

Most people avoid contact with the police. The days of the flat foot pounding the neighborhood beat are gone. As police have become motorized, citizen encounters with cops are relegated to calls for assistance and receiving unwelcomed traffic citations. The circumstances for idle conversation are no longer there. At the same time, however, the proliferation of police shows indicates an audience which is captivated by the TV image of what police presumably do. This audience is not confined to any one age group but attracts viewers from all levels. It is the thesis of this chapter that citizens are given false expectations of law enforcement. When the police do not perform to the satisfaction of the public, the police and the public become increasingly alienated. This research focuses on two areas of police imagery: (1) what we know about TV police shows in terms of the images they project, and (2) the distortion of TV police in terms of actual law-enforcement procedures.

Our criticisms in this chapter are not directed at law-enforcement agencies, but at the policing image fed to the public in the television police shows. As Charles Silberman recently noted, the police are the most familiar government agency known to the public aside from public schools, although the public still knows little about law enforcement.[1] While the preinted media have contributed to the glorification of the crime-fighting aspects of policing, today television has popularized policing for the nonreading audience. Starsky and Hutch need only fifty minutes to apprehend several criminals. At least Agatha Christie's Hercule Poirot required several months.

Law enforcement is a hazardous occupation. The failure of the juvenile justice system, the accessibility of drugs and guns, and the mobility of the general population are a few of the factors which have increased the complexity of policing in recent years. One response we see to this in the real world is the number of police officers who are adversely affected by their profession in their personal lives. The police have a higher suicide rate than the general population. Alcoholism, divorce, and cynicism take their toll on cops as well. Starsky and Hutch will never fall victim to the bottle as do Wambaugh's officers in *The New Centurions* or on "Police Story," nor would Baretta take his life because of his personal failure to survive on the job. The supercop image of the police is as misconceived as their effectiveness on TV.

The Impact of Television

There is no shortage of disagreement over the value of television. A good deal of attention has been directed to its effects on children, specifically the influence of commercials geared for the five- to ten-year-old audience, and the possible causal relationship between TV violence and children's acceptance of violence as a normal problem-solving method. In the much publicized trial of fifteen-year-old Ronald Zamora, an overdose of TV violence was rejected as a defense for Zamora's murder of an elderly Florida widow. In a case with far-reaching implications, a civil action was filed in San Francisco Superior Court in 1978 to determine whether or not a local TV station could be held negligent in the rape of a minor girl. The teenager was assaulted several days after the screening of "Born Innocent," in which the key character was attacked in the same manner. The case was dismissed. There are enough examples of kids and adults who are motivated by TV shows to engage in illegal behavior to substantiate the negative influence of TV on the behavior of susceptible viewers. Over twenty years ago, a psychiatrist writing on the influence of television noted that it was frequently used as a nonchemical sedative in many hospitals and institutions.[2] This tranquilizing role becomes more important when it is combined with the effects of TV as a socializing agent.

For better or worse, TV is the most popular form of mass communication today. According to former Federal Communications Director Nicholas Johnson, the average male viewer watches TV for a total of 3,000 entire days, or about nine years of his life.[3] Another observer has noted that there are almost twice as many TV sets in American homes as the combined daily circulation of all American newspapers. With 97 percent of U.S. homes having one or more sets, the distribution is about the same as indoor plumbing for homes.[4] Historian Daniel Boorstein rates TV second only to the automobile in terms of its impact on American life.[5]

TV Police

Television gives the consumer conflicting views of the police. Although some are pictured as supersleuths, others come across as little more than bumbling idiots. More importantly, however, in the more sophisticated shows the viewer is invited into the inner world of policing from which we are generally excluded in real life. Thus within the confines of one's own home we become privy to be complexities and frustrations of police duty. We glimpse personality clashes, problems in race relations, the burdensome task of selling professionalization to a reluctant public, crime prevention, criminal apprehension, and a host of other situations. In addition, the message is always subtly conveyed that if you violate society's values you will be punished. Thus the police are portrayed as guardians and enforcers of the accepted values and norms. Or the viewer may be given a conflicting value situation where the police deliberately violate due process guarantees to apprehend a criminal rather than risk the chance of losing the guilty through some legal technicality.

Jack Webb's "Dragnet" was the most popular police show of the 1950s. Officer Friday's standard line, "Just give us the facts, ma'am," illustrated early on the desired view of police efficiency. Portrayed as a stabilizing force in a society running headlong into chaos, "Dragnet" was ladened with heavy moral overtones and the obvious reminder that the police were performing the thankless task of keeping our moral compass intact. "Dragnet," no longer in production but still popular on local stations, remains as a period piece of the 1950s, when there was no gray area between the choices of black and white. Webb's imagery of policing in Los Angeles has since been transferred to his popular "Adam-12," a "Dragnet" approach with contemporary, humanistic overtones.

Although the wooden policemen of "Dragnet" were replaced by a more con-genial team on "Adam-12," the portrayal of cops in both shows is the same—efficient, dedicated, and, above all, professional. This point of view is deliberate. Jack Webb is an advocate of the Los Angeles Police Department and the department has had an active role in the Webb shows by having officer-consultants oversee the scripts. A new Webb production (shortlived, as it turned out) centered on a police dog was reviewed by two sergeants. A department memo on the show stated, "Except for some deviations in the concept from true-life situations the scripts are technically correct and, more importantly, do not portray the department in any way except favorably." Regarding the role of the police supervisors, the memo continued, "They understand that their role is to protect the department's interests and to oversee the production to the extent that police officers are portrayed properly and consistently with departmental policy."[6]

In one comparative study of TV police shows and the reaction of the police themselves, Professor Alan Arcuri found that "Adam-12" received high marks from his New Jersey police sample because the show portrayed policemen as professionals.[7] Important to the police was the fact that the "Adam-12" team did not go by the book, as was the routine on "Dragnet," but their conduct was professional nonetheless.

A contrasting point of view to the Jack Webb image of the Los Angeles police is presented by Joseph Wambaugh. A former detective with the LAPD and author of several best-selling novels on police, Wambaugh objects to the false imagery he perceives in the Webb-type cop programs. Following the success of his novels *The New Centurions* and *The Blue Knight,* Wambaugh oversaw production of "Police Story," a series of vignettes about policemen and the consequences of policing on individual officers. Wambaugh's focus was on how being a policeman affects the personal lives of individuals, and how that, in turn, affects an officer's performance on the job. If Wambaugh deemphasized professionalism by Webb standards, he did so to provide viewers an insight into cops as mortals faced with a job they could never resolve to the public's satisfaction. The officers on "Police Story" had marital and extramarital problems, abused alcohol, and questioned their efficacy. Although the series received critical acclaim, Wambaugh severed his relations with the program when he was instructed to promote action and lessen the interpersonal aspects of policing. Wambaugh acknowledges the value of the Jack Webb police image but feels that that image needs to be reworked: "Propaganda was needed back then because everyone thought of cops as low-life. But now it's time to show policemen as real people, and that's what I have tried to do. . . . The L.A.P.D. is the best, but it isn't perfect. And that's what I write about."[8]

If one accepts Webb and Wambaugh as repesenting opposite ends of the TV police spectrum, then there is a plethora of shows which fall in between. The main ingredient in police dramas is action—the apprehension of criminals through violence. Little attention is devoted to crime prevention or the public service aspects which used to be associated with law enforcement. In terms of approaches to policing, most shows conform to what James Q. Wilson has described as the "Service" style. Table 16-1 illustrates contemporary police shows according to his three policing typologies.[9]

As is apparent, the trend is away from the single hard-nosed approach characterized by the "Watchman" style. The "Legalistic" style is one of strict enforcement of the laws. The Watchman does this as well, but the Watchman also emphasizes the maintenance of order. The Service approach is responsive to citizen calls but there is more discretion in the enforcement of the laws. A young troublemaker might be punched around a bit by a Kojak, arrested on "Hawaii 5-0," or given a fatherly warning and referred to a job training program by a Baretta. Wilsons's typologies are constructed for real police departments and their application for TV police is limited. A more instructive method for capturing the imagery the shows convey to the public is to analyze them according to the following variables which are treated in the scholarly literature on law enforcement: social-

Table 16-1
Police Shows Categorized by Wilson's Typologies and by Approaches to Policing

	Watchman: Emphasis on Maintaining Order	Legalistic: Emphasis on Strict Enforcement of the Laws	Service: Emphasis on Enforcement of Order but with Wide Discretion
Individual	Kojak Bert D'Angelo The Blue Knight	Joe Forrester Columbo	Baretta Toma Bronk
Group		Dragnet S.W.A.T. Hawaii 5-0	Policewoman The Rookies C.H.i.P.s Adam-12 Starsky and Hutch Ironside Streets of San Francisco Police Story Barney Miller

ization, role and function, accountability, politics, and minorities and law enforcement.

Socialization

Arthur Niederhoffer has aptly chronicled the socialization process for police from (1) the recruitment process through (2) academy training, (3) a probationary period on the force, and finally (4) acceptance as a regular cop.[10] In brief, the process turns the idealistic recruit into a cynical, suspicious officer. Because of the priority of action on TV shows, this important aspect of policing is treated rarely, although Wambaugh's "Police Story" did focus on this topic. The cynicism of TV cops is directed at situations rather than at the public. "The Streets of San Francisco" used the older, streetwise cop paired with a young cop with a sociology degree as a vehicle for blending the old style with the new, but the characters were used more as foils for each other than as examples of contrasting schools of thought.

Role and Function

The role and function of TV police are combined by a unifying theme—fighting crime. Police activity in this country began with the nightwatch system, where citizens assumed responsibility for the safety of the community—checking for unlocked doors in commercial areas and sounding the alarm for fires, for example. As we became more urbanized, the police departments became more established in the eastern cities and the focus on public safety shifted to crime-related activities. The TV police do tend to noncriminal matters, but they are generally shown as a wasteful use of police talent. In reality, however, police departments are deluged with service calls for assistance of a noncriminal nature.[11] Community relations issues may be the topic on some program segments, but they take a back seat to the crime-related concerns.[12]

Accountability

This aspect of police work is handled in two ways on TV: (1) not at all and (2) by way of the bad-apple approach. The debate over the merits of internal versus external review boards is scarcely mentioned. In terms of socializing the public on police misconduct, the TV cops are more efficient at cleaning their own houses than police in reality. This image runs counter to the Knapp Commission findings and those of various fact-finding boards since the Wickersham Commission in the 1930s. When a corrupt cop appears on TV, he is found out by his fellow officers, who are successful in drumming him out of the department. Although Westley and others find police violations of the law commonplace,[13] on TV blame is laid to personal defects rather than being placed on the institutionalization of corruption. Indeed, the viewer who watches the TV cops hold their own accountable can only be impressed with their high degree of professionalism. Any rationale for citizen review boards will not find its way onto TV police shows.

Politics

TV police do not suffer the political interferences that plague most departments. Politics is most visible in two forms in real-world departments—the internal politics and community politics as they affect the delivery of police services. TV police uniformly apolitical, although a cynical grudge against "the system" in general is commonplace. One result of the police versus the system dichotomy is reinforcement of the common view that only the police know how to deal with the criminal elements. A number of pertinent issues concerning cops and politics are left untreated, including the politicization of departments, the consequences of police unions, and the police acting in a political capacity in the selective enforcement of the laws.

Minorities and Law Enforcement

This is a sensitive area. Most police shows focus on "street crimes" for which minorities are more often apprehended and convicted rather than on the white-collar crimes usually committed by Anglos. In terms of displaying an integrated police force, TV shows sparkle.[14] On five shows— "Ironside," "The Rookies," "Carter Country," "Barney Miller," and "Chips"—non-Anglos play major roles, although we have yet to witness a non-Anglos cast as the central figure or in a supervisor capacity. While "Policewoman" centered on a female lead, her success could be attributed to charm and feminine intuition rather than to general competence. Rarely are women portrayed as equals with their male officers. The impact of minorities on TV police shows is more cosmetic than substantive.[15] Blacks and Hispanics are differentiated from their white counterparts only by appearance. Similarily, women TV cops are most acceptable when they adopt the agressive attitude of the male cops.

Some of the more glaring inaccuracies fed to the public on the police dramas include:

An Overemphasis on Violence and Action in Solving Crimes: TV viewers want action on their shows. On police shows, this generally translates into violent action. In a report issued by the National Citizens Committee for Broadcasting, the ten most violent shows included six police programs. Only one, "Barney Miller," was listed among the ten least violent.[16] Most arrests made by the police do not involve force or violence, although certainly many in the viewing audience would be disappointed by the methodical manner in which investigations are usually carried out. We have a real appetite for violence which most people satisfy through spectator activities—watching boxing, auto racing, and contact sports in addition to police shows on TV. The behavior of motorists who slow down at the scene of a traffic accident illustrates a curiosity about violence which is difficult to explain. Most travelers fear auto accidents, yet we view the carnage with deliberation.

Overemphasis on Technological Sophistication in Solving Crimes: Technological advances have enabled law-enforcement agencies to perform their roles with much more sophistication than in past decades. However, many of these advances are too expensive to perform for a "high-grade" misdeameanor or a "low-grade" felony. One of the most accepted investigative techniques used on police shows involves the ritual fingerprinting at the crime scene. Many viewers believe that if fingerprints are obtained, the perpetrator of the crime is as good as apprehended. In reality, fingerprints are only of value in placing a suspect at the crime scene or in possession of an object. It is difficult for a police officer to explain to an irate citizen why his stolen car which was recovered abandoned is not going to be "dusted" for prints since TV officers do it as a matter of routine. Even the use of radar to apprehend speeding motorists may be beyond the budgets of local law-enforcement agencies. Or, as in California, political pressure on the legislature by the teamsters has successfully prevented the Highway Patrol from having funds authorized for the purchase of radar equipment.

The Inconsequential Role Played by Citizens in Helping the Police: Most crimes have a definite, identifiable victim. In these cases, the police act as fact-gatherers at the scene of the initial investigation. The success or failure of the investigation may well depend upon the facts recorded by the investigating officer. Most crimes are not observed directly by the police. Television portrays the police as efficient enough to solve crimes and apprehend criminals without much aid from citizens. In reality, the citizen is the primary source of information to the police.

Success of the Police in Apprehending Criminals: Television police capture criminals quickly and efficiently. In some circumstances, of course, real police are able to match the expediency of their fictional counterparts; however, in others, such as the Jimma Hoffa disappearance or the Hillside Strangler in Los Angeles, the police can do little more than follow up leads reported by the public or informers. The dogged determination shown by Kojak or Columbo in tracking down culprits can hardly be matched by detectives in the real world—there are too many cases, not enough information, and a lack of personnel to spend much time on a particular incident. Police efficiency is undermined most often on the private detective shows where cops have to be given everything but the smoking pistol before a case is closed.[17]

Overestimation of Violent Street Crime Which Serves as a Justification for the Police to Resort to Violence: Police use of violence on TV may be another way in which the public is socialized to tolerate police violence in reality. On television, it is difficult to sympathize with most of the dregs of society whose only livelihood is crime. And, since most crimes on television involve violent action on the part of the perpetrators, it is not surprising that they may be roughed up a bit when apprehended. Police brutality does exist, of course, but on television, it is not brutality but a justification for violence. The emphasis on violent crimes has increased viewer anxiety about lawlessness. People who watch the crime-oriented dramas tend to overestimate the amount of violence in society.[18] Law students who monitored the crimes shown on the three major networks during a one-week period in 1977 concluded that the net prison sentences would amount to 3,633 years.[19] Given this situation, the viewer can only applaud some of the police violence in the wake of increasing criminal activity.

Overemphasis on "gimmickry" to Make the Improbable Seem Routine: In recent years, TV cops have employed a number of gimmicks to attract a greater viewing audience. "Ironside" gave us a San Francisco police chief who operated from a wheelchair with the help of a sexually and racially integrated crew to perform the actual legwork. Also in the same city, "Macmillan and Wife" presented Mac-Millan as the police commissioner who must have had few administrative duties since most of his time was spent in the streets with his wife, apprehending felons.

"Starsky and Hutch" rubber-top most of the streets of Los Angeles in their undercover car, which appears ready for the final elimination runs of the local hotrod club. On "Baretta" we saw a master of disguises who lived in a seedy apartment square in the bowels of an East Coast slum. His roommate, a large white cockatoo, often perched on Baretta's shoulder while the latter mingled with the low-lifes. What was most surprising about Baretta was not his disdain for ordinary police work, but that his supervisors had not committed him to Bellview. Actor Peter Falk made "Columbo" as well known as Joe Friday. Columbo's trademarks were his raincoat and car, both of which would be refused by any reputable charitable organization. Little needs to be said about the likes of "McCloud," the New Mexican cop from Taos who rode the streets of Manhattan on his horse. The list of improbables could go on, but the point to be made is that, aside from the gimmicks these officers use, they are successful in their jobs. They evidence that standard police techniques are not productive. Our argument is that law-enforcement officials are often hamstrung in their jobs, though not for the reasons these shows suggest.

Contempt for Constitutional Rights: As Arcuri's police sample reported, policemen visualize themselves as being unable to respond with the same efficiency as cops on TV do. One result of the TV police crime-fighting success may well be an increased public acceptance of the police officer's circumventing constitutional due process guarantees to apprehend criminals. On TV the police increasingly ignore the Bill of Rights with impunity.[20] In one report, two observers found forty-three instances of flagrant disregard for the public's constitutional rights during one week of police dramas on television. These included twenty-one instances of clear constitutional violations, seven ommissions of constitutional rights, and fifteen instances of policy brutality or harassment. Yet, as viewers are comforted to know that law-abiding citizens have little to worry about, for the police only violate the rights of lawbreakers. As Arons and Katsh concluded, the overall effect of such illegal police actions may have a "softening up" effect whereby viewers are dulled to the gravity of the violations.[21] In reality, police do violate constitutional rights of citizens while some of this may be prevented, most violations are not deliberate. If a cop is so inclined to administer his own back-alley justice, he will probably come to the attention of someone in a position of power to discipline him, at least in the more professional departments. Police officers are expendable; there is little reward for a supervisor in keeping a bad cop on the force. The lack of respect for constitutional rights by TV police bothers some officers who object to the negative image given policemen by such behavior as well as the impression such violations are routine.[22]

The TV police reassure viewers that the weakness in the criminal justice system is not in law enforcement but in the judicial arena. In reality, there are sufficient deficiencies throughout the system to cover virtually all actors and institutions. On TV the police may be harried in their professional role, but they persevere nonetheless. The cops are cognizant of social and economic disparities, but law enforcement is a reaction to social problems, not part of them. As one retired San Francisco officer addressed the situation of cops today, "They are very uptight. They don't enjoy their work anymore. It's an ungrateful job. They don't live in their community anymore. They come in for eight hours, kick everybody's ass and then go home to their cul de sac."[23]

What's Missing?

The three major aspects of the criminal justice system have been the subject of TV shows for many years. Lawyer shows ("Perry Mason," "Judd for the Defense," and "Petrocelli," for instance) have all been popular. These shows strengthen the notion of the adversary system and reassure viewers that the innocent and the guilty are properly discovered. Television's treatment of the burdensome role performed by judges has centered almost exclusively on situation comedies in which judges are little more than courtroom jesters toying with the legal problems faced by hapless citizens.

Police shows clearly dominate in television's treatment of the criminal justice system. The police are depicted as the most important part of this process, with lawyers and judges playing almost incidental roles. There are few connections in the world of television among the police, lawyers, and judges. The police are typically shown doing their jobs efficiently and effectively, while judges and defense attorneys receive the blame when criminals do not get punished, or do not get punished enough. Whether or not the police do an excellent job of apprehending criminals, the TV shows give a grossly oversimplified picture of the total criminal justice system. Approximately 90 percent of the criminal cases in the United States are resolved through plea-bargaining between representatives of the defense and prosecution. The district attorney's office has wide discretion as to who is prosecuted, and on what charges. Social conditions which produce crime are left largely to the documentaries. The world of the police show on TV is a world of black and white.

As children are conditioned by TV to violence as a problem-solving method, so too are adults fed this same diet on cop shows. The resort to violence is not only accepted but expected. All of this reduces law enforcement to little more than a war of sharpshooters.[24]

TV police are deceptively efficient. As consumers of police shows we demand this same productivity from our own cops; if the criminals are not apprehended immediately, then fingerprints, blood samples, and license plates provide the clues necessary for arrest. A frightening extension of public perceptions of police efficiency may well be in the expectation of cops to act as robots in crime solving. And we have been subjected to this in at least one show, where a human-appearing robot cop could be programmed for efficiency.

Conclusions

In spite of the misperceptions fostered by TV police shows, it may well be that we encourage their proliferation out of a need for reassurance that today's lawlessness can be controlled. By assuming the police are responsible for the prevention of crime and apprehension of criminals, citizen responsibility for conditions that encourage crime is lessened. A show which emphasizes the boredom of policing has little appeal. "Barney Miller" pokes fun at the bureaucracy of police work, but without the levity of the multi-ethnic cast there would be little attraction for viewers. And, obviously, law-enforcement pressure groups would resist any show which downplayed professionalism, focused on police inability to deal with crime, or analyzed the political cleavages which exist in most departments.

Not all of the inaccuracies of TV police shows lead to negative consequences. The obstacles which face TV cops—public apathy and lack of resources, among other things—may have the effect of promoting more respect for law-enforcement officers. In turn, citizen acceptance of law officers as professionals can result in higher pay, more selective recruitment standards, and the recognition that the police are much more limited in their official capacity than we realize.

Notes

1. Charles E. Silberman, *Criminal Violence, Criminal Justice* (New York: Random House, 1978), pp. 200, 202.

2. Eugene David Glynn, "Television and the American Character—A Psychiatrist Looks at Television," in *Mass Media and Mass Man*, edited by Alan Casty (New York: Holt, Rinehart and Winston, 1968), p. 79.

3. Nicholas Johnson, *How to Talk Back to Your Television Set* (Boston: Little, Brown, 1967), p. 13.

4. Douglas Cater, "Introduction: Television and Thinking People," in *Television as a Social Force*, edited by Richard Adler (New York: Prager, 1975), p.1.

5. Daniel Boorstein, *The Americans: The Democratic Experience* (New York: Random House, 1973), pp. 392-393.

6. *Los Angeles Times*, December 18, 1977, VIII:2.

7. Alan Arcuri, "You Can't Take Fingerprints Off Water: Police Officers' Views towards 'Cop' Television Shows," Stockton State College, New Jersey, 1975 (mimeograph).

8. *Los Angeles Times*, December 18, 1977, VIII:2.

9. James Q. Wilson, *Varieties of Police Behavior* (New York: Atheneum, 1970).

10. Arthur Niederhoffer, *Behind the Shield* (Garden City: Doubleday, 1967), chpt. 2.

11. Elaine Cumming, Ian Cumming, and Laure Edell, "Policeman as Philosopher, Guide and Friend," *Social Problems* 12 (1965): 276-286.

12. David Bordua and Larry L. Tifft, "Citizen Interviews, Organizational Feedback and Police-Community Relations Decisions," *Law and Society Review* 6 (November 1971): 180-181.

13. William Westley, "Violence and the Police," *American Journal of Sociology* 59 (July 1953): 31-41.

14. See Bernard Cohen, "Minority Retention in the New York City Police Department," *Criminology* 11 (November 1973): 287-306, for a case study of that department's attempt to increase minority representation.

15. Marleme W. Lehtinen, "Sexism in Police Departments," *Trial* 12 (September 1976): 52-55.

16. *Los Angeles Times*, July 31, 1976, II:11.

17. M.E. Granander, "The Heritage of Cain: Crime in American Fiction," *Annals of the American Academy of Political and Social Science* (January 1976): 57.

18. Kas Kalba, "The Electronic Community: A New Environment for TV Viewers and Critics," in *Television as a Social Force*, edited by Richard Adler (New York: Praeger, 1975) pp. 146-147.

19. *Los Angeles Times*, May 13, 1977, IV:30.

20. Stephen Arons and Ethan Katsh, "How TV Cops Flout the Law," *Saturday Review*, March 19, 1977, pp. 11-18.

21. Ibid.

22. *Los Angeles Times*, March 23, 1977, II:7.

23. *San Francisco Examiner*, December 26, 1974, p. 4.

24. See Richard W. Harding and Richard P. Fahey, "Killings by Chicago Police, 1969-70: An Empirical Study," *Southern California Law Review* 46 (1973): 284-315.

Index of Names

Index of Subjects

About the Contributors

Gerald Caiden received the Ph.D. from the London School of Economics and Political Science, and is currently a professor of public administration at the University of Southern California, having previously taught at universities in Australia and Israel. In 1976 he was a Visiting Fellow at the National Institute of Law Enforcement and Criminal Justice. The results of his work are published in *Police Revitalization* (Lexington Books, 1977).

John H. Culver received the Ph.D. from the University of New Mexico (1975) and is an associate professor of political science at California Polytechnic State University. He has published articles in the area of police and judicial accountability. He is coauthor of *Power and Politics in California* (forthcoming, 1980).

Scott H. Decker is an assistant professor of administration of justice at the University of Missouri-St. Louis. He is presently assessing the impact of the 1974 Juvenile Justice and Delinquency Prevention Act in Missouri. His published works have appeared in several edited volumes as well as the *Journal of Criminal Justice* and the *Journal of Police Science and Administration*.

Robert Friedrich is an assistant professor of government at Franklin and Marshall College in Lancaster, Pennsylvania. He received the B.A. from the University of Colorado and the M.A. and Ph.D. from the University of Michigan. His major research interests, in addition to police bahavior, are statistical research methods and electoral politics.

Kingsley W. Game is a Ph.D. candidate and teaching fellow in political science at the University of Houston. He received the M.A. in political science from Louisiana State University, was a scholar of Lincoln College, and received the B.A. in politics, philosophy, and economics from the University of Oxford.

Doris A. Graber is a professor of political science at the University of Illinois, Chicago Circle. Her article is part of a larger study of "The Impact of Crime News on the Public." Her recent publications on the impact of communication include *Verbal Behavior and Politics* (1976), and *The Mass Media and Politics* (1979).

Harlan Hahn is a professor of political science at the University of Southern California. He is the author of numerous books and articles in the areas of urban politics, inter-group relations, and criminal justice, including *Urban Rural Conflict, People and Politics in Urban Society, Police and Urban Society, Corruption in the U.S. Political System,* and *American Government: Minority Rights vs. Majority Rule.*

Woodrow Jones, Jr. is an assistant professor of political science at San Diego State University. He specializes in urban politics and public policy. He received the Ph.D. from the University of Oregon at Eugene. His research interest is mainly in the area of resource allocation and efficiency.

Kenton L. Knight is a graduate of California Polytechnic State University and a twelve-year law-enforcement veteran. He has recently written about the problem of the drunk driver in California.

Nicholas P. Lovrich, Jr. is an assistant professor of political science and director of the Division of Governmental Studies and Services at Washington State University. His teaching and research interests lie in the areas of criminal justice policy, urban politics and administration, ethnic politics and public personnel management. His articles have been published in *Social Science Quarterly, Western Political Quarterly, Public Administration Review, Teaching Political Science,* and *Urban Affairs Quarterly.* He is currently conducting research on the impact of L.E.A.A. grants in American cities.

John E. Monzingo is an associate professor of political science at North Dakota State University, Fargo, North Dakota. He received the Ph.D. from Claremont Graduate School in 1976.

Elinor Ostrom is codirector of the Workshop in Political Theory and Policy Analysis and professor of political science at Indiana University in Bloomington, Indiana. She has had a long-standing interest in questions related to the effect of organizational arrangements on the output of urban public agencies and in the measurement of that output. She has written numerous articles on these questions, particularly as they relate to the area of law enforcement.

Roger B. Parks is an associate director of the Workshop in Political Theory and Policy Analysis at Indiana University. He is author of several recent articles dealing with questions of police organization, police relations with victims of crime, and police performance measurement. Work in progress includes an attempt to specify the way in which variations in police organizational arrangements are related to variations in police performance and to estimate the magnitude of the specified relationships.

Stephen L. Percy is a research associate at the Workshop in Political Theory and Policy Analysis at Indiana University. He is the author of recent articles concerning police response time, evaluating police organization, and citizen coproduction of urban services. Current research includes an attempt to measure the effect of citizen coproduction of community security and safety on individual and neighborhood outcomes.

Donald Phares is an associate professor of economics and associate director of the Center for Metropolitan Studies at the University of Missouri-St. Louis. He is author of *State-Local Tax Equity: An Empirical Analysis of the Fifty States,* co-author of *Municipal Output and Performance in New York City,* editor of *A Decent Home and Environment: Housing Urban America,* and author of articles appearing in *Social Science Quarterly, Proceedings of the National Tax Association, Annals of Regional Science, Journal of Regional Science, Economic Geography, Journal of Drug Issues, Journal of Psychedelic Drugs, Urban Affairs Quarterly,* and *Nation's Cities,* and sections in several books and government reports. His research deals primarily with housing and neighborhood change, state-local finance and governmental structure, and drug abuse.

Dorothy Rudoni is a professor of political science at Ball State University. She has contributed to articles in *Youth and Society, Law and Public Policy, Police Administration Review,* and the *Policy Studies Journal.* Her major interests are the presidency, sexism and women's politics, and the politics of the criminal justice system. She has presented papers to all of the major political science conventions.

Wesley G. Skogan is an associate professor of political science and urban affairs at Northwestern University. He is the editor of *Sample Surveys of the Victims of Crime* and the author of several articles and monographs on crime. He is currently completing a book on crime and the elderly.

Russell L. Smith is an assistant professor in the department of political science at the University of Missouri-St. Louis. He is currently engaged in the evaluation of decision rules used in CETA programs in St. Louis. He has published in *Administration and Society, Midwest Review of Public Administration,* and *State and Local Government Review.*

Thomas M. Uhlman is an assistant professor of political science at the University of Missouri-St. Louis, specializing in the field of public law. He has completed a book entitled, *Racial Justice,* and his articles have appeared in the *American Journal of Political Science, Western Political Quarterly,* and *Social Science Journal.*

Stephen L. Wasby is a professor of political science in the Graduate School of Public Affairs, State University of New York at Albany. During 1978-79, he was program director, Law and Social Science Program, National Science Foundation, Washington, D.C. He is the author of several books on the judicial process, most recently *The Supreme Court in the Federal Judicial System.* He is also a member of the editorial board of *American Politics Quarterly, Justice System Journal,* and *Policy Studies Journal.*

Gordon P. Whitaker is an assistant professor of political science at the University of North Carolina at Chapel Hill. His research and teaching concern public service performance measurement and the relationships between administrative structure and service quality and cost. He is currently completing a study of the activities of police officers on patrol. He has served as consultant to police and other public agencies and is coauthor (with Elinor Ostrom and Robert Parks) of *Patterns of Metropolitan Policing* and *Policing Metropolitan America.*

About the Editors

Ralph Baker, a graduate of the University of Illinois, is a professor of political science at Ball State University. He is coauthor of *The Criminal Justice Game: Politics and Players,* coeditor of *Determinants of Law-Enforcement Policies,* and has contributed to articles in *Law and Public Policy, Police Administration Review,* and the *Policy Studies Journal.* Dr. Baker's major research interests are the politics of the criminal justice system and public law. He has given papers at all of the major political science conventions.

Fred A. Meyer, Jr., a graduate of Wayne State University, is an associate professor of political science at Ball State University. He is coauthor of *The Criminal Justice Game: Politics and Players,* coeditor of *Determinants of Law-Enforcement Policies,* and has contributed to articles in *Law and Public Policy, Police Administration Review,* and the *Policy Studies Journal.* Dr. Meyer's major research interests are the politics of the criminal justice system and urban politics. He is president of the Indiana Political Science Association.

About the Editors